A DAY'S RIDE

FROM

DE BULLION

Order this book online at www.trafford.com
or email orders@trafford.com

Most Trafford titles are also available at major online book retailers.

Note for Librarians: A cataloguing record for this book is available from Library and Archives Canada at www.collectionscanada.ca/amicus/index-e.html

Printed in Victoria, BC, Canada.

ISBN: 978-1-4269-1238-2 (sc)

ISBN: 978-1-4269-1239-9 (dj)

ISBN: 978-1-4269-1240-5 (e-book)

Our mission is to efficiently provide the world's finest, most comprehensive book publishing service, enabling every author to experience success. To find out how to publish your book, your way, and have it available worldwide, visit us online at www.trafford.com

Trafford rev. 10/30/2009

 www.trafford.com

North America & international
toll-free: 1 888 232 4444 (USA & Canada)
phone: 250 383 6864 ♦ fax: 812 355 4082

A DAY'S RIDE
FROM DE BULLION

A Memoir

by

ROBERT KARMAN

DEDICATION

For my Dad

Acknowledgments

Always in my thoughts as I wrote this book was my dad, who unfortunately left us at an early age. I am deeply indebted to Yvonne Nelson for her unfailing help and her computer knowledge. Yvonne also helped in formatting my line drawings and pages in their proper order.

I thank Rick MacMillan most gratefully for the tireless hours he put into this. He read and edited my work for typos and other glitches. Rick did everything a good copy editor would do.

I do wish to acknowledge and thank the many people I've met in my life for making my stories interesting. Bill Waldie, an exceptional friend through the years, was a great help with the book cover. Another book that has brought back memories about Montreal is a small gem by Mordecai Richler called "The Street." It's very much about the Montreal I grew up in. Almost anything by Mordecai is recommended. Last on this list I must mention what a great help one gets looking up dates and facts from the newspapers and the Internet.

CONTENTS

Part One: GROWING UP IN MONTREAL

What a street!

A lot of things happened to me as a kid growing up in the '30s, but not necessarily in the order I've written it here. After all, I was still a kid, probably only 9 or 10 years old, eager as hell to know everything immediately. I couldn't wish for a better place to grow up than on De Bullion St.; of course, my mother didn't share that thought with me. She was certain that I'd turn into a hoodlum overnight and my older sister, Ann, would probably get married at age 15 and run off with Hungarian gypsies and never be seen again!

Now, my dad, to me was a genius. He could fix anything, even without tools; all he had was a screwdriver, pliers and a hammer. The hammer was used to adjust things that were out of whack. If the hammer didn't work, he had the axe. But whatever he had to say around the house didn't count. My maw, all five feet of her, was the boss and the brains—always. My dad went along with that. And thinking back now to those times, I believe he made the right choice; it was a lot safer for him. I think. Like me, my dad was happy on 3694 De Bullion, and another plus for him was the low rent. I was a kid and didn't know what rent was. I also didn't care. But the street! What a street!

My parents had come from Hungary when they were very young, so all of our meals were goulash or some other Hungarian dish. Maw didn't have one recipe in the house; everything was in her head, including the wonderful thousands of cakes and pies. Most of these pastries and cakes had Hungarian names, so I couldn't spell them or for that matter even say them properly. We had seven-layer cakes, rum cake with real rum, cheesecakes, little but fat pretzel-looking things with varnish on them—everything better than any gourmet bakery could whip up. Every kid's parents on the street were hard-working immigrants and spoke their own language and ate funny food. Some also smelled different than the others. But that was okay. What did I care?

My maw says I was born at home, but not on De Bullion St. I think I would have liked that, but I was born over a fish market on St. Lawrence St., known as The Main. I think that's kinda neat too. The house on De Bullion was a two-storey, and we lived on the top floor. De Bullion St. is like most streets in Montreal; the houses are all attached to each other in one long row from one corner to another. If you went up into our attic and onto the roof, you could go from Pine Ave. to Prince Arthur. We kids loved the roof. One of our favourite pastimes was to throw water bombs, made from party balloons, at the pedestrians below. Also, every house had a copper wire strung up to serve as an aerial for better radio reception. Television wasn't around yet. To enable us to run faster from one end to the other on the roof, we cut down all the copper wire.

Before this time, apparently when I was still a baby, the guys where my dad worked at the Chrysler plant had a raffle. Tickets were

2

10 cents and the prize was a used Indian motorcycle. My dad won; I told you he was a genius. My dad had never been on a motorcycle in his whole life, and for that matter, had never driven a car. After a five-minute lesson in the parking lot, he drove it home. In those days, one didn't need insurance or a licence. Now that he had transportation, he quit his job and became a house painter. According to family stories, he built a huge box on the side of the bike with lumber he found. Now he was able to carry his extension ladders (with a flag at each end) and tools and paint, to the job site.

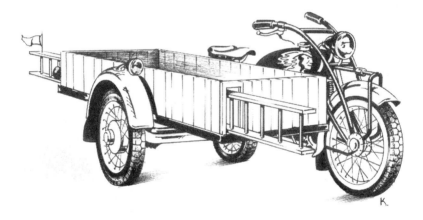

On many a weekend, my family and my cousin Doug (also a baby) and his family would go to Crystal Beach for the day. My dad drove the bike, my maw held me behind my dad. Dougie's father didn't know how to drive so he went in the box with the others. Doug's father was an okay guy because he had his own barbershop and used to cut our hair for free, except I didn't like it when I had the chicken pox. He would put a board across the arms of the barber chair for us to sit on, which boosted us higher. Then he'd get out the electric shaver and give me a bean shave, off with everything, including the chicken pox. Dougie's mother, his sister and my sister also got in the wooden box. This made a total of eight people on the Indian bike and in the paint box, plus a bunch of sandwiches, soft drinks, towels, toys, umbrellas and quart bottles of Black Horse Beer. And it wouldn't have been a picnic without the basket of peaches or plums, and always a watermelon. This too was back in the days when two families on a motorcycle was legal. If it rained, everybody got under the dirty paint tarp, except my dad of course. My maw and Doug's maw always put together wonderful picnic food they would find at the market. In my maw's day, I think my maw and everybody's maw was a good shopper and bargain hunter.

The vintage Indian bike with home-made side car.

I was slowly getting older and smarter (street smart) and the painting was still going well for my dad, until someone came along and invented the paint roller. Soon, people started painting their own houses. When this started, my dad went to Eaton's and bought two magazines on house improvements and a decorating magazine. In that same week, he tore out the pages he wanted, bought a cheap scrapbook at Kresge's 5 and 10 Cent Store, another 5 cents for school glue, and made himself a Sample Book. Within another day or two, he had his new business cards that read "Frank Karman, Painter and Decorator."

My dad always told my sister and me that he had three years' high school, and he had this funny smile on his face when he said it, but Ann (Annie back then) and I believed it. Why not? Our dad was our hero. Eventually, as we got older, he told us with that same wonderful smile, that he'd only done Grade 3 public school back in Hungary.

My whole life unfolded on wonderful De Bullion St. The street had everything a kid needs: drunks, prostitutes, people who worked, and people who wouldn't work, the Sisters (nuns) who lived across the road from our house and, most importantly, every nationality under the sun. But in those days in Montreal, if you didn't speak French then you might as well get out of town. I was beaten up so many times it became a way of life. Years later I remembered reading something about the poet Irving Layton's son telling a story about himself and his dad. Irving's first-born, Max, asked his dad, "Dad, Anthony is Hungarian and Tony Tiber is German and Ronnie is half Irish and half French-Canadian. What am I?" His father drew himself to his full height and said, "You, son, are a descendent of the oldest and noblest people on earth. You, son, are Jewish!" "Oh goody!" said Max, who went running outside to tell his friends. They promptly beat the shit out of him, and that was the side of Montreal he knew best. The side I knew best was getting beaten up by the French.

With that beginning, I became the fastest runner that Montreal ever saw! By the age of 9, I realized why the Frenchies were always in a gang. Alone, they would run away when they saw me, but they weren't fast enough. I'd beat the crap out of them, but, of course, the next day it was worse for me. But I sure could run—ask my best friend Schnutzer. It was time for a bunch of us to start our gang, but we didn't like the name "gang" so we called ourselves the Black Hawk Club Members, after a comic book action hero, and I was the leader because the clubhouse was in my mom and pop's coal shed. The coal shed was across a wooden walkway leading from our kitchen, which was on the top storey of our house. It was perfect because there was an outside staircase in the back lane leading to it. Our clubhouse space was beside the coal pile. We usually had four members, sometimes five, until one moved away and we became the "Black Hawk Four." There was me, a Hungarian, Nacum, a Jew, Schnutzer, a German, and Cyril, an Italian.

We had a lot of other kids on the street and that was good when we played ball. We needed enough guys for two teams. We always tried to get Moishe on our team. He was good. We also wanted his kid brother, Moishele, to go to the other side. He always ran stupidly, fell down a lot and cried. That can hold up a game. Another meshuggene I never wanted on our side was Hymie, a real putz. Hymie lived with his bubbe (which means grandmother in Yiddish). There were other kids too, of course. Girls too. Especially Natalie. She had big ones.

One of the favourite games on the street was touch football. The ball was made from socks. Hockey socks were best. You rammed into one big sock five or six other socks, and then got your maw to sew the end closed. The whole idea behind the game was to pass the ball to someone on your team and not have the other guys touch you when you had the ball. Of course, with all the throwing, the ball would often go down the sewer at the sidewalk, and I was always the one delegated to go down the sewer. I think that was because I was the only one who knew how, and nobody else would do it. After you got the manhole cover off, and about 10 feet down in the slime water, you would find the sock ball. It never sank because there was so much muck down there. And usually a dead cat or rat, so it was pretty smelly too. Now, what you had to do was put your back against one side of the sewer and your bent legs to the other side, then slowly slide down, grab the ball, throw it up to the guys, and hope they caught it on the first throw, or you got it back in your face! Then using your legs and back you made it back to the top. To this day my mother couldn't figure out how a little boy could get this dirty so quickly, and stink! I think every sewer in Montreal had to have at least one dead rat in it.

One of the habits of most parents on De Bullion St., when coming home late after shopping or a visit to a relative, was to make a noise after opening the door. The idea was to scare the rats or mice back into their hiding places. Also, when the kitchen light was flipped on, you would usually see the cockroaches run for cover. In all those

7

growing-up years, I will always remember the yellow powder (poison) around every baseboard in every room, especially the kitchen. You could kill every nasty critter in your house, but more always came in from the neighbour's. My maw had a different tactic. She would enter quietly, flip on the kitchen light, and, in a flash in front of your eyes, jump on two mice on the run, take off her shoe and whack a bunch of cockroaches and then plug in the kettle for tea. All this while my dad was still putting the old '38 Pontiac away. My dad stayed a Pontiac man for a long time, until years later in Toronto when he bought a '47 Ford five-passenger coupe, a car that started him saying SHIT a lot and swearing in Hungarian.

These cold-water flats, as they were known, all had a coal stove in the kitchen, so in the winter the other doors in the flat were all left open so the kitchen stove could do its best to heat the house. I slept in the hall and it was still cold. In winter, maw cooked everything on the coal stove to save the electricity. The one problem with the kitchen stove was that my sister Annie or I had to sift through the ashes to check if any coals hadn't burnt through yet, so we could use them again. Maw would give us a noogey across the head if a hot one fell on the linoleum. As far as food went, nothing was ever thrown out; we ate everything. The wax paper from the sliced bread packaging was used for my sandwiches over and over, and finally when it was well worn out, maw would polish the top of the coal stove with it; the stove always looked new again.

We had the usual hot water bottles for bed and took turns washing in the same pan of water. Some families without the proper facilities would go to public bathhouses. In the summer months, I would go to Schubert's Bath House for a swim. A bunch of us kids would line up outside Schubert's waiting for the doors to open. Then we were allowed a free swim for about 20 minutes before the "everybody out" whistle would blow. We'd put our pants on over our wet bathing suits, go stand outside again in line, wait, swim for 20 minutes and do it again and again till it was time to go home. A treat on the way home was a visit to a small deli that sold halvah, and that stuff was heaven. You'd give the man your saved-up six cents; on a scale went a small square piece of wax paper and then six cents of halvah. To make it last, you ate it slowly and ended by licking the wax paper till it looked new again.

Years later, our families were picnicking somewhere outside Montreal when I jumped off the bridge into deep water. My mother screamed in Hungarian; she didn't know I had learned to swim at Schubert's.

Our street was not much different than other nearby streets. Henri Julien, Clark St., St. Urbain, Colonial St., etc.—they were all noisy with horses pulling wagons, the ragmen, milkman, breadman, coalman, and, of course, the iceman, who would carry this heavy block of ice up the stairs and put it into our wooden icebox with the oval porcelain basin under it, which was always full to the very top when we emptied it. The thinnest horses always belonged to the ragman or the tarman. We loved the tarman; his horse pulled that black iron stove burning wood that melted tar. We kids always chewed tar because someone told us it would make our teeth white.

Playing

Everything we played with was homemade. The football, as I said, was made from socks. Lengths of rubber from old car inner tubes made wonderful slingshots. Our personal best was the scooter. You first got one of those great wooden orange crates. (They all had a picture at one end, such as a purple mountain with an orange sunset, or a cowboy on horseback with a dangling cigarette and holding a big orange.) You nailed the box (upright) to a piece of 2 x 4 with nails that were too long, but then you'd just bend them over. A short broomstick gave you handlebars. Two soup cans on either side of the box (with labels removed) gave you chrome headlights. The open end of the box would face you on the scooter; to this you nailed a curtain so nobody could see your stuff. Last and most important were the wheels; one roller-skate divided into two pieces finished it off beautifully. Now, to make it go fast, you painted the sides of the box with speed lines or flames.

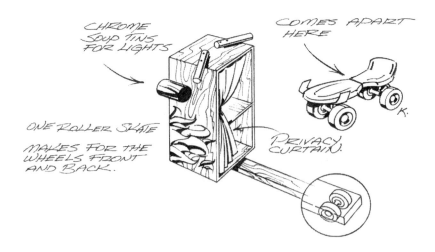

CHROME
SOUP TINS
FOR LIGHTS

COMES APART
HERE

ONE ROLLER SKATE
MAKES FOR THE
WHEELS FRONT
AND BACK.

PRIVACY
CURTAIN.

The invisible wire was another favorite. In every radio, there is a coil or transformer. The invisible wire is in one of these. You and your best friend face each other on either side of a sidewalk, both of you holding one end of the invisible wire. Then when somebody comes along, you hold up your hand as if you're scratching your head, still holding the invisible wire. Then the person walks into the invisible wire with their nose and you run away. Good, eh?

If we found some dead critter, we'd tie a gray thread to it, hide it under the first step leading up to someone's house, and run the gray thread along the crack of the gray sidewalk, and then under a parked car, then we'd hide on the other side and wait. Just as the person would step up or down, we'd pull the dead thing and watch them jump or scream. Rats worked the best. Schnutzer was my best friend, but I didn't see him every day because he lived on another street. My other friend, Nacum, from a poor Jewish family, lived nearby. So we were together a lot. All the Jews in our area were poor. The poorer seemed to live east of St. Lawrence (us). The more affluent lived west of St. Lawrence, such as on St. Urbain St. where Mordecai Richler lived. Now Mordecai was two or three years older than I was and studying the Talmud. His parents thought some day he would be a rabbi. (A good read of his, with Montreal thrown in, is St. Urbain's Horseman (1971); it won the Governor General's award. Another must-read is Barney's Version (1997). Around 1959 to 1972, he went to Paris, then England. During his years in England he wrote home saying, "No matter how long I live abroad, I do feel forever rooted in St. Urbain St." In 1972 Richler returned to Montreal, not to St. Urbain St., but to the eastern townships of Quebec and London England. When he wrote The Apprenticeship of Duddy Kravitz, he sold only about 1,000 copies in Canada, but when the movie appeared in 1974 sales of the book took off in Canada and around the world.

In the early years, when I was about 7 years old and Mordecai would be 9, my dad had an upholstery shop on Pine Ave. Directly across the street from the shop and on the opposite corner at 100 Pine Ave. stood a synagogue. Five streets from De Bullion was St. Urbain St., the synagogue roughly in the middle of these two streets. When I wasn't in school, I spent a lot of time in my dad's upholstery shop. Now my dad's way of working was to empty one of those little boxes of bluish carpet tacks into his mouth, then with his tongue, one by one turn the heads outward so that his upholstery hammer with a magnet at one end would hold the little tack while his other free hand could pull the material tight, and bang went the little hammer again and again. I did have a tendency to ask a lot of questions, and for my pop to answer he'd have to spit the tacks into his hand. What always followed was that he'd say, "Go play!" So, across the road I went into the synagogue.

What an interesting place—all those guys in black with big black hats. Nobody sat; they all stood around the walls talking and a lot of hand moving went on. Many had scraggy beards, long and not combed. From under the hats, the hair hanging down was the same. I always thought the hair came with the hats. I'd ask my dad about a lot of this stuff. He'd spit the tacks into his hand and say, "Go play." He also spat on the floor a lot; he said the blue steel of the tacks tasted funny. Now, many years later, I wondered if this was the synagogue that Mordecai went to. Today at 100 Pine Ave., the site of the synagogue building is now the Theatre of Quatre Sous (Four Penny Theatre).

I always figured the synagogue to be a more fun place than our Catholic church. At the synagogue, the men all stood around the walls making deals, and in our church we had to stand and sing, then kneel and pray, then stand, kneel, sit, kneel again, and pray for stuff we never got. This would go on for two hours in our church. We kids never sat with the parents. We also sat at the back, and of course, kids being kids, we talked. When you got caught talking, the priest (Father Debeld), who had to be 300 pounds and 6'9", would stop his sermon, call out your name (which embarrassed your parents), and after church you stayed kneeling for another hour. This only happened to my sister and me once because my maw, on the way out of the church that Sunday, let Father Debeld have it. I remember maw had to look straight up, he being so big and maw so small. She told him while aiming her crooked forefinger at his nose, "Don't you ever call out Robert or Annie's names in church again; if Robert or Annie need disciplining, they will get it at home." While other kids still got whacked, thanks to our maw, from then on Annie and I were untouchable.

Back in the '30s, most of these parishioners came from the same small town in Hungary and all settled in the same area in Montreal like other ethnic peoples who leave their homelands do. Father Debeld was big and frightening. My public school (St. Louis De France) was on top of the Catholic church. This too, in some ways, had its drawbacks. The school was run by nuns. If you were bad, you were sent to one of two men teachers for the strap. Mr. Hock or Mr.

Schneider would take their leather belts off and strap the open palm of both your hands. Then you were marched downstairs to the church and knelt on the wooden floor for an hour. We always wore short pants, so kneeling on hard wood in bare knees really hurt. Once a month, a class at a time would go downstairs in single file for confession. In confession, Father Debeld would sit behind a small portable screen. On the other side (your side) was a board to kneel on. Then, in turn, you went up to this portable barbaric thing, knelt, and started with two prayers to God. After that, we were to confess our sins for the past month, be forgiven, and could then go out clean and do it again if we wanted to.

Father Debeld would sit sideways on the other side of the screen and twirl his rosary. Occasionally, he'd ask a question like, "Have you had any evil thoughts? Did you do anything bad that would offend Jesus?" Of course, we all said "No" to everything. How could we tell him that we wanked if we found dirty pictures, or that we smoked, but first had to steal the cigarettes, and that we played "church on fire" every time a new kid started school and didn't yet know the game? The new kid was the "church on fire" and had to keep his eyes closed.

We, the firemen, would run all around making fire truck sounds, run up to the new kid and all together pee all over him. So you see, there was no way you could tell the priest stuff like this at confession. You'd get whacked across the head, then he'd tell your parents and you'd get whacked again at home. We may have been bad, but we weren't stupid! You'd have to be stupid to confess stuff like that.

Poor Andrew Wolf. At every confession he would make mistakes in the opening prayers. Father DeBeld would slowly lift himself off his chair, lean forward over the confession screen, and give Andrew a backhand across the head that would send him flying across the terrazzo floor. Andrew cried at every confession. This happened every month for years and Andrew never got to give his confession. Too bad Andrew didn't have my mother! My maw would have put a stop to this on the first day! Needless to say, you could see why we kids were very nervous around the son-of-a-bitch.

You learn an awful lot of stuff when you're a kid. Did you know if you wanted to run faster in your brand new rubber boots, all you had to do was turn down the top of the boots about five inches and paint wings on each side? Did you know that to taste rain, all you did was tilt your head all the way back, open your mouth, stick out your tongue and all the rain went right into your eyes? Did you know that at the hockey games in the Montreal Forum they didn't have glass on the boards until years later? Did you know that when you were bad in class the teacher always sent you to the cloakroom, where you could go through all the other kids' pockets? Another great discovery was that you could hear through a wall if you put a glass to your ear. Did you know if you put your hand under your armpit and pumped your arm up and down, it makes great farting noises? Did you know you could light a fart? Finally, what I didn't know was, how come so many women teachers in public school never married? I still don't know.

When you're a kid you also see stuff grownups don't see, like gum under tables and hiding places all over the house that only you know about, except for the cockroaches that live there.

Directly across the street from Saint Louis De France school was a corner cigar and candy store. The old couple who ran the place were Marvin and Gladys Tannenbaum. Besides selling the usual popular candies like bubble gum, and those small yellow shaped ice-cream cones with the white icing top and filled with sugar guck that gave you pimples overnight, there were cinnamon hot balls and wax lips with a liquid inside that tasted like anti-freeze. But you could chew the wax all day. Another favourite was licorice made into what was then called (in those less sensitive times) nigger babies. There were also candy cigarettes and wax coke-shaped bottles with a drink inside. I believe the reason why so many of us kids went into the store was for the homemade popsicles that Marvin and Gladys put together in little juice glasses. They made lime, lemon and lemon- lime but all three tasted the same. There was also orange, grape, root beer and cherry. Each had a round stick in the middle and cost a penny. Above the door hung a bell on a spring, which rang when you opened the door, making it difficult to nick something.

When there wasn't much to do, we would take the corks out from the back of bottle caps, put the caps on the outside of our sweaters and the cork on the other side. Now we had badges. In every comic book there were ads for neat stuff, like sending away for a book on how to get X-ray vision: "Learn how in your free time at home and then see through everything." Wow, imagine watching the girls' basketball team play, or spending the day at the beach, or going to find Natalie with the big ones. My mind became quite busy when I read about this, and I remembered that stores like Eaton's had those x-ray machines to measure your foot size, but everything was purple and fuzzy including your bones. The whole thing looked weird, so I decided I didn't want to see Natalie's tits after all. I was now going to learn how to throw my voice across a room.

From 3694 De Bullion I had to walk north of Pine Ave. to my school. Going the other way brought you to Prince Arthur. Prince Arthur St. used to be called Bagg S. after Stanley Clark Bagg, one of the biggest landowners on the Montreal Island. They renamed the street Prince Arthur in 1890 after the third son of Queen Victoria, who was at the time the Governor General of Canada. In the 1960s, people moved into the area because the rents were still low. This changed drastically around 1980 when the restaurants on Prince Arthur were doing well and able to pay higher rents. The city of Montreal helped this evolution by establishing a pedestrian mall in 1981. Colonial St. was one street west of De Bullion.

As the years progressed, the Portuguese community kind of took over, and that still continues today. There are self-renovated houses in a variety of colors with many touches of Portugal, such as the ceramic plaques at door entrances or building facades, which are very nice indeed. Some of the richer class, not that any lived on De Bullion St., moved to Westmount. If you lived in Westmount, you have done quite well. Westmount even had its own police force. In the '30s when I was on Colonial St., it looked very similar to De Bullion but with a little more class. I periodically had to do an errand for my dad to Mr. Kemerle's house to pick up a gallon of homemade whiskey. Mr. Kemerle had his own still in the house. I'd see all this copper piping and the shiny copper vat with a lot of other stuff bubbling. To me it looked like Mr. Kemerle was making a monster like in the comics. No one ever stopped or approached me. It just looked like any kid delivering a gallon of vinegar. I'd take it to the corner (not far) on Pine Ave. to my dad's upholstery shop where he immediately hid the bottle. I took a swig once on the walk—a big mistake, I had the worst hiccups of my life!

—The Gallon Bottle

St. Lawrence Blvd.

After Colonial St. came St. Dominic and then the famous St. Lawrence Blvd., which has always been the important street in Montreal, the dividing line for the city. Addresses for the east and west streets begin there. It seemed Anglophones lived west of St. Lawrence and francophones lived east. In English the street was known as "The Main," partly because it was the main street of the Saint-Louis district. I guess that's why my school was called "Saint-Louis de France."

The street was around in the early 18th century during the French regime. In 1850, mansions lined Sherbrooke St. It was a middle-class area inhabited primarily by English-speaking businessmen and trades people. A new wave of working-class immigrants came to the area when pogroms in Russia started a stream of fleeing Jews in the 1880s, and by 1920, Yiddish was heard everywhere around Saint-Laurent. Wealthy Jews established textile factories in the area. Most Jews were poor working people and struggled to survive. The factory owners hired the cheapest labour they could find. Getting closer to around my time as a kid in the 1930s, the Jewish community started slowly to move northward past Mont-Royal Blvd. After the Second World War, the Jews moved further again. The Greeks followed. They settled first on St. Lawrence near Sherbrooke, and later more northward. Park Ave. became popular to the Greeks. Many other ethnic groups settled along "The Main": Hungarians, Slavs, Portuguese, etc. made this area an exciting place for shopping.

In these present times, more upscale, trendy products are taking over on St. Lawrence. Large, airy lofts are inviting to artists, designers and a bunch of wanna-be's. New chic clothing stores have moved to the street, along with, of course, the marked-up prices. With all this hype and new tenants, rents were climbing very quickly. More than likely, it's possible the lovely ethnic flavour that has always made the street my home, will be lost forever. Without the Jews, would we have the delicatessen? Probably, but would it be as good? And all the appetizers that go with a deli. Would they have the same chutzpah if they were run by an Irishman or a Yugoslav? I don't think so. Who made the best smoked meat? Was it Sid Kravitz or Solly Berman? This always came up on "The Main," St. Lawrence Blvd.

In the late '30s and '40s, we would walk north on St. Lawrence from Prince Arthur and smell the spicy smoked meat aroma from the many delicatessens, each with its own flavours and spices to add more to the best brisket of beef. Then the owners would argue who brought the first smoked meat to Montreal from Romania. Many delicatessens were around in the '30s but I'm now told that in 1959 there were only three left on the St. Lawrence Main. This happened mostly because the Jews started moving away to nicer areas, thanks to more gelt. So they left the poorer, shabby streets of St. Lawrence Main and the Greeks and Hungarians moved in where the Jews vacated. The indestructible (been here forever) "Schwartz's," which was there in the '30s, is still there today at 3895 Boul. St-Laurent (was St. Lawrence before), not far from De Bullion.

Now, in these present years, we've all heard of the French language police. They insisted the exterior sign be changed from "Schwartz's" to—are you ready for this?--"Chez Schwartz Charcuterie Hébraïque de Montréal!" Do you believe this? Everyone still knows it as "Schwartz's." The deli is a no-frills, narrow place that still serves the best smoked meat. Vegetarians will not be happy here. This is Jewish haute cuisine. Reuben Schwartz was a Jewish immigrant from Romania who first opened the place in 1927. If Schwartz's Deli is not your thing, go somewhere else and have some québécois baked beans with tourtiere (meat pie) and a piece of sugar pie.

Just recently, after 98 years in the deli business, Ben's Delicatessen closed. They say Ben introduced the smoked meat sandwich to Canada. Bens hit the big time in the 1940s and '50s when Montreal was known as the sin city and the deli sandwiches were 15 cents. It is said Bens served to Ed Sullivan, Jack Benny, dancers, jazz musicians, ventriloquists and their wooden dummies, hockey players, Pierre Trudeau, Leonard Cohen and many more. Bens was opened on St. Lawrence Blvd. (now St-Laurent) in 1908 by Ben Kravitz. Apparently, a strike by employees and other things helped the family decide on the closing, in 2006. The deli has always remained in the Kravitz family. Montreal will miss Bens. It almost made it to 100.

During the 1940s, a columnist wrote, "Whether you're looking for a gal or a gun, haircut or a hustler, a hock shop or a hamburger, you'll find it on St. Lawrence Blvd. These days the Vietnamese and new immigrants from Hong Kong have taken over much of St-Laurent between Viger and René-Lévesque. On festival days such as August Moon, there are dragon dances, martial art demonstrations, Chinese chess and, naturally, firecrackers. I guess this also explains why the wonderful delicatessen on St-Laurent isn't as popular as it once was.

One event that changed things dramatically in Quebec was the passing, in 1977, of Bill 101, brought in by the Parti québécois. All

English on signs had to be changed to accommodate the French. With the new language code, English was permitted providing the lettering was only one-third the size of the French lettering. This new language code has certainly led to some very idiotic changes. The owner of an Indian restaurant is told he has broken the law by having coasters for "Double Diamond," a British beer. The language activists protested the existence of an English language option on Quebec phone lines, where callers are told to press nine for English, for example. Strange that after pressing nine for English, the caller is served in French in most instances. There should be no cause for surprise that over 40,000 people have moved from Quebec since 2006. Some time ago, a sign went up at the Dulles airport near Washington, D.C., and saying, "BIENVENU... Welcome to the Province of Quebec, where the unrestricted use of the English language is against the law. When visiting Quebec govern yourselves accordingly." "This is a civil rights movement we're fighting," says Howard Galganov, a Montreal radio talk show host who helped raise money for the ads.

As things stand now, children attending English schools in Quebec must learn French from the first grade on. But the francophone children wait until grade five before taking English, which we're told isn't great. As a result of this, only about 35 percent of French Quebeckers are bilingual. Now, living in Quebec, speaking English certainly isn't necessary to earn a living. But try leaving Quebec if you speak French only and see what the job prospects are. The Italians, one of the largest communities in the province, have the right idea. Most Italian families send their children to an English school. This way they learn to speak English every day, take a French class starting in grade one and carry on speaking Italian at home, therefore learning to speak three languages. Some say trilingualism is gaining ground, but slowly, much to the humiliation of the hard line nationalists.

The language police still wander around the streets, measuring the letters of billboards, and every year another wave of English Quebeckers leave for other parts of Canada or the U.S. How about the struggling Pakistani couple who worked seven days a week, 18 hours a day, in their Montreal convenience store and were ordered to learn better French as required by Quebec law or else? Or the Greek immigrant who had a van on which he advertised his work, "Bill's Plumbing and Heating?" He would not pay the fine and his truck and tools were seized and auctioned off. Another who made gravestones for a living was attacked because the epitaphs were not bilingual. One of the silliest targets was a rural Quebec couple whose family business had been selling maple syrup for the last four generations to Americans and Western Canadians. Their seven-year-old web site is in English because they export 99 percent of their syrup to Americans. They have hired a lawyer. We wish them luck.

In the meantime the Québécois are flooded by U.S. television programs from across the border, but nobody in Quebec, where the mother tongue is French, has complained. Not a soul of the seven million people plus has as of yet suggested an electronic jammer to stop the cultural intrusion from south of the border. Lately thousands of young French Quebeckers are thinking a little different about English because it is the international language of business. An undercover survey in Montreal showed that almost 100 percent of

French speakers were quick to offer English in directions when asked and at the same time it was found that many English gave directions in French when asked. Let us hope, that little by little someone has finally seen the light at the end of the tunnel.

As Mordecai Richler said about the Quebec police around that time, they never made the headlines by pouncing on a drug deal with hundreds of pounds of cocaine worth millions on the street. But they made headlines the world over for other reasons, even in the Los Angeles Times where a headline read, "Police seize 15,000 Dunkin Donut bags in Montreal because they weren't bilingual."

The "zoot suit" first showed up in the late '30s, before the war. It was around at the time of the jitterbug and a few bad characters gave the zoot-suiter a bad name. The zoot suit was banned in many parts of America because of the riots in 1943 in Los Angeles. In America, the sailors were beating up the Mexicans. Britain had a similar problem but not as bad as the States. The Brits had the Jamaicans, who loved the zootable look. Around 1944 in Montreal, large-scale brawls were happening everywhere—service men, especially sailors, against the zoot-suit civilian youth. What was causing all this fighting? Was it the smart-assed youth who didn't want to serve his country, here and in America? The zoot suit? Was a memorable fashion statement too much for a young man in the '40s?

A zoot suit consisted of a long, loose coat with wide, padded shoulders, ballooning pants worn very high above the waist, like all old men like to do today. Also an over-sized (and I do mean over-sized!) bow tie, a wide-brimmed gangster hat and, to top all that off, a very long, hanging watch-chain. All this was meant to attract attention. And how could it not do exactly that? This flamboyant group was referred to as "zoot-suiters" or "zooters." All too often, when a young lad put on his zoot suit, he became somebody else. He took on this youthful defiance and was ready for fighting and drinking. Considering the tense wartime atmosphere in Canada, and the zooters' unpatriotic outlook, in the eyes of many caring Canadians, especially those brave lads in uniform, it was easy to see why the zooters' social values clashed with wartime moral views.

Now we had in Montreal the youth with their "uniforms" and the servicemen in their uniforms. These two groups, both aggressive and in their own clothing, were on a wartime collision. The newspapers began carrying stories of minor clashes all over Montreal between the zooters and the Canadian military. Major fighting took place during the night of May 27, 1944, in St. Lambert, just across the St. Lawrence River from Montreal. La Presse said the zooters were mostly of Italian origin, though there were also French Canadians with them. On May 31, another fight took place that spread to the south shore of the Jacques Cartier Bridge. There, a group of about 60 mainly French-Canadian soldiers were attacked by a band of 200 zooters. In another terrible incident, a sailor and his wife were beaten by zooters on Dorchester St. This attack so upset other sailors in Montreal that they immediately began plotting their revenge against the zoot-suiters. The well-organized sailors divided into many groups of 75 to 100 men and began to hunt down the zooters. Groups of soldiers and airmen joined in the hunt. They descended on nightclubs, bars, restaurants, dance halls, pool rooms, etc. As soon as a zoot-suiter was found, the Naval mob beat them and stripped them of their outfits, which were promptly torn to pieces. The beat-up zooters were left in their underwear until rescued by the police.

Serious fighting broke out along Ste. Catherine St., mostly at the intersection of Bleury and a few blocks further east. Violence was also happening in La Fontaine Park. For many years my friend Schnutzer and I played in La Fontaine Park—it wasn't far from De Bullion St., just 10 or so streets east to the park. Around this terrible time, a sailor was found drowned face down in La Fontaine Park. How he drowned was never explained. But it didn't look good, so Schnutzer and I never went near the place again. Around this time, 100 angry sailors made their way to the Verdun Dance Pavilion located by the City's waterfront. There, some zooters, some not, were set upon by the mob. Bottles and clubs were used by both sides. The Verdun Messenger printed the following story:

"The zoot-suiters barricaded themselves within the dance hall while the young sailors tore up concrete park benches, which they used as battering rams to clear a way into the building---they ordered all the girls off the premises, with the exception of two who were wearing the feminine equivalent of a zoot suit, and they also expelled all young men who were not zoot-suiters. They then proceeded to tear off the clothes of the luckless zoot-suiters, including the two young women who were caught in the Naval net. Some (zoot-suiters) climbed to the rafters of the building, but were soon pulled from their perches---and many were bruised and exhibited black eyes."

The *Montreal Star* and *La Presse* both referred to the fighting as "vicious." News of this sort continued until the more serious news of fighting in Normandy took over the headlines in newspapers.

Eventually, the zoot suit was made illegal. It's grotesque dimensions called for far too much fabric. With the riots going on and wartime pricing, the Trade Board issued a stern warning to tailors, reminding them of the permissible lengths and widths of men's clothing, and said that suits "shall have no belt, bi-swings or pleated backs, also shall have no vents front of sides, no buttons on the sleeves." One tailor was fined $400 for making a zoot suit. The zoot suit problem in time did quiet down, but the fighting between the servicemen and civilians continued.

Scrapping between the members of the three branches of the armed forces was not unheard of. A prominent venue for this was "The Music Box," a bar in the basement of the Mount Royal Hotel. The soldiers, sailors and airmen could find plenty of girls to dance with and, of course, to quarrel over. If a wrong word was said or misunderstood, then the fight was on. An airman might take a swing at a sailor and the army figured this was too good to miss and the whole place was out of control. It could be as simple as, "Is this chair being occupied?" Most of the girls tried to get out of the fight, but a few would remain to scream encouragement to their fellas. Chairs would break, drinks were spilled, a few unlucky ones got their heads bashed in, but the following day everything was forgiven and life went on. The zoot suit went on for years, but like most fads it, too, eventually fizzled out.

De Bullion St. stayed the same throughout my childhood. We continued on with the street pranks, some new, some old. Another fun game we all enjoyed playing on the street began with a broom handle, with a five-inch piece cut off the end. You had to taper off both ends so that when you whacked the short piece lying on the road, with the broom handle, it would leap up off the road. Then, while it was in mid-air, you'd whack it again down the street. The one who got to the other end first was the winner.

Montreal had many whore houses with lots of variety, depending on how much money you had. The quality prostitutes worked in places uptown, like the one at 150 Milton St. where the government Ministers and politicians went. Now the poorer working man went for the much cheaper prostitute. De Bullion St. was well known for its many brothels, so much so that every second house was a whore house. The prostitutes weren't so busy on our street; it was much lower down on De Bullion where they occupied the houses numbered 910, 912, 930, 934, 936, 948, 956 and 958. Many more were on neighbouring streets, and this whole area was known as the red-light district.

A woman called Mme. Beauchamp owned at least 24 houses, 16 of them on De Bullion St. On top of all this, all forms of gambling were taking place all over Montreal: horse-betting, roulette tables, blackjack, baccarat, craps, etc. Gambling was illegal in Canada but in Montreal everything was wide open. Of course, you had to know the right people and whom to send the thousands of dollars to (regular payoffs). These payoffs went to the police and civic officials. The police raids came often—the public demanded it—but there always was a warning first so the owners could leave before the raid. The collector was a guy named Harry who distributed the graft to the municipal officials and police. As the years passed, illegal slot machines found their way to Montreal and the suburbs.

Montreal was a wide-open town in a straight-laced Canada. In 1939 King George VI and Queen Elizabeth came to town. This was the first time royalty visited Canada. I was 7 years old and knew nothing about George and Liz. What mattered to me was I didn't have to go to school that day. The limousine with the King and Queen would drive about 20 or more miles through Montreal. The authorities were warning people not to overload their balconies along the route of the royal couple for fear that if the balconies collapsed they, the householders, might have to face lawsuits.

The politicians in Ottawa were worried about the behavior of some in Quebec. For instance, Premier Maurice Duplessis: would he be drunk or sober? It was less than a year before that he had ordered his car to stop in front of the Reform Club, rushed in and in front of all its members (all political enemies) unbuttoned his fly and pissed into the fireplace. Also, there was the unpredictable Camillien Houde, then mayor of Montreal. Three short months previously, Houde had said in a speech that if England would go to war with Italy, Quebec would side with Mussolini. The big worry for Ottawa was: How are the French going to treat the English King? For the poor, the cheapest flag at Eaton's cost 45 cents. The city was still in a great depression. Forty-five cents for a family man unemployed represented two days of what the government gave him for food. On May 18, the Canadian Pacific Railway's proudest locomotive arrived at Quebec City with a crowd of 100,000 people cheering. When the train came to a stop, Mayor Houde sprang forward to greet them. The mayor was a fat man with a nose like W.C. Fields and bulging eyes. A year hence Houde would be arrested by the RCMP and locked up for telling the Quebec people not to register for military service. My dad always referred to him as Mayor Hood. At one of the dinners with the royal couple, Mayor Houde said to the King and Queen, "I thank you from the bottom of my heart. My wife thanks you from her bottom too." So much for class from the bozo.

While all this was going on, we sat on the front steps of 3694 De Bullion drinking Kik Cola, five cents for five or six glasses. Another favourite, even cheaper and in a bigger bottle was "Jumbo" drinks. They made orange, lime, grape, etc. It came in a beautiful bottle with an elephant embossed on it. Very good, but it made you burp a lot. We drank Pepsi-Cola too, but not as much as the French. The Frenchies or pea-soups as we kids called them, loved their Pepsi. First, It was cheaper than Coke. There was a radio commercial that went, "Twice as much for a nickel, Pepsi-Cola is the drink for you." Another jingle went, "Pepsi-Cola hits the spot, 12 full ounces, that's a lot." The word Pepsi became a derogatory slang word for a francophone Quebecker. This slang word didn't seem to bother the French, possibly because all around us on De Bullion we already had "The Krauts,"the Germans, "Limeys" were the English, "Potato eaters" the Irish, "Dagos" the Italians and of course many more.

This was also a time of great movies, but kids were not allowed into movie theatres. My parents would dress me up in a suit, white shirt with tie and shiny black shoes. Accompanied by my parents, I usually got in. Most of the flicks were mushy, the kind of stuff my parents wanted to see. You know, Cary Grant, Jean Arthur, Claudette Colbert, Jimmy Stewart, etc. I wanted John Wayne fighting the enemy, whoever they where. He could do it all, and by himself. What a lot of horse shit that was too. My cousin Dougie and I went to a serial flick every Saturday morning to see Flash Gordon or Buck Rogers. Even though you could see the strings holding up the rocket ship as it flew crazily across the screen and landed on the moon (where the mud men live) with a thud and the rocket flame would go "pletch" and go out. Each show had a cliff-hanger at the end, so you had to be back the next Saturday. In these days, if you went into a phone box there was always something scratched into those nubbly zinc walls with a key. "Kilroy was here" was very popular. "Gitel Sugarman bangs," "See the promised land at Mrs. Resnick's." "Manny has a big tuchus," "For a good time, go pull your petzel," and many more. The first thing you did when you went into a phone box was put your finger into the slot, to see if anyone left some change. We kids would ram Kleenex up into the slot, wait a day or two, come back, pull out the Kleenex and hope for a few nickels and dimes.

On most corners of every street would be a small variety store that sold everyday stuff, from groceries, fruit, one-cent candy, cigarettes, newspapers and so forth. We kids would ask for an item we knew was kept in the back of the store. While the shopkeeper was busy going to the other end, we would hop up on the counter, reach over and nick a pack of cigarettes. Sweet Caporal was a favourite, not only for the smokes but also for the picture cards inside of airliners.

Montreal had, and still has, those charming outside staircases. Most are welded metal and curved one way or another. The idea of having the staircase on the outside of the building was to make more room on the inside of the house. The bad part of this thinking was that in the winter, with Montreal's snow and ice, it became very dangerous. French-Canadian families had many children, 10, 15, some had more. The first floor was for the family and the upstairs would be rented. The alleys behind the houses were for the horse-drawn carts delivering wood and coal. In the summer the street could be rather noisy at times, with a row of balconies on both sides of the street and the people carrying on a conversation from one side to the other. Added to that is they're all speaking in a language other than your own.

Occasionally we could have a Bar-Mitzvah or a Polish wedding on the street and that would mean, for us kids, cake, chicken wings and with luck a nicked bottle of Mogen David or Slivovitz. Between Pine Ave. and Prince Arthur on De Bullion we had it all. A few prostitutes moved in with the drunks down the street so that offered us another education we didn't even dream about. Two doors over from 3694 lived Walter, a young kid with Epilepsy who had many attacks. His mother showed us how to hold his tongue forward with a pencil so he wouldn't choke. We did what his maw said because he was little and it seemed serious.

She also told us to never put our fingers in Walter's mouth to hold his tongue down, because he would bite them off. Now, the prostitutes were a different matter and more exciting. There was one girl we called "The Semi" because she was still learning. She never wanted anything to do with us because we were kids and I guess kids

33

don't have money. One of the kids said that his brother heard from somewhere her name was Esther and she had syphilis. It was decided we didn't want anything to do with Esther now, because we were told if you got the syph, you'd get holes in your thing and pee in nine directions all at the same time.

We had great stuff to play with. I think every kid had a chemistry set, or should have. They came with test tubes and bottles of stinky stuff you mixed with other stinky stuff that made even stinkier stuff. The microscope gave you little glass swatches that you put different bugs on or a hair from your head to look for cooties. Another fun thing was to find a piece of broken glass, preferably a thick one. The bottom from a pop bottle was good. This made a good magnifying glass. With the sun shining through it at the right angle you could start a pretty neat fire with a pile of leaves or sneak up behind someone, aim it at the back of their neck and in seconds they'd be off the ground.

Okay, now here's the secret behind invisible ink, You get a lemon from your maw, squeeze out the juice into a small glass, then write the secret message on a piece of paper using a nib with the lemon juice. The lemon juice is invisible on the paper, until the guy you sent it to holds a candle under the paper, a few inches away, and the secret message appears. Pretty good, huh?

In the early days of public school, we had Chiclets gum. They came 12 in a box. If you read the letters on the box back to front, CHICLETS stood for Stingy Teacher Eats Lousy Chiclets In Her Class. Pretty good, huh? Also when the box was empty it had a small cellophane window at one end. If you blew into the other end, it made a nice horn.

If your parents had the money, you might be lucky enough to get a Meccano Erector set, or toy metal soldiers, or pick-up sticks. And remember the Bolo Bat? That was popular and cost 10 cents for a cheap one, 25 cents for the deluxe model. The Bolo Bat was a paddle you held in one hand, with a long, grey elastic attached and a sponge ball at one end. The other end was stapled to the Bolo Bat. The idea was to whack the ball into the air as often as possible without missing. My grey elastic had been broken so many times and knotted together that it ended up being only about 10 inches long. The original length must have been at least three feet. The Big Little Books were popular, but not cheap. Then there was the prize of all toys, actually not a toy at all. It was the Red Ryder BB Gun. No one I knew had one or could afford one. Not only that, your maw said you could shoot your eye out. My dad said we didn't have any money to spare because of the crash of '29. I never did know what that meant or what I had to do with it. I'd only been around since 1933.

Popular Science and Mechanics Illustrated magazines showed us with drawings how to make things like flying machines, or how to explode things, big or small. They also included long articles on new cars, explaining better engines like the Strato-Streak V/8 or how Turbine Turboglide works, why a car with a Power-Flite Range Selector is a good item to have, or what Hydra-Matic and Torsion-aire suspension were. On top of all this, there were articles on why we need or don't need more chrome on all the cars.

Remember the yo-yo? We kids all had a yo-yo, and every one of them was made out of wood. Not like today; everything is plastic, providing you can even find a yo-yo. What was and is still good about

35

the yo-yo was the tricks it could do. In the beginner's book of tricks, there are over 35 listed, but my favourites were maybe just five or six. Number one had to be "The Sleeper." In The Sleeper, the yo-yo is at the end (bottom) of the string, and stays there spinning until a little tug sends it back up to your hand. "Rock the Baby" is another winner that requires two hands, "Walk the Dog" and " Around the World" were a bit hard on the various hardwoods of a yo-yo because the two discs had to survive hours of being whacked against cement sidewalks.

No one can agree as to who was first in inventing the yo-yo. It may have been the Chinese, Greek or Filipinos. The Asian historians say yo-yo toys originated in China around 1,000 B.C., consisting of two discs made from ivory, connected together with a central peg and a silk cord. Greece has evidence of the yo-yo in existence around 450 to 500 B.C. Either way the yo-yo is (they say) the world's second oldest toy; only dolls are supposed to be older. Napoleon's army played with yo-yos. The Flores yo-yo was introduced in 1928, and in a year or two the company was producing over 300,000 yo-yo's every day. Flores ads said, "If it isn't a Flores it isn't a yo-yo." How does a yo-yo work? Well, it's sort of a toy flywheel that goes up and down. And why does it do what it does? I don't know. I think you should buy one (probably plastic) and figure it out yourself.

Hardly a day went by when we weren't running away from the Frenchies. Occasionally we would see one of the pea-soups alone, then chase him and beat the crap out of him. At home our mothers would insist we eat everything on our plates because some poor kid in Europe was starving. I could never figure out what I had to do with it. Sometimes in the evenings, we kids would have this discussion about

Tarzan and whether he was some kind of pervert, you know, hanging around the jungle all day with a bunch of monkeys. And did he ever have a woman or ever see a naked woman? Johnny Weissmuller, who famously played Tarzan in the film series, could go from one village to another without ever touching the ground, thanks to all the jungle vines. He spent the whole time swinging from vine to vine yodeling. I think that was his way of saying, "I'm coming through." Also, this way, not once did he ever step into elephant poo.

After we tired of all this kind of nonsense talk we (mostly Schnutzer and I) would go hide under the Burghardts' front steps and porch. It was very dirty under the porch but it had a basement window (also filthy) that looked into where a few drunks and two prostitutes lived. How come in places like this, under steps, there are always spider webs everywhere, around the windows, above your head, everywhere? At night we could look in through the filthy glass and nobody could see us. The two girls weren't beauties but had long legs and wore black tiny panties and black brassieres. Sometimes they would scratch their private parts and that's when Schnutzer and I would get a hard-on. Around this time, Schnutzer and I started talking about how to get a girl and what a guy had to do, and what to say to look good. Now we knew it was tough to impress girls in school wearing our funny corduroy britches, or a leather hat with ear-flaps and a chin strap. Wearing glasses didn't help either. Wearing galoshes turned you into the school jerk, and when you put Brylcream or Wildroot cream oil on your hair, your maw would say, "And what the heck are you up to now?"

It was very hard to be grown up when your maw was around all the time. This was still in the days when we would go visit a relative across town by streetcar, and before my maw would knock on the door she would have to clean my ears. The way this was done is you first wrap a hankie around your finger, then spit on the hankie a few times, and then push as hard as you could push the hankie into your ear until it feels like your maw is trying to push your eye out.

Lately my mother had started asking, "How is school going?" I always answered back with confidence, "Fine, no problems at all." Truth is, I didn't do well with school. I had difficulty with concentrating, and doing homework was a punishment on its own. Going to school every day I imagined was similar to spending time on Devil's Island. I enjoyed art class and recess. I never took to any of the men teachers, because they could see through the bullshit and crap you might come up with. The lady teachers might say something like, "Come and sit beside me dear, and we can go through this together." Also, they smelled better.

Larry Briscoe stopped coming to school one day. We thought he was expelled because he came to school with a picture of a naked black girl he got out of a National Geographic magazine. We all liked it even though it was a bit torn from being folded so many times. Maybe he was expelled because he wanked and his nose was always running.

Now, under the school system at Saint Louis De France, every month you had to take home your report card and have one of your parents sign it. The report card showed a ranking system. In my class we had 33 kids and I was usually ranked 32 or 33. My mother asked, "What does this number mean?" I told her that if I was ranked 33, I would be at the top of my class. My dad would add to that, "That's very good, go play." Often, if something went wrong in school and the teacher wrote about what you'd done in the report card, that made things very difficult when it was time to have the report card signed by your parents. This didn't create any problems for me because I became very good at signing the thing myself.

On Sundays we usually had chicken. That was also the only day of the week I saw my father unless I went to the upholstery shop. On weekdays he left for work before I was up and was still not home when I went to bed. Luckily he could walk to work, which wasn't far. But those long days did make him look very tired. My mother always believed in fresh chicken, not some bird that's been hanging in a store window. Maw always bought a live chicken at the market, and then went to the coal shed and wrung its neck. Dessert was always homemade apple pie, and absolutely the very best apple pie in the whole world. To this day, I have not had an apple pie that has ever come close to my maw's.

3694 DE BULLION ST.

Living in the kitchen

At 3694 De Bullion we had a big kitchen, and that was good because we pretty much lived in the kitchen all year round. Our kitchen had wall-to-wall linoleum. The original pattern was pretty much worn off in front of the stove and sink. On the wall near the stove was one of those tin boxes that held the big wooden matches. Next to it was a plaster head of a cook with a tiny hole in his mouth. A ball of string was in his head and the string hung out of his mouth. On the wall directly over the kitchen table was a large calendar of Jesus with his hands over his chest holding his heart, and his heart was on fire. This was printed on very shiny paper so you could wipe the kitchen grease off it when necessary. This was around the time when auto part dealers gave away calendars every year of sexy girls draped over car hoods or kissing a spark plug, all on this shiny paper. My dad got the Jesus calendar from Schlep the butcher. Schlep always gave us the salami ends to chew on when we dropped in. I liked Schlep.

My dad knew another butcher, a German guy from the old country. Around this time of year we always made sausages. The German guy always gave my dad a deal and would deliver to our house, upstairs into the kitchen, a whole pig. This dead pig, with its slit-open belly, was thrown on the kitchen table where I'd be having my breakfast. Also the open belly was always facing me. It ruined the taste for me of my chicory and hot milk coffee. Saturday my maw and paw would use this portable meat-grinder, with a handle you turned, bolted to the kitchen table. Then you attached this long condom about sixty feet long to the front of the grinding thing and filled the condom with sausage meat. I couldn't believe it, we were still making blood puddings late into the night when on the radio you heard, "And now Lux presents Hollywood" introduced by a guy named Cecil B. De Mille. Imagine calling your kid Cecil?

Those Radio Days, what a great time! TV wasn't around yet, so how could you miss it? It didn't exist. We had "The Shadow Knows," "Mr. Kean, Tracer of Lost Persons, "Fibber Magee and Molly," "The Fred Allen show" and lots and lots more. I never missed an episode of "Terry and The Pirates" or "The Green Hornet." Now, how could you not love "Superman?" Here was a guy who had this beautiful damsel tucked nicely under one arm, and with the other free arm he would swoop down and grab this crippled kid off an ice-flow that was inches away from going over the falls. I used to think, I'd love to be an action comic book hero. Just think, you hang around the house all day sitting in your tight fitting silk panty hose, your name in gold letters across your chest and your secret phone would ring, and off you'd go to save this gorgeous and really built woman with big kabungas on a roof top. Or how about, she's all tied up in a trailer she lives in and the whole works is about to blow because the fire is inches away from the propane tank? And what about the kittens inside?

In Montreal, we had what you would call the separate school system. Protestants and Catholics were educated separately. The same went for us. The English-speaking children and the French children were also educated separately. I think this just added to the hostility of each other.

Natalie was always popular on De Bullion St. How could you not remember Natalie? She was the girl with the big ones. Well, the word on De Bullion now was that Ziggy Schwartz was stupping Natalie. We all hated Schwartz now and figured Natalie was a tramp. Naturally we all felt this way because we weren't included in the good times. Of course Natalie and Schwartz were older than we were. So what? We still wanted to see under Natalie's blouse. When we were bored, we would phone a person at random and ask for Sammy. The person who answered would say, "You have the wrong number, there is no Sammy here." We would call again and again and always get the same answer, "There is no Sammy here, you have the wrong number." We figured by now the guy must be going crazy, then we'd have another one of us call back and say, "Hi, this is Sammy, any messages?"

Since the prostitutes moved in, things started to become more interesting on De Bullion St. Late one night, Nacum, Hymie (the putz) and I were playing on the street when one of the prostitutes came staggering home. It was very late and you could tell straight away she was drunk. Next thing that happened was her legs gave out and she fell, and started to fall asleep where she dropped on the sidewalk. Her legs were apart and she didn't have any underpants on. This was the very first time we three had ever seen a woman's parts. Luckily no one was around on the street and we could look as long as we wanted. The three of us got very warm in the crotch and it showed. We told Hymie (the putz) he should touch it. After a minute or two, he did, and that's when she started to pee. We all ran home. In the days that followed we talked of this exciting night again and again. Of course, the story got better each time.

Around this time Hymie's bubbe (grandmother) got sick. She was very old and had been confined to her bed for many years at this point. The doctor said she would only last two weeks. Because it was winter and the ground was still frozen, Hymie said we would have to keep bubbe alive till spring when the ground was softer. The doctor came back in two weeks and saw that she was still alive, said he would be back in another two weeks and gave Hymie's family the bill. Hymie's father said, "She will be much better off when she goes and so will we." The doctor came back and said he couldn't believe his eyes that the old woman was still alive, and gave Hymie's father another bill and mumbled, "I'll be back in two weeks." Hymie said his grandmother was definitely on her way out, because the Rabbi began to come every day. Hymie's father said, "Sure he comes, the food is free."

As bubbe got sicker, more and more people came to pay their respects and to see if grandma had anything worth taking. They came from far and near. The out-of-work actor, the meshuggene lawyer, his wife, the princess covered in jewelry made from glass and a face still wet from paint. Hymie said you should have seen her before she had her nose fixed. He also said that his grandma didn't recognize him or anybody anymore, she just lay there and said things in Yiddish like "Oy Vey," farting at the same time. Hymie's father said it was the medicine. Like a good grandmother she left this earth in the spring when the ground was soft. The relatives were called, they came bringing nothing and went right into the kitchen. The next day was the Sabbath, so everything was put on hold till Sunday. In the meantime everybody was drinking from the gallon bottles of Mogan David wine. Hymie said by the next day, you could see, they were all showing signs of pimples. At the funeral, the custom was to open the casket and throw dirt on the face. Hymie said he wouldn't do it or even look. The out-of-work actor was to say something appropriate to the deceased but couldn't remember his lines, so he talked about the rising cost of bagels. Many people came to pay their respects, including the doctor with his final bill payable in 30 days. Then they all went one more time to Hymie's house to eat.

Mr. Burghardt lived down the street from us with his three sons, Jacob, Peter and Hans (Hansey). Mr. Burghardt had a glass eye he would take out and put in a glass of water when he slept. He also worked very hard all night as a dishwasher at Murray's restaurant. Because of this he slept in the daytime. When we knew he was asleep, Hansey and I would roll ourselves some cigarettes with his makings. His favourite tins of tobacco were Sweet Caporal and Old Chum. Another thing we did was look into that hole where the glass eye was, with a flashlight. Soon after we got tired of that so we just smoked and talked about Natalie, the tramp.

Around the age of 10 or 11, girls started to look pretty important. Not just to me, but all the guys I hung around with. Guys like Schnutzer, Nacum (Noo-chem), Arthur (Aut-tuh), Cyril, Arty, Bernie, Moishe, all were now interested in girls. We were finished with touch football, scooters, comic books, unless it was Sheena of the Jungle. Hymie used to say, "Girls are no big deal," but Hymie (the putz) wanked more than anybody else. We were told if you wanked you'd stop growing and lightning would knock you down. Well Hymie didn't get hit with lightning, but he was a little fart. We noticed the girls in school were now wearing brassieres and using lipstick. Also, when they walked they sort of moved their asses from side to side more than they ever did before. Mind you, a lot of these girls were older than we were. Molly, from De Bullion St. was starting to sprout tits. I always wanted to play doctor with Molly. We used to talk about it a lot and she thought it was a good idea too, but we had nowhere to go and be alone. We boys in the clubhouse would talk about some books we heard about, books like "The Art to Making Love" and "How to Kiss a Girl in Different Places." We wondered if they meant, like in a car, or at the movies, or did they mean in different places? Arty took a few good books from his big brother's hiding place and brought them to the coal shed. Some had drawings to show where your thing goes and other parts. At the end of the meeting, Arty had to sneak the books back home, but said he'd bring them back again sometime.

The girls seem to be interested only in the older guys. I guess if a guy had a driver's licence, his dad's car, and if he was working and old enough to buy beer or wine, he probably looked a little better than a kid who had his own scooter made from a box. Hymie always said "Fuck 'em" to everything, and we said, "How?" When I think of all the nickels I spent on Molly, and all I got from her was, "So what's news which you?" Or, "Gee, thanks for the black cherry soda, I have to go home now." It was really tough being a kid, but as Hansey's big brother always said, "Hang in there kid." What the hell does that mean?

It was Schnutzer who always said, "You haven't lived until you've had it with a Japanese girl, because theirs, you know, is built sideways like their eyes." Some of the guys dated girls who already had jobs. How lucky can you get? Schnutzer always bragged, "Let me have just one night with a girl and she'll come back begging for more." I thought, What a lot of bullshit, Schnutzer, who's nose had been running for the three years I'd known him and wiped his nose on his arm sleeve. No girl was going to go for that.

The war with the Germans was still going on. Montreal welcomed its wartime hero, a pilot named George Beurling. He was young and a fighter pilot in Europe. Also, he had shot down 29 German and Italian planes at 20 years of age. Prime Minister Mackenzie King gave a speech about what a hero he was. In one day in his Spitfire he shot down four Fokkers. Those fokkers must have been lousy pilots. My dad used to tell me stuff all the time. Montreal sent thousands of soldiers to battle on the beaches of Dieppe, and many never came home again. After the war Buzz Beurling was restless and the only thing he knew was flying, so around 1948 he signed up to fly for the Israeli air force to fight Arab States. He took off from Rome in a small plane heading for the Middle East and crashed after take-off. During the war with Germany he crashed many times but this one killed him at 26 years of age.

In 1942 the French ridings in Montreal voted no to going overseas and fighting for the English, and said if we must go to war, we shall do it on Canadian soil only. Meanwhile in the rest of Canada, 80% voted yes, giving Mackenzie King a clear go-ahead to send young men to overseas duty. The zoot-suiters continued their usual havoc by not joining the service and aggravating the military. Police were kept busy with the riots and looking after the gambling and whore houses, which were still very profitable. Young women were volunteering with the Red Cross, others took home-nursing classes, and some knitted socks to send overseas. Many others learned to be air-raid wardens during blackouts. Others entertained young soldiers at dance parties. To look and be fashionable the girls would paint their legs and draw a thin line up the back to look like a seam. Boy Scouts called at thousands of homes and collected pots and pans to melt down for the making of tanks and guns. Bones were needed to make glue. Lead, toothpaste tubes, your Brylcream or Wildroot hair cream tubes were also needed. It was said that the empty tubes sent in helped build 845 engines for bombers. Anything made of rubber was particularly valuable.

One of the landmarks in Montreal is the 764-ft. Mt. Royal, the hill for which the city is named. Another is historic old Montreal (Vieux Montréal). Montreal is an island city surrounded by the St. Lawrence and the Ottawa rivers. It was originally a gathering place for Native American tribes. The Mt. Royal's public park to a 9-year-old was simply the mountain where we played. Schnutzer, Nacum, Arthur, Hymie, Cyril, Arty, Moshe and on some occasions, Natalie and Molly.

We had a natural vine hanging from a tree up there. Only a few of us knew where it was. We could swing way out over a ravine and back with this vine like Tarzan. Fortunately it never broke, we never even considered something like that. Of course, you could have broken your back or head and died on the spot. I was called "Toothpick" on the vine because I could swing further out than the others. The most fun was when the girls came, when it was their turn we would go down into the ravine a little way, and when the girls would swing out we could see their underwear. It was great. I think they knew we could see everything. I'll always remember, the knickers were made of that terry cloth material and usually pink. The winters on the mountain were best. We'd toboggan on a flattened cardboard box. Everything was fine up in the mountain, until the snow melted and a little girl's body was found. The newspaper said she was murdered. We were scared now and never went back that winter.

Montreal has always had the best of jazz, hockey too. The jazz was really for the grown-ups, but for me, even though I was only 9, it didn't matter. I loved jazz first, even before hockey. I was only 9, but I was hooked on the jazz magazine Down Beat. My favourites were Stan Kenton and Stan Getz, also Basie, Dorsey, Armstrong, Fitzgerald, Billie Holiday, Lionel Hampton and a whole bunch of others.

Born in a limestone house on Delisle St. in August 1925 was our very own Oscar Peterson. In the years that followed, Oscar studied with an accomplished classical pianist, a Hungarian named Paul De Marky who taught Oscar technique and fast fingers. He also convinced Oscar he had something special to give to the world. In high school (Montreal) Oscar played with Maynard Ferguson (another great). While still in his teens Oscar did performances on CBC radio for the show called The Happy Gang. Oscar always wanted to be a Jazz piano player, and as the people say today, "The rest is History."

City of churches

Montreal is and always was a city of churches. As a Catholic kid, I did not like church, and later as an older Catholic kid, I still did not like church, while attending my Saint Louis De France school, the catholic school over the catholic church. The nuns took us kids to many churches, but not by our choice. The very beautiful Notre-Dame Basilica has the most astonishing interior you have ever seen: stained glass, carvings, paintings, statues, the most magnificent organ, etc. The cost of all this was not a big problem, thanks to the poor people's money. Then there is the Marie-Reine-du-Monde, finished in 1894. This Roman Catholic cathedral was 1/3 the size replica of St. Peter's in Rome, down to an exact copy of Bernini's Baldacchino over the altar. Even at this 1/3 scale the church is overpowering and was extremely expensive to build. The Notre Dame de Bonsecours building dates from around 1771, and its facade dates from 1890 to 1998. The decor is simple but very elegant, with a nautical flair to older days as The Sailor's Church. From school, in large groups, we would go to the sailor's church with the Holy Sisters and gaze at the hanging lamps that all had the look of sailing ships. This chapel was always called The Sailor's Church because so many seamen came to worship here. This wonderful church was founded by Marguerite Boureoys, a nun and teacher who was made a saint in 1982. The original foundations go back to 1675. Historically, sailors saved at sea came here to pray and give thanks. If you should be lucky enough to get there, by all means, climb the tower as I did as a kid, for a great view of The Port, and the Old Town.

A must while in Montreal is a visit to Saint Joseph's Oratory. Here you'll learn about the history of Brother André, who it is said performed actual miracles. Frère André's real heart is well guarded in the oratory, and when I was up there (still a kid) I remember people praying in front of his heart. The heart was kept in a glass box with some kind of yellow liquid in the box to preserve it. After the short prayer the Catholic believers would kiss the glass. All that went through my head was, what about the germs? You can still visit the original chapel, the crypt, the basilica and the museum. Simply attend a few different masses and services and don't forget to put some money in the dish.

SaintJoseph's
Oratory of Mount-Royal

St. Joseph's Oratory is perched high on a hill of Mont Royal and is the largest church in the world dedicated to Joseph. You may also want to climb the more than 300 steps that lead up to the front of the church. The stairs in the centre were designed for the pilgrims, who would climb to the top on their knees and pause to pray on each step, often in the rain. The immense oratory was put up on the same site as a church from around 1916 in honour of St. Joseph, who is now a patron saint. Oratory St. Joseph is the second largest church in the world, after St. Peter's Basilica in Rome. Montreal certainly does have a lot of beautiful churches to see. I may not be a religious person now for some of the reasons I've previously mentioned, but religious or not, the architecture of a great building is worth seeing.

So, thanks to Brother André, Saint Joseph's Oratory of Mont Royal, we have this wonderful church devoted to Saint Joseph, the spouse of the Virgin Mary and the foster father of Jesus. Work on the Basilica was begun in 1924, but due to construction costs as well as a recession it took several years to finish. Unfortunately, due to Brother André's death, he never got to see the roof or the magnificent dome. Today believers from around the world attend celebrations of all kinds at the Basilica. The dome itself is the highest point in Montreal.

In later years as I got older, I would spend time in places like The Gaspé. As a painter, I would get my easel set up, out came the oils and folding stool and a stretched canvas. No matter where you set up, in front of the Gaspé rock, a farmer's field, a street, the French kids showed up with a thousand questions. But everyone was very well behaved and quite serious. The most often asked question was, "Why are you doing that?" After giving your best answer, you got back a,

"Why?" and answering that one got you another, "Why?" And that's how the day went. I would interrupt the kids with my own questions. "What do you want to be when you grow up?" The answers were always the same. First and most popular was, "A priest." "Why?" " Because they have a nice home, a new car, eat well and don't go to work." The second popular answer was always, "A policeman." "Why?" "Because he drives the police car home and his police clothes are free, also he's the boss."

Not one of the kids said, "I want to be a fisherman like my dad." I asked why. They were shy at first, but then they opened up with, "My dad has to get up very early and is gone from home for days, and in the winter too. His job is dirty and you work very hard when you're out in the ocean, and because you're fishing all the time you come home stinky. All fishermen are poor and some dads never come home again because they die. The dads who come back are paid very little for their hard work and are now asked to give some to the church every time they get paid."

So you see, some of these kids are pretty grown up after all. Can you blame them for wanting to be a priest, or policeman? Wait till they get a little older and smarter, they may want to be a politician.

Winter games on De Bullion St. were the best. Street hockey had to be the favourite. To every kid in Montreal there was only one team, the Montreal Canadiens, with greats like Maurice Richard, Jean Beliveau, Elmer Lach, Toe Blake, Boom Boom Geoffrion and many more. We had snow every day, and lots of it. The snowplow didn't get to De Bullion St. often, so our snow got higher and higher. If we got tired of hockey, we'd hang onto the bumpers of cars when they slowed down at the corner and hitch a ride (sliding on our shoes) for many blocks, then let go and do the same to get back. One day Moishele got the belt from his coat caught on the chrome bumperette and somehow got himself turned around and began sliding on his bum. Everything was fine until the car got to Pine Ave., where the road was clear of snow. Boy! What a lot of yelling went on with the friction on his ass. The driver could hear Moishele and people were pointing to the back of the car. The driver stopped, unhooked poor Moishele and started to lecture him with, "So Liss'n you little boychic asshole," and a lot of other nice Yiddish words. All the while Moishele just cried.

The Catholic nuns lived across the road from our house, and they had the biggest house on the street. As a bonus to this charming stone building, they too were the only ones for blocks around who had a huge front yard. The yard was more of a park to us kids, it had trees. Nobody else had trees. Now, the good news was that we were allowed to play in the yard. I remember one winter that could not have been better, with tons of snow. We built snow huts, all connected to each other with tunnels, and here and there an open fort, so we could throw snowballs at cars as they drove by. On occasions we used frozen horse dung to make the perfect snowball. Some drivers, obviously very angry, did stop, but with the help of the tunnels we'd be at the far end and free in a minute. Now at the far end was a high link fence (one of those Lundy fences). On the other side of the link fence was the lane to freedom. The escape tunnel led to the link fence, so we got the heavy-duty wire snips from somewhere and cut a big hole in the fence and continued the tunnel on the other side. Spring came, the snow melted and we were never allowed in the yard again.

Because the sidewalks on streets like De Bullion were never shoveled and the snow could be as high or higher than three feet, we kids took the opportunity to cut a big hole in it with an axe and shovel, fill it with water, cover the top with cardboard, add snow on top, then go hide and wait. This was one of our better pranks, and it worked each and every time.

Mr. Leonard was his name, he drove a delivery truck for a drug store and he lived on our street. Those were good times, when Mr. Leonard and his wife moved onto our street. He and his wife didn't have any kids. Many times if he saw us playing on the street, he'd invite us into the house and his wife made us hot chocolate. She was very nice and had big ones, she also gave us those store-bought cookies of chocolate covered marshmallow with the red jam in the middle. Mr. Leonard was always a happy guy, and he would often give his wife's ass a pinch or a feel. She'd be at the sink and he would rub himself against her and grab her tits. We would start to eat our cookies slower and just watch. The best occasion was when Mr. Leonard went over to the sink where she was bending over, and lifted her dress up. Mrs. Leonard didn't have any pants on and we saw it. Moishe, Nacum and I got a little warm and got hard. We three talked about this for a long time and always waited for Mr. Leonard to come home from work and maybe have hot chocolate and cookies again. It never happened, Mr. Leonard moved away and we never saw Mrs. Leonard again.

It was still winter and nearly Christmas. At school, our teacher (I think her name was Miss Sullivan) asked if I could stay after school for a few minutes and help string up some crepe paper, red and green for Christmas decorations. I held the old wooden ladder for her and she would twirl the paper and push thumbtacks in above the blackboard. I would look up her skirt when I knew it was safe to look, saw her panties and had an erection the whole time. Miss Sullivan must have known because she stayed up on that ladder a long time. Also when we were finished she smiled a lot and looked down at my pants and said things like, "My, you are a big boy."

When I look back now to those days when I was a kid, it sure was a nice time in my life, but I just wish I had known more and not been so frightened and shy. But I guess I was no different than any other kid. Maybe I had it better than some of the other kids. After all, how many kids are lucky enough to grow up on De Bullion St.?

Christmas was also Eaton's and the Santa Claus parade. Santa and his elves had their first parade in Montreal back in 1925, paid for by the Eaton's department store. It apparently cost Eaton's $100,000. Eaton's would also tell us that "Santa-grams" are coming to us from the North Pole and Santa would soon be at the Eaton's store. This wonderful tradition went on till 1950 or so. Every kid went downtown with his parents to see the mechanized Christmas window displays. But of course the big thing was the parade, which always took place in Toronto first and a week later in Montreal. In Montreal it was always cold, every kid had a muffler (scarf) around his neck and nose, plus mitts, a snowsuit, boots, etc. When they got all this stuff on, the kids couldn't move.

The parade would stretch itself out to a mile and a half, with floats, marching bands and about a thousand volunteers wearing the most colourful costumes you've ever seen. You could volunteer, but then you waited three years for your turn. Eaton's always picked up the tab for the entire production and had a year-round staff to create the parade. Thousands of people lined the parade route (including my dad and me) and another 30 million across North America would watch it on TV. With so much importance riding on this day, plus the money it cost, Eaton's took no chances. Santa being the most important guy, Eaton's figured if something should happen to Santa we'd better have a stand-by Santa, plus a doctor and a nurse. The humble beginning for all this started in Toronto. It traveled from Toronto's Union Station to the store, a short distance away. This was back in 1905.

In 1948 Eaton's introduced Punkinhead, the sad little bear who eventually gets to star in the Santa Parade. Punkinhead did well for years with storybooks, records and TV commercials. Each year Eaton's published a new Santa Parade Christmas book. Sadly in 1969, following the FLQ bombings, the Montreal parade came to an end and never returned. One of my wonderful memories, aside from all the parades I attended every year, was going with my maw to the downtown Eaton's store. I believe it was on the fourth floor where they had Toy City. At Toy City you got on a train that took you around the fourth floor and the ride would end at "The Land of Dreams," where the Christmas Fairy gave you a present. Yes! Thanks to Eaton's those wonderful memories remain to this day. Ironically, decades later I would start my art career working for Eaton's as an artist on the Eaton's catalogue.

Now, after 92 years, the catalogue is gone and the T. Eaton Company, which declared bankruptcy in 1997, is no more. It was sad to say good-bye to that wonderful, magical time: Santa, the Christmas Parade, Punkinhead, the Elves, the Eaton's Christmas Colouring Book, the Train ride on the fourth floor, the Eaton's windows, Eaton's Toyland, Santa calling out your name on the radio, and getting a letter from Santa. And last, and most important, the Toy Section in the Eaton's Christmas catalogue, which we kids would leave open so our parents couldn't miss it.

Lili, queen of the strippers

I'm not sure how old I was in Montreal when I discovered or heard about Lili St. Cyr, queen of the strippers (1918-1999). When the first European sailors docked there, they weren't overly excited by just earning a good living from the beaver pelts. They were introduced to the sexual practices of the hookers in Canada. The sexual activities and horizontal gyrations of some of the Montreal girls were different than back home, or so it seemed, or maybe because they were away from home. Montreal guaranteed its reputation as a sex capital before and after World War II, thanks to performers (strippers) such as Lili St. Cyr.

Lili worked at the Gayety theatre at 84 St. Catherine St. One of the city's by-laws at the time was that a performer could not come off the stage with less clothing than what she had on when she arrived on stage. So every evening Lili would go on stage fully naked, climb into a huge bathtub full of bubbles, and after the act leave the stage totally nude, the way she arrived. When Lili started at the Gayety I was 11 years old. The year was 1944 and that year was Lili St. Cyr's seven-year reign as Montreal's most famous stripper. As the musicians played their parts, Lili did her part better. She allowed her clothing to fall off slowly, revealing what was probably the most sensuous and voluptuous body the Gayety had ever witnessed. As the music became louder and reached its climax, Lili and her nakedness moved with a quickened frenzy and she would end the dance with a large key unlocking her chastity belt and hurling it backstage. The fans came from nearby and out of town, women too. They came for a good show and that's what

59

they got. Ventriloquists, comics, jugglers, etc., but they were all there to see Lili St. Cyr. I saw Lili do a number called "Jungle Goddess," where she made love to a large stuffed parrot. You're probably wondering how such a young lad got into the Gayety theatre. I will explain, but first a little backgrounder on Lili.

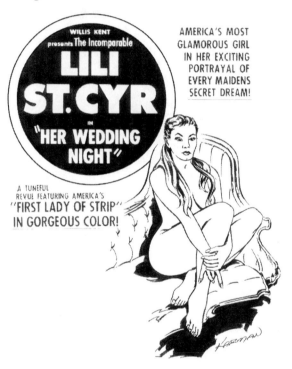

Lili St. Cyr danced in New York, Miami, Los Angeles, San Francisco, Vegas and many more places. But she seemed to love Montreal the most and said it was her favourite city. The French thought Lili St. Cyr was French and they came in the thousands to see her. She even wrote a book in French about the striptease, with the help of someone else. Lili went on to let the French think she was one of them, but in truth, she knew not one word of French. Lili St. Cyr was born Marie Klarquist in Minneapolis, of Swedish-Dutch parentage.

Lili loved the men and the men loved Lili. How could you not? She was five foot six and certainly looked a lot taller. She was 36-24-36 and built to please. But it was her seductive moves that made her a big star. It was the bathtub routine with the bubbly froth clinging to her naughty bits that got one aroused, especially one who was only 11. Naturally I never saw all her acts, but my very favourite was the "Jungle Goddess" skit with the parrot. The things she did with the parrot. I often wished I could be the parrot. Lili St. Cyr was the best ever, and justly so, right up there with Gypsy Rose Lee, Blaze Starr and Tempest Storm. Now there's a name for you, "Tempest Storm." That name alone should make you go and see the show.

Lili had many lovers and romances with the likes of Orson Welles, Victor Mature and well-off businessmen who looked after her very well with gifts of jewelry and furs.

She would meet hockey players like Boom Boom Geoffrion. At the El Morroco she met Jimmy Orlando, a hockey idol who became the love of her life but cheated on her with chorus girls, so Lili dumped him.

Lili knew boxers like Rocky Marciano, wrestlers and many gangsters. She often said, "I've broken hearts and emptied wallets, what's the use of being beautiful if you can't profit from it?"

Lili got a break in Hollywood after she was charged with indecent exposure for her bathtub act. When she beat the charge, the publicity got her a movie contract, all low-budget films like Son of Sinbad (1955) and Mobster (1958). She was also in a flick called The

Naked and The Dead (1958) where she had nothing to do with being dead. Her debut was at The Music Box, in an Ivan Fehnova production. The producer loved her looks, but the act was a flop, Fehnova didn't fire Lili but gave her a chance in a new act. At the end of her dance, a stagehand would pull on a fishing rod, which was attached to Lili's G-string, and the G-string would fly into the balcony as the lights would go dim. This wonderful, successful act was known as "The Flying G."

The first time I saw Lili St. Cyr, I got into the theatre through a side door (stage door) that hadn't been locked. Everything was quiet, nothing was going on at the time, no show, no comics, no knife throwers, nothing. I remember people were slowly starting to arrive and being seated. Customers would come early to get the better seats up front. I hid backstage amongst some props from another show. But I knew I had a great view of the stage from this spot. That was the very night that Lili did the "Jungle Goddess," the exotic number with the parrot. Another time I tried to get in and found all the doors were locked, but just as I was going to leave, a truck pulled up at the back to unload some stuff. I pretended my dad worked here at the Gayety and I helped unload some smaller boxes. When I saw my chance, I went and hid. Later, when the lights went out and one of the comics was on, I made it to the back where nobody went and hid in one of the seats.

I don't remember what Lili did that night, but it sure was good. I must admit, I was chased away many times, but I got lucky many times too.

It seems Lili St. Cyr got married at least six times. She also got married just for the thrill of getting married. Though she's not well known today, her name was in the news often, stories of her many husbands, brawls, and her attempted suicides. The cult movie The Rocky Horror Picture Show has a scene in which Janet Weiss (played by Susan Sarandon) is swimming in a pool, singing an ode to decadence. A line in the song goes: "God bless Lili St. Cyr!" It kind of goes unnoticed except for the true fans of the movie, who know every line.

But not everyone in Montreal was a fan of hers. A well-known priest, Father D'Anjou, did his best to run Lili out of town. Every time she danced, the Holy Father wrote things like, "The theatre is made to stink with the fowl odor of sex." Soon the public morality committee became involved and a week later Lili was arrested and charged for immoral acts, obscene and indecent. At the trial, the judge was irritated by the fact that the prosecution's most vocal witnesses had never seen Lili St. Cyr dance. On top of that, on the night of her arrest, some housewives had been to the show and had seen nothing morally wrong with her act. The judge found Lili not guilty on all charges. In the morning, one of the paper's headlines read, "Bravo Lili, this dancer is a national treasure. She stimulates the young and comforts the older man." The article was full of praise for Lili. It also warned the businessmen that if the puritans got their way, Montreal would cease as Canada's capital of nightlife, and millions of tourist dollars would be gone.

Lili's many years of working at the Gayety eventually came to an end, as she headed for Las Vegas. A new resort opened in the desert and vaudeville and burlesque were on the way out. In a few years the old Gayety was no more. Lili St. Cyr always wanted adventure and to be somewhat mysterious, and she succeeded. While still in her 20s she dated boxers and gamblers in Montreal. In Hollywood she was with Franchot Tone in his mansion. By the 1950s the adventures were winding down, and the great seductress was becoming extinct in Montreal and elsewhere. Lili started a lingerie business offering costumes for strippers and excitement for housewives. Her catalogues featured photos and drawings of her modeling articles for sale. Like so many in the sex business, she dropped into the drug and alcohol scene. In her last years she remained mysterious and alone by choice, tending her cats till she passed away in 1999.

Cleaning up the streets

In Montreal there was a long understanding between the police and the prostitutes, and also the gambling around town. The brothel-keepers saw to it that the police got their cut of the graft and the same went for the gamblers, but of course the politicians came first. In the whorehouses, if trouble started with a customer the police would be called in because on many occasions a prostitute would be treated too roughly. Just as soon as the call went out to the police radio, many of the cars would race over to the disturbance, knowing that by being first and breaking up the quarrel, there would be a big tip by the house madam—if not cash, you got a freebie from the girl of your choice.

The public, and mostly the church, began to ask daily, "Why isn't somebody cleaning up our streets?" The president of the Canadian citizenship association laid the blame on the police, but more so on the ones higher up. The higher ups (the officials) believed that prostitution was needed so depraved men wouldn't attack our own women on the streets of Montreal. So for a while the De Bullion St. houses stayed as they were. Around 1925 judge Louis Codere, after studying the prostitution problem, wanted certain people in office booted out or demoted. He insisted on names, which he made public and which added to how important it was to stop this activity in selling flesh so openly. By the 1940s, two decades after judge Codere had done so much, nothing had changed. Judge Codere pointed out how 10-year-old boys were hired to go down to the port with business cards and phone numbers to hand out to sailors who had just arrived. Codere was angry that children were getting an early education on the prostitute business. I for that matter, at age 11, thought everything was exciting.

The prostitutes would lean out of the windows and call out in French something while holding up two fingers to indicate $2. To a kid like me, it was the same as $200. There were three types of hookers: There were the low-budget types you would find around De Bullion St. Then you had the in-between type on the Main, which wanted a reference before you were welcome, even though they weren't fussy. Last came the top hooker, and she accepted only lawyers or politicians or policemen, anyone who would be good to know if something went wrong.

The bribes and the bordellos worked well together. In 1944 some of the houses started to close their doors, since the Canadian army weren't coming to the red light district like they used to. A great number of soldiers were coming down with syphilis and gonorrhea. The war effort was now in danger. The military said that if the civic officials didn't close the houses down, the entire city would be out of bounds to all in the military, army, navy and air force. The military had no quarrel with gambling. After four years of internment during the war, Camillien Houde was re-elected as mayor of Montreal in 1944. At a city council meeting, Councillor Stan Allen said that Montreal was known at that time as "the most lawless city in North America." Whenever the public outcry became too loud, the head man of the morality squad was fired and a new guy brought in.

In 10 years there were at least seven heads of morality fired for doing nothing, and that is exactly what they were hired for. After the last one was fired, an unknown lawyer named Pacifique Plante went to chief Dufresne and asked for the job and told Dufresne he could clean up Montreal. Plante told him he knew all the ins and outs of the gambling world, their bosses and their protectors. So if he were put in charge he'd see to it and change things immediately. Dufresne gave Plante the job, adding, "It's not going to be easy and will be very dangerous. Also if you run into any trouble, don't come back to me, you're on your own."

After a short time getting used to his new job, Plante was ready for his first raid, and this time there was no advance warning by a snitch. Plante and a group of policemen burst into the horse-betting house on Bleury St. and arrested all, including Mr. Big, the owner Julius Silverberg. Plante's picture began to appear in the newspapers and he soon became Montreal's hero and saviour.

Plante figured, to show he meant business, that he'd go after Harry Ship, who was one of the biggest gamblers in Montreal. Harry started in the business as a young lad and before he had reached the age of 30 he owned the White House Casino in Cote St. Lac. Other casinos soon followed. His best bookmaking enterprise was on St. Catherine St. And then he bought Chez Paree, the nightclub that headlined entertainers like Frank Sinatra, Dean Martin, Sammy Davis Jr. and many more. Harry Ship bet for big stakes, half a million a week was not an unusual thing. In September 1946 Plante and his squad broke down the door and arrested all inside, including Mr. Ship. In about four months' time, when the trial got under way, Plante was ready with 17,000 pages of depositions. Ship was ready too with four of the best lawyers headed by Joseph Cohen, who was known for winning acquittals with serious criminals.

When it was all over, Plante was the winner and Harry Ship got six months in the slammer.

Gambling was soon at a standstill, so Plante started to clean up prostitution. The war was over, the bawdy houses had opened again. There were too many for Plante to raid, but a start was made in any event. He began with the elegant bordello operated by Madam Eva Nadeau, who had many friends in high places and in the police department. It seemed risky for Plante to raid Eva's but he and his men did anyway. Plante arrested Eva and closed the place down. Eventually came lotteries, even bingo was on Plante's list. The church thought he was going a little too far with his importance. There were weekly bingos in Catholic churches, all making money and illegal. Through the papers, Plante announced he was declaring war on the church bingo, and before the week was over they were all closed.

Most Montrealers thought the little lawyer was going too far, but in less than a year Plante had done what the whole police force hadn't done in half a century. Not a single word of encouragement or a pat on the back came from city hall or the chief of police, though. It seemed the people in high places were pissed off at losing their graft. The underworld bosses offered him money to look the other way, but he turned them all down. Then he received threats and on one occasion was shot at. Plante's most determined adversary was a man called Albert Langlois, the new chief of police who didn't care for Plante's impulsive ways and detested all the publicity Plante was getting. Something took place in 1948 that gave Langlois an opportunity he'd been waiting for. It turned out that three policemen in the morality squad, in the process of trying to make a case against some prostitutes, had slept with them. Later the three policemen all said it was their idea and Plante knew nothing of this. But, with all the publicity that followed, Langlois found reason to suspend Plante, and two months later he was dumped from the police force.

Within a short two days, gambling nightclubs were re-opening and eight whorehouses were working overtime. Montreal was returning to its old self instantly, as if nothing had changed. After all his hard work, Plante wasn't about to go away and lie down. He didn't have a job but he decided to fight the civic establishment another way. Fortunately, when he left the police department he had accumulated a huge file dealing with vice in the city. The daily Le Devoir agreed to publish a series of articles using Plante's name. These were ghost-written by a young reporter who one day would become the ambassador to France. The paper headline was, "Montreal under the reign of the underworld." The first article was published in November 1949, and in the following three months another 62 appeared. One of the most damning was, "Here are the guilty parties."

The public now knew how the gambling casinos and whore houses worked in the 1940s. One of the articles was about how chief of police Albert Langlois did whatever he could to get rid of Plante, including stories that Plante was a womanizer—which proved to be completely false. Plante's list of the city's worst went into Le Devoir. These names included J.O. Asselin, chairman of the city's executive committee, and Chief Langlois and former Chief Dufresne were right there at the top of the list. Another long list of officers was accused of protecting dozens of criminals, and yet another of being under protection—owners of whorehouses and a bigger bunch of gambling bosses. The editors at Le Devoir were the object of libel suits. To look after this, the paper hired Jean Drapeau, still young but moving up quickly (he would one day go on to be mayor of Montreal). From the start the civic officials and police did everything possible to confuse and stop the inquiry.

Plante's petition was over 1,000 pages and contained the names of more than 15,000 charged against the city council and police department alone. In the next four years (on both sides) everything was done. Plante and Drapeau subpoenaed a long line of witnesses from the seamier side of the city, employees from the brothels and gambling-den employees. The court heard how the average prostitute could service eight to 10 clients on a day shift. One of the more interesting witnesses was a close friend of police chief Dufresne. Dr. Charles Bayard was owner of several houses on De Bullion St., which he rented to brothel keepers. He said prostitutes were good tenants, they kept the houses in good shape and occasionally made improvements. Dr. Bayard was not upset that the prostitutes in his houses had venereal diseases while at the same time he worked at the city of Montreal's health department as superintendent of the contagious disease branch.

The gambling bosses each had a turn to speak: Max Shapiro, Harry Ship, etc. Captain Arthur Tache, who earned around $3,000 a year, was asked if he could account for his lifestyle, which included a $3,000 car, a $2,990 diamond ring, another few items worth $3,500 and property valued at $10,000. Tache, who had been the head man of the morality squad for only nine months, told judge Caron he had been earning extra money helping people do house cleaning.

In April 1953, the hearings were over and judge Caron had the task of going through all this stuff over the next year and a half before he would air the city's dirty laundry. After 358 sessions, 374 witnesses and 50,000 documents, he was ready. Judge Caron started reading at 10:30 a.m. and finished four and a half hours later. He pointed out that the police department could have and should have suppressed gambling and prostitution, but decided to permit and protect it. Police director Albert Langlois was fired and fined $500. Former police director Fernand Dufresne and former assistant director Armand Brodeur were fined $7,000. Many other police officers were fined and others fired. When it came to mayor Houde's turn, the judge imposed no penalties but decided to leave it up to the voters. Camillien Houde later announced that he would not seek re-election, and so in October 1954 Jean Drapeau very easily became Mayor of Montreal.

Within days of Drapeau's election, The Herald reported that "questionable ladies" were leaving for New York. Drapeau's first order of business was to bring back Pax Plante to the police department, and within the year Plante became its director. The taxi drivers said the tourists used to come to Montreal and stay two weeks; now, with the sex trade almost at a stand still, they wouldn't come at all. With big-time gambling in limbo, the big spenders never showed up. One waiter said he'd often get a $50 tip in the old days; now the ladies bridge club would come in, order Shirley Temple drinks and at the end of an evening leave a dime.

Every big city needs a little wickedness to survive and remain interesting, but Drapeau and Plante were closing down everything. As Al Palmer, a columnist in The Herald said, "The old lady has lost her girlish laughter." He wrote, "Now it's Montreal the good." The church thought maybe it would be good if only a hand-full of brothels stayed open to protect the decent women from being harassed and molested. The church was and always has been against divorce, masturbation and birth control. To make your marriage work, the answer was for the wives to be respectful and obedient, stay sweet and have patience. Nothing was said for the male. Montreal in 1941 had a million people, of which 10,000 were priests and nuns.

I can remember my very early days at St. Louis De France school, where everything worked around the church. A lot of our schoolbooks told stories of saints, angels and miracles. Any books of adventure always included missionaries. I spent many hours in the church below the school before heading upstairs for the morning class. Parents and their children went to church together on Sundays and attended church functions as a family, picnics, bingo, etc. Some children would get up at 5 or 6 a.m. to attend early mass, all before going upstairs to class. Thanks to my mother, I only went when I had to. I did have to study my Catechism but I didn't use the rosary like some did. When Lent came along, we were supposed to do all kinds of extra stuff, but again I never did, even though Father Debeld said we might turn to stone—and forget about going to heaven. Women were told not to practice birth control or they'd fry in hell. In a Catholic hospital during a difficult childbirth, if only one life could be saved it was to be the baby.

The Catholic church needed more young souls to baptize. The depression was still a memory and that was very apparent among the poor. The church was far from being poor but needed still more donations in the Sunday plate. My dad had it tough like many others, but rather than sit around saying "poor me" every other day, he taught himself how to speak Yiddish. In the area where we lived, Yiddish was widespread, and he had the accent down perfectly. In the earlier years when he was still a house painter (before the upholstery shop) I would go with him into a hardware store to buy paint. My dad would speak Yiddish and we would get everything wholesale. Another gift he had was, no matter where we might be, if someone was talking with a hint of an accent, he immediately would whisper to me, "He's a Jew from Poland" or "He's a Dutchman" or "He's trying to be an Austrian, but he's a German." He was very good at it and of course at many other things (all self taught). Not bad for a guy who only got as far as grade three. I told you he was a genius. Another time my dad said, "That man's a survivor of the holocaust." I said, "What's a hollow cast?" He said, "Go Play."

Living at 3694 De Bullion sparked the best memories for a kid. As I said before, my maw made the best apple pie in the world. Sundays could be goulash, chicken paprikas, schmorra, schetcka knadel (my favourite), palichenda for dessert, or seven-layer cake, or rum cake (when you put your fork into it, real rum ran out). Maw had hundreds of recipes in her head and not one recipe on paper. I could go on and on about just the food in the house, but then this would turn into a cookbook.

Speaking of food, I'm reminded about an old Jewish joke. There is a Jew eating in a restaurant, his table heaped with food of every description. Outside, a poor Jew watches him eat through the window and finally forces himself to go in. "I haven't eaten for days," he pleads. The Jew turns to him and says, "Force yourself." When I was growing up entertainment was the radio; television wasn't even talked about yet. This was the 1940s, and we had Jack Benny, Edgar Bergen & Charlie McCarthy, Henry Aldrich, The Inner Sanctum, Flash Gordon (every kid's favourite), The Green Shadow, Superman and a bunch more. We had Bulldog Drummond and Saturday-night hockey if the Canadiens were playing. There were plays on the radio with actors like Lorne Green and Christopher Plummer. By the 1950s, when we were living in Toronto, television had come along, but everything was still in black and white. We had shows with Milton Berle, Red Skelton and many more but what I missed was what radio gave me: you had to use your imagination and listen. Somehow in your head you saw a lot more.

De Bullion St. is still there in Montreal, but it certainly has changed. Gone are the noises as I used to call them, and I sure do miss them. The noises were the different accents of the ethnic people. Along with that were the smells from the cooking of European dinners. I miss the condensed different languages all within one block. I miss my mother's old brass-barreled washing machine with the two hard rubber rollers on top for wringing out the water. The drunks and prostitutes are gone. Even the mice have left.

I'll get the lights

To De Bullion Street

The move to Toronto

I'll never forget those last days in Montreal, when I got to be 14 and my dad said, "We're leaving De Bullion St. and we're moving to Toronto. Wow! That was like telling me I'll never be 15. Everything flashed through my head in a instant: I'd never see Natalie's tits, the street I knew so well, my friends, the clubhouse, my street education, my comic book business that took years to build up. All I could think of was that the sky was falling. I was into comic books in a big way. I started collecting them when they were only in black and white. My action heroes were guys like Captain Marvel, who through the day was a crippled boy. Batman was alone at the beginning and Robin came much later. There were so many, and all were a dime. Then, "Holey Moley," "Great Willakers," colour comics were born. Batman and Robin, Superman, Tarzan, The Torch, Submariner, Sheena of the Jungle, Mutt and Jeff, Li'l Abner and on and on. Yes! I had them all, and in crisp condition.

For my comic book business I would lend out four comics and in return be paid back one comic I didn't have. The only rules were that no one was allowed to read the comics while eating or to turn (fold) the covers back. When all the super heroes went into colour, I had them all starting with number one (the first issue). Of course I had all the black and white comics before that, comics like Bulletman and Bulletgirl with their trusty dog Bulletdog. The problem here was how to move all the comics to Toronto from De Bullion St. All the family possessions were going to be moved in my dad's 1938 maroon Pontiac. This would take many trips. My sister and her husband Steve were already living in Toronto. I had well over 1,000 comic books, all in mint condition. The problem was that there was no room for comic books in the Pontiac. Now we all knew the Pontiac was going to die soon, and often it did just that: it was old and the tires were terrible. You couldn't buy tires because of the war and so on. The tires looked smooth like the tubes, except the tubes were covered in those little red-hot volcanized patches. One couldn't buy tubes then and what my dad had were so bad that he just threw two of them away and soaked many potato sacks in water, then somehow hammered them tight into the tire. It sort of worked, but the tires got very hot and we had to stop a lot. The comics had to stay in Montreal, one thousand and something of them.

Later on highway No. 2, on one of the many long drives moving furniture from Montreal to Toronto in the 1938 Pontiac, the rear differential universal joint blew apart. Now the rear seating area of the car held some of the dresser drawers with family clothing. What happened next in simple terms was that the drive shaft, with parts still attached, going around and around faster than a speeding bullet, came through the car and into the drawers until everything was splintered wood and rags. Now I figured this could have caused two very different disasters. First, what if people had been sitting back there? Second, and I shudder to think, what if we had brought my comic books with us? In time I forgot about all my action heroes and discovered girls. My dad was having a rough time about now, money had been scarce in Montreal and the dream now I guess was Toronto.

A lot of years had passed since the comic book caper, when, not too long ago, I heard about an auction in New York that included comic books. The number one Batman and Robin comic in colour (which I of course had in mint condition) sold at auction for $65,000 American dollars. In February 2009 The Globe and Mail ran an article about an upcoming auction of the first Superman comic going up for sale. The experts figured this June 1938 Holy Grail of comics should go for around $126,000. It sold at auction for $400,000. I remember it well. I had this Acton Comic. The cover had Superman lifting a wrecked car from an accident scene. Now imagine, I at one time had more than 1,000 of the super hero comics. All I can think of now is, "Sometimes shit happens."

Now I'm older, but I do fondly remember my Montreal days and very often find myself reminiscing about things like my first bicycle (used), a C.C.M. One bit of custom work involved adding an empty cardboard cigarette pack to the spokes. With the help of a clothespin you attached the cardboard to the front forks of the bicycle, which gave you a loud "brap" sound. On one particular day it was raining hard and I was fascinated by the water shooting out at the top of the front fender. I had my head down, and the faster I pedaled the more water shot out from under the fender. That's when I ran into a parked car, went over the handlebars and took two pieces out of my two front teeth on the car trunk. The schmuck (owner) was sitting in the car when it happened, and he was out like a shot with, "Oy Vey, you fershtinkena meshuggene putz, look what you did to my beautiful car!" Mrs. Resnick (I think she was Ukrainian) was sitting on her porch when this happened, and bless her, she jumped up and saved my life with a sentence that started with, "Liss'n dollink tuchus face, you leave the little boy alone or Mr. Katz from next door and mineself are going to give you such a kick in the petzel, you won't know from up." I never knew Mrs. Resnick had such chutzpah. The shmuck drove off and I picked up my bicycle. I thanked Mrs. Resnick and asked if I could do something for her. She said, "Liss'n dollink, the next time you see me shlepping groceries like you usually do, you could help shlepp.

Boy, was I going to miss the street: Mr. Katz, Mr. (one eye) Burghardt, Sugarman at the corner store where we got cigarettes, Ginsberg's horse who had his own hat, Feldman, Bernie Segal, Maxie Waxman (another tuchus) and, of course, all my best friends that I grew up with—Moshe, Nacum (noo-chem), Arthur (aut-tuh), Schnutzer, Cyril the Italian, Ignacz, Hymie (the putz), Nathan, Arty and, most important, the girls, including Esther, Rachel, Natalie (with the big ones) and Molly. Everyone taught me something different. Yes! It was going to be tough to leave all this, and to leave winter hockey (we used frozen horse droppings for a puck, and when the horse first dropped his dung all steaming, the birds were there first for their warm breakfast).

There was so much to remember, that, for many years, new memories were added to the old ones. All this I owe to one street called De Bullion St.: my dad and his quart bottles of Black Horse Ale, chewing gum with hockey cards, bootleg whiskey, the strap at school. I remember silly stuff like, when flushing the toilet we had to use water that was kept in a varnished box mounted high on the wall near the ceiling, and you pulled a chain to flush. Montreal's slushy streets, chiens chauds (hot dogs) or Le Roi des Frites (French fries) and Montreal's rye bread (it's said that it's the water that makes it best). Life was salami, pickled herring, strudel, a corned beef sandwich with a dill pickle, my maw's coffee made with chicory and hot milk. There was watermelon, pickled eggs, smoked meat on rye bread, the Indian motorcycle that took us all to Crystal beach. I really miss the Italians, the Jews, the Yugoslavs, the Ukrainians. I miss Schnutzer, who wanted to be a big-shot lawyer, but how could he with a name like Schnutzer and still wiping his nose on his arm? I miss seeing Lili St. Cyr do her act with the swan and the better act with the parrot, and here I'm leaving De Bullion St. At age 14, still a virgin.

There was a time before De Bullion St., earlier in Montreal, when we lived on Hutchison St. My dad was superintendent (janitor) of an apartment building. The building occupied a lot of Jewish people. A typical orthodox house never switched on a light or turned on the kitchen stove on the Sabbath. Obviously a guy who took Talmud classes and was a good orthodox Jew would also never date a shiksa, eat pork and drink non-kosher booze. So on religious days I was asked to come upstairs to their apartments and turn off the stove, or at other times turn on the stove. In payment for this I got bagels, and boy, did I get bagels. The only thing wrong was that these bagels tasted like they were made in the '20s and had become completely fossilized. In the lane behind the building of Hutchison St. one time I found a real gun in the garbage can. It was shiny with a round barrel that had six holes in it for six bullets, also it was heavy and it was mine. I played with my gun until, a few days later, my dad said something like, "Hey! What have you got there?" Like all kids, I said "Nothing." He said, "Let me see that" and next thing I knew the police were there and took my gun away. Then, of all stupid things to do, my maw made them tea. I remember saying to my maw, "Let's give them some of my bagels for their tea." Maw said, "NO." After tea, I showed them the lane where I found my gun and they left. I was a bit upset with the whole thing, so my dad gave me a quarter.

I bought a shiny tin peashooter with the money and went roller-skating. It wasn't a nice day on Hutchison because of the rain, and I had my shiny tin peashooter in my mouth, doing about 160 miles an hour on my roller skates when I crashed into a parked dump truck. The peashooter became stuck into the back of my mouth and bent forever. I pulled it out and the blood came gushing out like a fire hose. I rammed my hankie into my mouth and ran the two blocks home with the roller skates on, including down the stairs of our building and into our apartment. All janitors live downstairs, even if there is no downstairs. That's the rule. My mother didn't understand a word because of the handkerchief. She yanked out the hankie and more blood came out. I didn't know I had 10 gallons of blood in me. Maw put a new hankie in my mouth and I went to bed for four years.

De Bullion St. was almost history for me by the time we finished the move to Toronto. Pretty much all the furniture was already there and we were on the last trip in the Pontiac. My dad did one more walk around the car checking ropes and kicking the rear tires with the potato sacks in them. Getting behind the wheel in front of 3694 De Bullion, he said, "Make yourselves comfortable, It's going to be a day's ride from De Bullion."

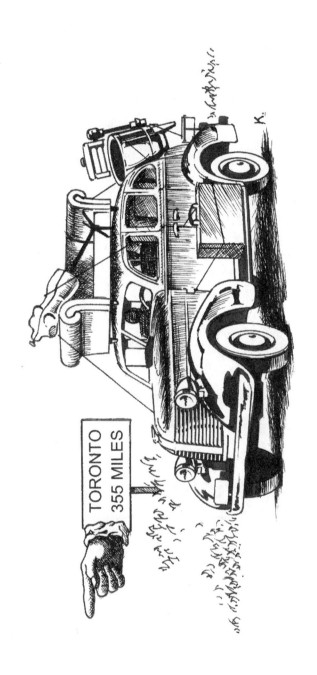

Part Two: The Art Studio

Super heroes

When I was a kid, growing up in Montreal, I remember sitting at the kitchen table for hours drawing and tracing all kinds of stuff. Mostly, the comic book heroes were my favourite; Batman, Captain Marvel, Bulletman, Bulletgirl—and of course where would we be without Bulletdog. The Bullet family had this U-shaped thing made of chrome that you held in one hand, with which you could catch and send bullets right back to the gangsters and crooks. Also, Sheena of the jungle was a favourite and fun to draw. When you drew Sheena, your mind would begin to wander, and on occasions you'd have to sit at the table until you calmed down. Other comic greats were Superman, Wonder Woman, The Torch, The Mariner and many more. During my early days of collecting, in the 1930s and '40s, a great many comics were still in black and white. Then colour became the only way to go, and as a plus they were a treat to copy. I hit the age of 14, then living in Toronto, and never bought another comic book ever again, because now girls started to look pretty interesting and voluptuous. A whole new world was about to open up for me, and I was ready.

My mum and dad and I had now moved in with my sister and her husband Steve, in their house in Thornhill Ont., on a street called Jackes Ave. The dirt street ran from Yonge St. to Bathurst St., with only seven houses perched on Jackes Ave. from one end to the other. Of course, we knew everybody in those houses. The only big inconvenience was that there were no conveniences, such as water or hydro, just a lot of mud. Some of our neighbours still lived in tarpaper shacks. As it turned out, over the next few days I started to get my sex education right there on that forgotten street. Directly across the road from us in a smallish tar paper shack lived the Fricker family: Daryl & Marie Fricker. Marie was an attractive woman, and each morning, Marie, at almost the same time, would open the front door, and without a thing on, would fling out a basin of dirty water. Occasionally she'd stand there for a moment, smell the fresh air, stretch and give herself a scratch or two. Not wanting to miss the show, I made a point of being up early every morning. My mother, now thinking I must really love school, wondered how come no one in the house had to get me ready for school anymore.

Another family on our side of the street was the Crocker bunch--and what a bunch that was. There was maw Crocker and sons Roy, Billy and young Mark. Across the road from them lived an older couple, Mr. & Mrs. Rodney Bekins, an odd couple who pretty much stayed to themselves and didn't talk to anyone, except that Rodney Bekins would go and live with maw Crocker from time to time. This went on until the police came and arrested old Rodney for stealing tires from the company that employed him. Now maw Crocker was sleeping alone, until, as my friend Billy told me, his older brother Roy began sharing the bed with his maw--because, he said, it was warmer that way.

These were our immediate neighbours, after that the view was nothing but fields. Occasionally on a Saturday night, Marie Fricker and her husband Daryl would invite me to go with them to the twin screen Dufferin Drive-in movie. The first flick of the evening would always start at dusk. The place would be jammed with cars early, people had to get themselves organized first with sandwiches, popcorn, beer, get the kids into their pyjamas and whatever else grown-ups do. We'd pile into the 1928 Model A Ford with Daryl driving. Beside him would be their two kids, I would get into the back seat with Marie and Roy Crocker. Once at the Drive-in and after the movie had been in progress for about 15 minutes, Roy had Marie's panties off and somehow got his cock in her. She'd be in the middle, sitting sideways with Roy behind her. This, of course, would arouse me, but being a kid I couldn't do anything about it but sit still and watch the movie. To this day, I don't know if Mr. Fricker knew what was going on or just didn't care. Also, I never did tell my parents about this, for fear they might never let me go with them again. I always figured Daryl must know what his wife was up to, because the back seat was always mucky and sticky on that side. I know now why Marie asked me along. That's so their two kids would sit up front with their dad. I found going to the drive-in was pretty exciting and went along every time I was asked.

The Hadley Girls

I was now going to Thornhill Public School and made new friends. My very best friends were Jack Forsyth and Jimmy Adams. We three hung around a lot and did most things together. Jimmy was an epileptic, so Jack and I did the best we could to look after him. Also, we three were in the same classroom. We were still 14 and virgins, until we heard about The Hadley Girls. It seems that almost every village, town or other small place has a girl or two who is mentioned in school as being easy or words to that effect. Well, we boys knew where Sharon and Sue Hadley lived, so as soon as it got dark, we'd bicycle back and forth in front of the house in hopes that one of the girls might come out. We obviously couldn't phone, we were only 14.

I don't know about Jack or Jimmy, but on one evening I was alone with my new Raleigh 3-speed English bicycle with the built-in headlight and generator, when quite by accident, the two girls were outside. We talked for a while, and the three of us decided to walk down the road to a field that didn't have any lights, and was out of view of houses around. Sharon, who was 17 and three years older than I was, walked out into the field first, while Sue, the younger sister, would watch my bicycle. I must admit, this being my first time, that it wasn't easy. When we were finished, Sharon stayed with my bicycle and Sue, who I'm sure had more experience than her older sister, headed for the field. Sue and I stayed longer. I had some trouble at first (being my first time) but Sue just sat on me and jumped up and down. My penis was red and sore for days. I was a little worried at the time, but as it healed, I felt good about myself. Imagine, 14 and two girls. The following morning my mother asked about the grass stains on the knees of my pants. For a minute or two, I didn't have an answer, but then I blurted out, "My bicycle chain broke last night out in a field."

At school, about two months later, it happened. Two men in suits knocked on the classroom door. Our teacher, Miss Hagarty, went out into the hall to talk to them. We could see them through the clear glass on the top half of the door. Whatever was going on out there, it sure looked serious, with Miss Hagarty's head nodding up and down constantly, and nobody smiling. Then Miss Hagarty came back in and said "Jack Forsyth, you're wanted outside in the hall." After a short time, Jack came back in, all pale looking, and said, "Jimmy, you're wanted outside." When Jimmy came back, he too was very upset and pale. After talking to Jack and Jimmy, the two men left. At recess we three got together immediately. Sue Hadley was pregnant. Sue Hadley had blabbed about everything and was also around our age. The men in suits said that when the baby is born, there would be blood tests done and then we shall know who is responsible for this atrocious and unspeakable thing.

A few days later, it was raining and Jack's father gave me a ride home in the farm truck. On the way, he said, "I know what you boys have done." and then he asked, "does your father know?" I answered, "No sir." I was worried now, because when my mother hears this, she is going to kill me. It was decided now that we three have to run away. I had a few dollars from working Saturdays at the Dominion grocery store and I still had my paper route, plus a bicycle to sell. Jack and Jimmy had a little saved up from working on the farm. The plan was to jump on a freight train and leave town. We decided to jump the train late at night while the parents are asleep, take whatever food we could carry from the kitchen, and leave a note saying we're off to see Europe and will write later. Love to everybody, dog too.

In the weeks that followed, we heard that Sue and Sharon's mother, Mrs. Hadley, had turned in Mr. Hadley because he had been having sex with the two girls for years. Also, it was Mr. Hadley who had impregnated Sue. The police removed Mr. Hadley from the house and we were in the clear, until Jack's father noticed this round ring shape on the leather of Jack's wallet, made there from carrying a condom. Until then we all carried one, but now it was time to throw them away. We'd had them for a long time and they were getting pretty old anyway.

For some unknown and wonderful reason, my name was never mentioned by the Hadley girls or Jack Forsyth's father. My parents never did find out, and my maw never killed me. The unfortunate thing about all this was that, finally, I had sex with a girl and now because of the recent mess with the sisters, I decided never to have sex with another girl again. I was too frightened. But maybe later I would.

I think it was about a month later that a girl named Jay moved to Thornhill. She had a great figure and knew how to tease by showing off her tits a little bit at a time. We would chase her around this little forest, pull off her halter, and chase her again, all laughing and giggling while her tits were jumping up and down. What a wonderful day we all had, and we would repeat this day many times over. This would always take place at the swimming hole in Thornhill, an out-of-the way spot that nobody ever visited. It was there that Jay would swim with us, all of us naked. (When I say us, it was always the same four guys.) All she asked in return was, no touching. That was fine with us, because we didn't want any trouble like we had with the Hadley girls and it was terrific just to watch. After the swim, Jay always invited me over to her house for a while. Her parents both worked so we were alone. Jay would tell me stuff about her past that would get me aroused, and other stuff about why they moved here. Jay got pregnant and had to leave school and then she had an abortion and it was best to move because everyone knew what had happened. She told me she still liked boys, but had to be really careful so nothing like that would ever happen again. I told her a little of my past with the Hadley girls and that's why I too didn't want anything to go wrong. So now, we just played doctor under the kitchen table—for a couple of hours or until it was time for me to go home

Brigden's

Then I hit the magic age of 17 and it was time to go to work. After a go at construction and—thanks to my dad, who at the time was painting a house for an art director named Bill Linden at Brigden's Ltd.—I got an interview with Mr. Bill Linden.

Now Brigden's was a very large company that did everything creative, and it was a great place for a kid who knew absolutely nothing to get his start. I was hired in the art department to work in the Eaton's catalogue section. I was going to be a RETOUCHER (whatever the hell that was, I thought at the time).

For at least the first year and a half I was not given a desk; instead I was given chores. I emptied water bowls for the other artists, delivered artwork to Eaton's in the annex building, and took on many other menial jobs. I was 17 and the education was coming very fast. On the many deliveries to Eaton's I always took the same route and passed the same stores daily on York St. One of the shops I passed never had anything of importance in the window but there were always one or two women sitting outside on stools or boxes, who said hello as I passed.

On one memorable occasion, they stopped me and wanted me to come inside and see "the black pussy." Well, there was a cat in the empty window, so I said "I can see the black pussy from here." Then the lumpier woman of the two said, "No, the other pussy is inside, but it will cost you a quarter." I told her, "Thank you but I only have 18 cents, and I have to deliver this Eaton's catalogue page to the annex building, so maybe another time when I'm not so rushed."

Of course, later on, my bigger mistake was telling the engravers at Brigden's what had happened'

The catalogue department had many employees. One in particular, John McGall, already an accomplished shoe artist, and I became good friends. Sadly, John didn't have any fingers on one hand. Also, he had fallen out of a tree when he was a child. It was said that the shock one goes through during such a trauma, from between the distance of leaving the tree and before hitting the ground, can do strange things to a person. Because of this, John lost all his hair and it never grew back.

Like most lads, John loved girls, but it did give him trouble dating. All was not lost though, as he did have a group of loyal friends at his favourite hangout, the Orchard Park Tavern. I met some of these friends of his, guys who were still carrying coal bags up flights of stairs into houses for a living. There was usually at least one of his buddies who seemed to have a drunken girlfriend in the car out back in the parking lot of the tavern. Now, if you were willing to buy a round of beer for the table, you could go out to the car and have a go. I was curious one evening, went out to have a look, said no, but not to hurt anyone's feelings, did come back, pretended, and bought a round. John was an important guy here with this lot. He had a brand new 1956 Mercury hardtop, bright red with a black roof, and also a new BSA motorcycle. This helped make him popular with the girls. Aside from being talented with his work and making reasonable money, his personality did help get him a girl or two. If John did have a flaw, it was his drinking. He also lived with his mum, a lovely Irish woman who did her best to look after her only son. When John drank too much, two of us would drive him home, carry him up the front stairs and push the buzzer. Mrs McGall would say, "Would you please hold onto Johnny while I first put newspapers down from here to his bedroom? Then you can carry him in. After that we'll have biscuits and tea."

At Brigden's we had two older women, both artists, who were

always on time and worked diligently. Both did detail on corsets and other garments. Back in these days everything was done by hand and one artist would start with the pencil drawing, then another would put the colour wash in. Another would just put in the faces and hands and finally the senior girls would put in the missing detail. This is where Miss Darrell and Miss Fitzy (both spinsters) would come in and do the finishing touches. At home John McGall, the fellow I mentioned earlier, had made the perfect penis in clay and put it in the top drawer of Miss Darrell's side table. Later that afternoon, we heard a scream from her cubicle, but nothing was said and we never heard a thing after that—and for that matter, we never saw the penis again. Someone said she took it home.

Even though Miss Darrell and Fitzy had never been married, they did come across as very worldly. Eventually I was given a desk in one of the cubicles, and Fitzy had moved in with me in the same cubicle. I had my dad's car one Christmas, and after work I offered Fitzy a ride home, which was on my way. When we got to her house on Fairlawn Ave. she said, "Why not come in and have a holiday drink with me." "Okay," I said.

Fitzy had obviously never mixed a drink in her entire life. In two large glasses, one with a decal of Pinocchio on it and the other Jiminy Cricket, she proceeded to fill them within an inch of the top with Seagram's rye whisky, and then added a quarter inch of ginger ale. It didn't take long for Fitzy to nod off, and I went looking for the front door. I already knew Fitzy had an artificial leg, and one day back at work she said that she was having a bit of trouble and would have to go to the doctor's soon. That day arrived, and off she went. She was back in a couple of hours, and I asked, "How did everything go?" "Fine," she said. "Would you like to see the new one?" I thought she'd lift her dress and I'd have a look at the new one. Instead she said, "I'll go and get it." "Okay," I said. She came back with a little blue box and said, "You sure this won't bother you if you have a look." I said, "No, I'm fine," having no idea what to expect. Fitzy opened the little blue box and there looking at me from the box was a perfect glass eye.

There were so many different personalities at Brigden's, and each is worth mentioning. One such individual was Gord (I can't remember the last name), a lettering man who at different times gave me a ride home. Gord was a married man and practiced the art of washing condoms at home over and over again. He would dry them on a little rubber clothesline in the kitchen, powder them with baby powder, and roll them up so they would be ready when needed. It must have worked, because he and his wife didn't have any children.

Stan Brown, besides being a little man and an art director for Eaton's, was also known as the perfect asshole. We worked on the entire Eaton's catalogue and every page required something in the way of corrections. The little fart was never happy with anything, and made it perfectly clear on every visit. On one occasion we had trouble with such a page. It was a full page of colour swatches of leatherette material. Photographs had been taken of the leatherette and we artists, using bleaches and dyes, would colour the photographs. Then each colour swatch was cut to a size of approximately one by two inches, and pasted on a mock-up page. Well, Mr. Brown did not think the Indigo swatch matched the material. We did it again and again and again. Finally, Ed Nicholls, our boss, carefully cut a piece of the real indigo material and stuck it down. Stan Brown, who was God at Eaton's, grew vivid and hollered things like, "You people are incompetent, you can't match colours worth a God damn. Next time I will use another bloody studio and never put up with this bullshit again.

Without saying a word, Ed Nicholls lifted the real piece of material off the board with his fingernail and handed it to Stan Brown. Mr. Brown said nothing but moved on to another page, which happened to be hardware. He now asked for a marking pencil, to make notes as to what he felt needed fixing. He also asked for a Pepsi Cola. Someone on staff handed him a marker and a Coke. Without turning around, he hollered, "I said Pepsi," and threw the marker over his shoulder adding, "I want a fucking pencil."

What a shame good people have to put up with little shits like this to earn a living. Unfortunately Eaton's was our only client. I think that's why when I got older and went into freelancing, I made sure I had many clients and not just one.

Brigden's had a driver called Spiegelman, who said he knew a guy we could buy suede jackets from for $12 each. Fifteen of us from work piled into the Brigden's truck and drove to Spadina and Adelaide, Toronto's garment district. When we got there, Spiegelman pulled into the lane behind a men's wear store, parked beside a big iron fire door at the back and explained the rules of shopping. Once inside, we had 10 minutes to pick a jacket and be out again. One more very important thing was that we were not to make a sound. Spiegelman knocked on the iron door and we were in. Spiegelman drove us back to work after this and 15 of us jumped out of the truck, all wearing the same new suede jacket but in different colours.

I learned a lot at Brigden's, it was here that young Larry, an apprentice, sitting in his chair beside me, threw his legs up in the air, lit a match, put it to his rear end and farted, launching a big swooshing flame. Larry excelled in this but not much of anything else. I drove a black 1950 Prefect (English) four-door car at around that time. It was grossly underpowered. With luck, if the wind were behind you, you could get up to 50 miles an hour in about 25 seconds. The Prefect had those very English turning signal indicators, on either side of the car between the door pillars (internally lit yellow plastic semaphores that would spring out letting the car behind know your intentions). In the back seat, on either side near the roof, it had cloth handgrips, the same as the older cars had in the 1930s. I believe back then they were called "ankle holders."

The 1950 Prefect

The one most serious thing about the Prefect was the brakes. They were controlled with cable rods (not hydraulic). In the winter, when they froze up, you'd have to get under the car with a candle and start thawing the damn things. A big hammer was essential for the ice. My dad bought this car so I could drive my mother and me to work in the garment industry area. First on the way we always picked up Ruth, a lovely girl a bit older than me who still lived with her mother, and who also worked at Brigden's. My mother sat in front, Ruth sat in the back. Maw got out first, and with Ruth sitting behind me, both of us alone, she used to put her tongue in my ear till we got close to work. I loved working at Brigden's, this was far better than the construction business. In construction there was just my dad and me and the cold winters.

Every year when the Eaton's catalogue season was over, the boss, Tommy Howard, would throw a stag party at his cottage. While we were at the cottage, north of Coboconk, Ont., we always ended up at the local Coboconk dance, which was in a big wood-frame building that was hard to miss, painted white and standing in the middle of a field,. And a great place it was. It was the kind of dance hall where the girls all sat in a row on one side and the boys on the other. Well, after a lot of heavy guitar music by the local lads and throwing back a couple of beers, I saw her. She was licking the back of her hands and wiping them on her cheeks, something a cat would do, I thought it was odd, but she did have stunning breasts. They were the kind you'd like to put your head in, and stay there until you nodded off. When she looked up and saw me, her eyes seemed to enlarge and sparkle. I now had the courage I needed and asked if she'd like to dance, while I waited for those sensual lips to speak. Then it happened, her lips started to part and out came, "Beat it you creep, my feet hurt." I did see her again later on the dance floor and had the urge to give her the finger, but didn't.

I was now dancing with Gloria, who was lovely. I felt like singing a tune from The Sound of Music, but this dump didn't seem to have the right atmosphere to give the song justice. She felt soft and had the smell of WD-40. Gloria later told me, WD-40 was good for her rheumatism. I wondered if she was a good kisser. I told her I'd been looking at her since I came in and finally got the courage to ask her to dance. She answered this with, "From the moment I saw you enter the room I couldn't keep my eyes off you. I hoped you'd ask me to dance and now my wish came true."

After hearing this I started to get warm all over. I was now hoping she may be thinking the same thoughts I had, which came from that Mae West movie She Done Him Wrong, when she says, "Is that a gun in your pocket or are you just happy to see me?" I mentioned that movie to her and the part about the gun in your pocket. She answered back with "Wha?" I finished the dance with Gloria and decided that for now I'd just work the floor. Next I was dancing with a girl who didn't speak a word of English. We danced cheek to cheek and the place was very hot. I remember we were dancing to the Beer Barrel polka. Our cheeks were sweaty and stuck together from the heat so I decided to pull my face away from hers creating a loud suction sound. I could feel the sweat running down the middle of her back and wondered where it stopped. I saw her mouth open and it was then she made a lunge for mine. Our teeth hit for a minute and then I felt her tongue reach for the back of my throat. I started to gag and figured the best thing for me to do was look at her breasts to forget the gagging. I next gently held onto one of her ears and kissed her again. I opened one eye to see if she kissed with her eyes closed. They were both open and reminded me of a cow's eyes. We were now dancing to a dreamy number and I purposely danced us towards Gloria. I overheard her dance partner say, " It's nice to dance with you," and Gloria answered with," From the moment I saw you enter the room I couldn't keep my eyes off you. I hoped you'd ask me to dance and now my wish came true." I was shattered. I wondered, do all the girls say stuff like this? I went outside for some air. A young couple were walking their dog. As they went by me, the dog passed wind.

This whole evening reminded me of a dance I attended to at Sauble Beach, on Lake Huron, years earlier. You had to admire the girls here. They sewed their own dresses and some of the girls, I think, must have arrived by tractor. They would remove their rubber boots and put on glittery shoes like Dorothy in *The Wizard of Oz*. It was then I saw her sashay into the room with her girlfriend. The girlfriend looked like she had sewn together a beautiful white gown from an old parachute. I knew it was a parachute because of the trailing straps following behind her. The girl who first caught my eye was dressed in what looked like sofa fabric, but I was smitten with the parachute lady. It was thoughtful to leave the arms bare so you could read the tattoos. One could tell from her appearance she looked after herself by lifting weights. She was built like a Buick. I didn't know whether to go over and offer to buy her a drink or a can of Simonize.

You could tell both girls were thrifty and bought their makeup at the Pratt and Lambert paint store. One of the girls had on beautiful green gold earrings that matched her ears. The other had what looked, from a distance, like a fibreglass flower stapled to her dress, and from up close, was actually a fibreglass flower. Volunteers were still putting up streamers and balloons, rubbing them on their heads and sticking them on the walls while people danced. Other girls were still arriving and all chewing gum with their mouth open. So far, the evening reminded me of the Titanic going down. Olga (the parachute lady) was starting to look pretty good about now and I thought we should be alone. I suggested we go outside for a while, but Olga said, "I can't leave Mavis alone." I suggested we take Mavis (sofa fabric) and lock her in a closet. We sat Mavis at a table with a glass of wine and told her we'd be back soon. I bought four beers at the bar and we headed out the door when Bruno the bouncer said, "Where the fuck do you think you're going with those beers." Olga answered,"Fuck You." We were told to leave just as the accordion player was doing a solo of "Who Stole the Kishke." I had enough of Coboconk, so said my good-byes to Olga and headed for Toronto. I wanted to spend a day or two in Chinatown and look at the little people.

I was still living with my folks on the outskirts of Toronto, north of Steeles Ave. at 54 Jackes, now changed to Crestwood Rd., where we experienced the worst inconveniences in the bloody winter. The backhouse usually had snow on the seat and was at least 50 ft. from the house, and the wind would knock it over every once in a while (once when I was in it.) The wood stove was fine until it went out in the night. The drinking and cooking water would come from a garage at Steeles and Yonge, about a mile away. We took turns pulling a wagon with two large milk cans tied to it. In the winter we used the sled. All the water for washing ourselves and our clothing came from rain in summer and snow melted in winter. In winter, we'd wash in an oval basin from the melted snow, all five of us. Since I was first home I'd get the fire going to melt the frozen water in the basin from the morning, so we could wash again. Occasionally, I would attempt to draw something at home. Well, when it was too cold, I'd put a sock over my hand to warm my fingers and then stick the pencil or brush through the sock.

For entertainment my dad brought home a great big car radio, the kind with glass tubes in it that light up. Attached to this was a six-volt car battery that gave us a few hours of our favourite shows. When the battery would start to die, we'd move the whole works over near the stove, and the heat would rejuvenate the battery long enough to catch the ending of a show like Jack Benny or Uncle Milty. After this the car battery went into the wagon or sled and we'd lug it to the garage for a recharge.

When summer arrived it was time to do something about the water problem, so my dad and Steve started to dig a well with shovels. They dug down a long way, at least it must have been a long way, because you couldn't see who was down there. Also, there was only room for one to dig at a time; the other had to pull up the pail with dirt, empty it, and send it down again. Mr Wooley, a neighbour, had dug down around 60 feet or so and still no water. One day he winched himself to the top to have lunch. While he was gone, water broke through and took with it his shovels, pail and pickaxe. Everything was gone. Some said, it was good Mr. Wooley wasn't down there at the time, because he would be gone too.

It was still tough going for my dad around this time. He needed a car badly so he could continue with his house painting. He now bought an old car with racks on the roof to carry ladders and other stuff. I remember when he couldn't keep up the car payments with the finance people, he would hide the car in different places and walk home. In winter it was good to leave the car somewhere else anyway, because the snowplow didn't come down our street most of the time. After all, with only seven houses from one end to the other, why bother.

To get to Brigden's I'd walk to Yonge St. and wait for the trolley that had a small charcoal stove in the middle of the car for heat, providing you were lucky enough to get near the thing. After the long shaky ride to the city limits one had to change cars to proceed downtown. Often the problem of being jostled from side to side on the trolley was, it gave you an erection, therefore giving you a problem in getting off.

I was determined to be an artist. I was 17 when I started at Brigden's and I wasn't given a desk at the beginning, so, to feel better, I went out and bought a beautiful black sample case like artist's have-- only in mine, I carried my lunch. Besides changing water bowls for the others I was finally learning other stuff, like how to mount the photographs with rubber cement for the retouchers. For the longest time I didn't know what retouching was, but now things were starting to look up. Some of the talented bunch I would work with later on included Bill Roberts, retoucher and painter; Colin Clark, retoucher and owner of a tiger moth bi-plane plus vintage English cars; Hal Sewell, retoucher and older fellow who went out and got married on his lunch hour; Ron Date, retoucher, who came to work with great sandwiches and always a cartoon in his lunch; and Don Rover, retoucher, who played chess every day with someone in Europe by mail. In the years to come I would meet and work with many more talented guys.

Basically, in these pre-computer days, retouching involved working on photographs with different paints to make the product look better than it actually was. In the earlier years we'd cover the glossy print in paint, then deliver it to the Eaton's annex for approval. If they saw a bit of shiny photograph showing, it was considered not finished and it came back for corrections. In later years when we started working with dyes and bleaches, no art director would accept your work if the smallest amount of paint was showing. The print had to look untouched even if you had worked on it for days. How the thinking had changed with time.

Brigden's had a lot of perks for a very old and big company. Fred Brigden, who was getting on in age and a bit feeble, would turn up every Friday. He would arrive in the same heavy green tweed suit and cane. Now, I'd been with Brigden's a good five years by this time and every Friday he'd come into my cubicle and say, "You must be the new fellow, I'm sure you will like it here." And every Friday I would say "I like it very much and appreciate the opportunity to work here."

Another perk was Ruth. She worked as a secretary in another department. As I mentioned earlier, Ruth was a little older than I was and would often visit my cubicle at lunch times. The others in my area always went out for lunch, mostly to knock back a few beers. So while I ate the sandwiches my mother made, Ruth would sit on my lap, stick her tongue in my mouth and wriggle her ass from side to side. I, of course got very aroused by this and Ruth knew it. This went on for years and never went any further than this. I had a big fear that if word got out, my art career , just nicely getting started, would be over.

Every year at Christmas, Brigden's threw a big wonderful party for the employees and their families. Mostly this was done for the employees' children. It always took place on a Saturday afternoon with one of the engravers playing Santa, and with the help of some elves (engravers) the party started. Santa would call out a child's name, the little boy or girl would run up on the stage and an elf would hand out a lovely present. Now, the engravers were always known as big drinkers, and were pissed as newts. That's when it happened. Santa had started drinking in the morning and with the hot suit he was wearing, the beard, the hot lights on stage, it was all too much, and Santa, smashed out of his mind, slid off his red and gold chair onto the floor, and instantly passed out. Santa weighted about 280 lbs., so it took four elves to drag him by his feet behind the plastic bushes. All was quiet at first, and then you heard a child cry out, "Santa's Dead, Santa's Dead." That's all it took before all the children were crying out, "Santa's dead, Santa's dead." Some were crying as the parents were now stuffing their kids into snowsuits and leaving for home. The following year Christmas was cancelled for good. (We heard later that on that same fateful day another engraver had gone and punched the president in the nose and broke his glasses.) It was a shame, and all because of "the Santa affair," as it became known. About 300 people and a lot of kids lost a good party.

Soon after the Santa affair Susan started working at Brigden's. She was young, pretty with flaming red hair and always sketching little erotic things on scraps of paper. I stayed after hours to either practice or do samples. Susan would come into my cubicle, the building now empty, sit at the vacant desk next to mine and hint at all sorts of suggestive things while doing erotic drawings. She had drawings of couples doing things I didn't know were possible. I was naturally very nervous about this, fearing someone would come in and see all the little dirty doodles. I told the older guys about this and asked what I might do about it. Well, they said, "Susan was a nympho, and the best thing would be to tell her to go away." Now, how does one tell someone to go away without making a scene or causing trouble? Also I wasn't sure what a nympho was. Luckily I didn't have to do anything. A few days later she was gone. Apparently she ended up in a home somewhere for help. I do remember though, they were lovely little drawings.

In the eight years I'd worked for Brigden's I moved with the studio three times. In that time some people would leave and new faces would arrive: Art salesman Bill Richards, art director Ed Nicholls who looked very much like movie star Zachary Scott, Betty Collins who was an assembly artist and at different times attempted suicide. Years later while, working at TDF Studios at Yonge and Temperance corner, over the Birks store, Betty was called into the boss's office, which happened to be on the fourth floor, and was told she was no longer needed. Without uttering one word, she took three or four steps to the window and jumped out. Down at street level, Birks was refurbishing and had scaffolding across the front of the store. Betty had landed on the plywood scaffolding, breaking both legs and her spine. Years later when I was working on my own, Betty, who was freelancing, came over to my studio in a wheelchair to help out. She seemed to have come out of her depression, but at one hell of a price. Also at Brigden's, was Gray Mills, another talented retoucher whom I would work with again at Pacesetters. Gray went on to do sculpture and painting.

There was always time for pranks. Some were silly and others real winners. The silly included rubber cementing the girls' working shoes to the ceiling while they were out to lunch. We all worked two to a cubicle. The bottoms of the cubicles were open about a foot, which was necessary for ventilation, and often the girls in the cubicle in front of you would lean against the cubicles to chat to one another. So while they chatted, leaning against the partition with legs apart, we on our side would tape a small hand mirror to a ruler, hold it down to the bottom opening, and see what colour panties they had on, if any.

Some pranks took more time, being more elaborate. Gray, who was very proud of his vintage Triumph sports car, usually got the full treatment from Colin Clark. Colin had brought back from Buffalo a firecracker device that could be wired to a car's spark plugs. After work, when Gray started his car, we first heard a minor explosion, followed immediately by a lot of smoke. Next, when Gray dropped the clutch out, nothing happened, because the back of the car was already on blocks. Unfortunately Gray was not amused. Earlier, on some of the other cars I had prepared something else. I got some old bicycle tubes, cut them into about eight-inch lengths and slipped about three inches over the end of the exhaust pipe. Believe me, if you own a car, start it up and hear this, you immediately think you have a big garage bill coming up.

After working in one place for eight years, I figured it was time to go and hopefully learn more about art than the Eaton's catalogue. My next stop was Pacesetters. This was a small studio on Adelaide St., within a stone's throw of Yonge St. Here I worked for two guys, Jack Elms and Bill Cameron. Cameron was a retoucher and colour blind. Gray Mills was already here. Lettering man was Bob Hines, who happened to be my next-door neighbour and who years later told all to my wife when I was seeing someone else. For some reason Gray always referred to Bob Hines as bear's ass. I think Gray was too kind. Tom Bjarnason, an illustrator, also worked at Pacesetters and later did sculpture in Port Hope, Ont. Today, Sadly, Bjarnason has Alzheimer's. Eventually Gray Mills would give up retouching and teach sculpture at the Ontario College of Art. Layout and designer, Bill Pulver, who went to Spain for a holiday with his wife, came back alone. Apparently his wife loved bullfighters and decided to stay. Last on the staff was Shirley Sanderson, who looked after the books and payroll.

Jack Elms, one of the bosses at Pacesetters (with no sense of humour), had a secret hiding place for his porn pictures. It was one of those large yellow Kodak film boxes and it was quite full. Gray and I found the hiding place and every now and then would add some new porn to the box. Nothing was ever said, but the hiding place would change and of course we always found it. Again we'd add a few new pictures. This went on for a time until we ran out of pictures. Jack never said a word. I was happy at Pacesetters until the night of the fire. I was alone that evening and doing freelance work. I usually listened to CHFI-FM, broadcasting from the floor below us. The disc jockey on that particular evening said something about putting on his last recording for the night and was now heading out the window because of the smoke. I looked out our window and, sure enough, the restaurant below us at street level was on fire. I too left, without locking up or putting the lights out.

The next day we were allowed up to salvage what we could. Damage wasn't from the fire but mostly from smoke and water. I did manage to salvage one or two of my samples. After things were cleaned up and things were back to normal, Gray and I had to come into work one Saturday along with Bill Cameron (the other boss). The three of us were in the small boardroom talking about something or other when Bill turned very pale and said, "I don't feel right." No sooner did he get those few words out when he started to head for the floor. I managed to get one hand under each of his arms, but knew I couldn't hold him, so I quickly spun him around to land him on the sofa. Gray was gone like a shot down the three stories to the street. He kept jumping in front of taxicabs until he finally got one to stop. We got Bill downstairs and into a cab, and Gray went with him around the corner to St. Michael's hospital. After three days of tests Bill was back. In time, Pacesetters moved elsewhere, and so did I. I heard a few years later that Bill Cameron had died from heart failure.

S&R Studios

I've decided to change the name of the studio here to S&R studios for different reasons, and loyalty to some of the people who worked there. In some instances I've changed some names, but not all. The studio had over 80 people on the payroll and many were the best at what they did in the city. Money was not a big problem at S&R. The two bosses running the show, let's call them Bert and Ernie, were only 19 and 20. The big money came from two other young guys (brothers) who were fortunate enough to be born into money. The family owned a conglomeration of department stores that pretty much covered Canada. These four young lads all met at university and when it came time to go to work, thought, let's start an art studio (with the brothers' family money), because it certainly sounded more exciting than opening a shoe store or some other everyday thing.

I joined S&R around the tail end of the '50s and into the '60s. I was to look after the small retouching department of six. We had our own room with one other guy named Cec Pentland, who did fashion drawings. Cec and I became very good friends for years to come,. I enjoyed going to work here every day, and a huge plus was the fact that I was paid more money than I had ever made before. (As a matter a fact, I was the highest paid retoucher in the city of Toronto.) S&R had every creative person that mattered: the best designers, layout people, photographers, illustrators and assembly people--and of course, the best bullshitters in the business (the salesmen). Right from the start, the more money that was spent on entertainment, the more work the company took in.

The studio would throw a party for one agency at a time, which seemed like a good idea. That way there didn't seem to be any favouritism to one agency. The younger boss (Ernie) was born to entertain. Bert, the other, came from a moneyed family and was more refined. In any event, Ernie was the one who spoke the same language as most of the agency art directors, so he fit in beautifully. Gifts to the right people brought in more work than usual. Booze was never turned down, along with great parties. Ernie knew a madam who ran a quality stable of girls who were always available for the correct fee, and a very attractive bunch they were, as I later gratefully found out.

Yes, it was a good time to be working at S&R. Whenever an agency evening party was to take place I stayed on, since I was considered necessary to represent the retouching art dept. If I had work on my desk that had to be done, I was paid time and a half. I would have worked for free on these nights just for the perks. We had topless girls serving drinks and hors d'oeuvres on trays. This was in the years when topless dancers hadn't arrived yet in bars and strip joints. On occasions when I was working alone because something had to be done for the morning, Ernie, being very thoughtful, would always send in one of the girls to make sure I had a drink. On one of those party nights, a lovely fair-haired Amazon came into my room with a tray of drinks and asked if I would like a drink. I asked, "What would you recommend?" She answered back with, " What I have now with me on the tray is, on the left, scotch and soda, on the right I have, rye and ginger ale." Because she was topless, I was momentarily distracted. Before I could speak again, she carefully dropped one breast in the scotch and soda and the other breast into the rye and ginger ale. After this she pushed both tits forward and in a soft voice said," Why not give each a taste and then make a decision." I did, and decided to try the scotch taste one more time. She was back in an hour and we did it again and later again till the evening was over. All this, and paid time and a half too.

KARMAN

These sorts of evenings went on until every agency had visited. When that part of studio introduction was over, other things would replace it. Christmas was always a wonderful time. Studios would always try to outdo the others with gifts, cases of booze, colour TVs, a holiday to the islands for two, bottles of Dom Pérignon and, if you weren't too important, a bottle of Canadian Club.

Ernie would occasionally set up a special evening with a beautiful girl, thanks to The Madam. I worked a fair bit of overtime in those days. The money was good. I also earned extra money doing retouching to Ernie's private porn collection for his album. Many of these shots he took himself. Also there were so many duplicates and triplicates that I could keep what I wanted. All these extras were passed on to Jack Reppen.

Jack Reppen, another good friend of mine, who earned his living as a cartoonist for The Toronto Star, and also worked for an insurance company, loved two things, painting and anything erotic. Jack and his wife bought a big house in Toronto's upscale Rosedale neighbourhood and immediately had one bedroom done in wall-to-wall mattress. In a short time he became a fine painter who had his work shown at Gallery Moos on Avenue Rd. Moos later moved to the Yorkville area. Unfortunately, Jack Reppen died very young from cancer.

A well-known painter around this time was Tom Hodgson. I would see Tom quite often at The Pilot tavern, a bar on the west side of Yonge St. close to Bloor St. The Isaacs Gallery was just north of the Pilot, so on many an evening you'd find a group of painters at the back of the Pilot tavern. On one of those memorable evenings back then, I remember meeting Tom out in the street. He was out of money and couldn't cover his beer tab. He sold me a line and wash drawing out on the sidewalk for $35, and then treated me inside the Pilot tavern to a couple of beers. I'd bump into Tom often at different functions around town, or out of town. Tom would always be at the Gray Mills annual party in Tullamore, a great place to go to and hear, see, drink and tell stories.

In one such famous story from a Mills party was that everyone had to bring along a lobster. Jon McKee, a cartoonist, attended the party and brought a small lobster, but without guilt he ate a big lobster. To this day, there are many people who have heard the lobster story but have never met Jon McKee. The Gray Mills parties were always memorable. Gray a sculptor and painter, as well as a perfectionist with tools, built a barbeque spit from old Ford Model A parts, including the transmission. You could put the biggest pig on this barbeque, and with a choice of three forward and one reverse gear, everything was possible.

Over on King St. E. the best was yet to come. Three small buildings, numbers 107, 109 and 111 on King near Church, were being built back in 1836-1841. The buildings miraculously survived the great fire of 1849. Behind 107 and 109 stood The Masonic Hall on Church St. It had its beginning as a hotel owned at one time by James Mink, and was built in 1841. Mink, a black man from the States who got into Canada via the underground railroad, made a lot of money and built the hotel. He had a daughter and wanted to make sure she found a decent husband, so he offered $10,000 for the perfect husband. The chosen husband then took miss Mink to America and sold her into slavery. James Mink and his wife travelled to Georgia, rescued their daughter and brought her home by way of the underground railroad.

My reason for referring to this is that it brings me back to Tom Hodgson. In the 1960s Hodgson moved into the upper floors of 107 King St. and made it his home and studio for approximately six or seven years. Tom was a member of the "Painters Eleven," along with Harold Town, Oscar Cahen, Jack Bush and William Ronald (more

114

later). On many Saturday nights Tom would throw parties and I, for one, attended whenever I could. All one had to do was bring your own drink and throw $10 or $15 into the pot for the evening's entertainment. A typical night could be two hookers paid to do an erotic show.

The girls would walk around naked and introduce themselves to you. If you happened to be seated they'd come by and sit on your lap. If you wished to keep one hand on your lap (palm up) that was okay too. From the very high ceiling hung a thick manila rope. On this rope there was always a pretty naked girl swinging back and forth.

These female guests never had to pay. Their admission was free. When it was time for snacks, someone else would roll out into the middle of the big room, a hospital gurney. On one occasion the gurney carried a lovely girl (naked) completely covered in cold cuts, with parsley, radishes and lettuce. Naturally, the cold cuts around the naughty parts went first. All this, to the music of Ray Charles, Creedence Clearwater Revival, Chicago, Santana and others.

Back at S&R, if I had a retouching job to do that Ernie himself had to take to the agency in the morning, I would deliver it to his place when I finished, no matter how late it was. It seemed to me whenever I went to see Ernie, to drop off some work, he usually had some agency types visiting. Some evenings I would stay for a drink or two, then get ready to leave. On one particular occasion, the bedroom door was opened and a girl with some small frilly thing on, said, "Oh!, I didn't know there were six of you," and added, "I'm sorry, I can't look after you. I'm running late and have to be somewhere else now, so would someone please phone a cab for me?" One never knew what to expect, but you were never disappointed.

Cec Pentland, who worked in our section, had a serious drinking problem, so much so that he drank every day, starting on his lunch hour, sometimes sooner. He'd return from his liquid lunch, wander into our little room, fall into his chair and in minutes be fast asleep. In the corner of the room where Cec sat, was a door nailed shut, that originally went into the photo studio. The doorknob was missing on that door, and one could (if you wanted) still look into the photo studio. Ralph, our production guy, did not like Cec. It was very obvious to everyone that Ralph always wanted Cec fired, but Ernie gave it a flat No. One day Ernie wasn't back from lunch so Ralph was going to take a Polaroid of Cec, drunk and asleep at his desk. Ralph had to run all along the outside of the building to get to the photo studio for the Polaroid. While Ralph was on his way back to where we are, Barry in the photo studio hollered at Cec through the little round hole to wake up. "Ralph is coming, Ralph is coming," he said. Barry now came along with a piece of plumber's pipe and stuck it through the hole, waving it up and down and sideways to get Cec's attention. Meanwhile, Ralph had been back long enough to witness all of this and just stood back to watch. Cec, by then in a sort of wakeful state, saw the pole and quipped," What the fuck," grabbing the pole and doing his best to pull Barry through the little hole. Ralph saw the whole fiasco taking place, shook his head, decided not to take a picture, and left. Cec was safe once again for another day.

Just outside our door is where the receptionist sat. She was wonderful at her job. No matter what was going on or what you did she never lost control, especially when she was on the phone. One time four of us came out of our door, each with his own big horse fly attached with a thin thread to a fly's leg. We had all four flies up in the air and walked past her while she was on the phone. She looked up with no expression at all, just as if we had done this every day. Another time soon after, we had some artwork to do for Sun-Ray glasses. The boys taped 50 pair of sunglasses all over my head, back and front, neck too, and out the door I went. Nothing, again nothing, until I did the holy grail of jokes. I airbrushed a very lifelike drawing on illustration board of a penis--and a good sized one it was too, it would have made anyone proud Then I carefully cut out the penis and tucked it into the top of my belt and pulled my shirt over it. I waited at my door till I heard Mary on the phone. Then, out I went. Well, she lost it and the control was gone. I think she kind of liked me more after that.

Orv Dunlop did layout, design and drank. He was very good at all three. Because he was very gifted in what he did, S&R gave him his own room. Orv liked working evenings, and quite often all night. The room had a closet in which he kept a folding bed. He was also comfortable working in his pyjamas, so now he could work, drink and go to sleep when he wanted--part of him in the closet. In the mornings when staff started to arrive, there was Orv, 2/3 in the closet and 1/3 (the feet) out of the closet. Often the studio had clients walking around, so it didn't look very impressive, especially when Orv was drunk. It became a big problem. On top of all this, Orv would walk around the studio in his pyjamas, and he was a bad drunk with a temper, which didn't help. Bert,(one of the bosses) on one occasion tried to calm Orv down. Orv, picked up Bert and carried him around the studio. They never fired Orv, I imagine because of his talent. He was needed. A few years later Orv died.

Another at S&R was Jane (not her real name). Jane did assembly and loved Yoga. We boys played dumb to what Yoga was, and how one practices Yoga. Jane was more than happy to educate us.

After explaining how Yoga helps one relax, Jane said, standing on your head in a corner was her favourite thing to do. Of course we all said, "Nobody can do that." Next thing you know, Jane pulled some wrapping paper from the cutting table, put it on the floor against the wall, and stood on her head for many minutes. Some of us were up on that cutting table so fast, to get a better view. Oh yes, Jane always wore a skirt and yes, she could do it.

Ken Craig was a very close friend through the years at S&R, and many years after that. At the studio Ken did assembly and with his time off turned out a small book on poetry every month. Most of the poetry was submitted by others. His books became successful and with that Ken ended up with two partners. Eventually the partners took over and Ken went on to something else. Also, he loved the ladies. At S&R he was dating three girls at the same time, until the girls found out. They decided to teach him a lesson, and very convincing it turned out to be. One of the girls went first, and asked Ken over for a lovely meal with candles and wine, and gradually when it seemed like the right moment told Ken she was pregnant. Another, weeks later, told him the same news at a pub. One by one they told Ken they were pregnant and needed money for an abortion.

Ken was now in deep shit and needed to borrow money, if he could find some. On top of all this, Ken was married and the father of two little boys. The girls let him sweat it out for a few weeks, and then told him the whole thing was a hoax and to fuck off, and soon after, fuck off he did. With his family he moved to New York and became a fashion photographer. He did quite well, bought a house in Queens, and life was good again. Eventually Ken's wife, Fran, thought it better if their two young boys went to school in Ontario, rather than the States, So back to Canada they came to start over once again. He continued working as a photographer, had a studio on Church St. and did well. He bought a house, plus 175 acres on the water in Honey Harbour up on Georgian Bay. The Honey Harbour property became a successful trailer camp. I wasn't living at home around that time, so I bought a house trailer and kept it at Ken's trailer camp. It was to be my cottage, and good as it was, I found I was using it far too much just to drink in. So I sold it. In time Ken and Fran broke up, and Fran kept the house in Toronto and Ken kept his trailer camp, until he sold it to some Chinese organization for $1.4-million,. Throughout all the years I've known Ken, he couldn't be without his beloved rum and coke. With all this money from the camp sale came new friends, a lovely girl and fun. The money didn't last long, and when it was gone, so were the friends, and the girl. With the few dollars left, he drank more, until that money was completely gone. On welfare, he ended up living in his mother's basement in Alliston, Ont. In the earlier years when Ken lived in New York, I never saw him happier. I often wondered how things might have gone if he and Fran had stayed in the Big Apple, where he had many talented friends. He was now obviously missing that life.

I went with Ken back to New York when he sold the house. There were still some items to wrap and bring back to Toronto. While we were there we visited a lot of his old friends. He had friends in the Chelsea Hotel and from their windows you could see wonderful sights of New York, like where Johnny Carson's Tonight Show took place every night. New York is famous as the city that never sleeps. If you should want a haircut at 4 a.m., then in New York you can have a haircut at 4 a.m. This is why Ken loved the city so much.

The Chelsea Hotel has a list of names on the wall of people who had lived there: Jane Fonda, Bob Dylan and so on. In the daytime we would go to his favourite bar and drink sake martinis. One day in the car he said, "You need a haircut." "No I don't." "Yes you do." And we were off to see a model he knew and her boyfriend, who had just recently opened a hair stylist place called Vertigo, in a warehouse somewhere in New York's east side. Well, I must say, this was certainly no barbershop. They had at least 20 big leather chairs, all with creature comforts, such as adjusting foot stools, your own phone and a side table to hold your coffee and cognac. Others had wine. Some, after the hair styling was finished, would have a neck massage and manicure.

After Ken had his hair pampered with by his friend Ivana (her name before they opened was Mary), Ivana invited us to the other half of the warehouse to show where she and Lance lived (his name before they opened was Freddie). The living room and entertaining room, or whatever label one can put on it, was very striking indeed. Sofas were placed randomly here and there, and around all this, a plethora of huge pillows on the floor. The main interest of the room was in the very centre. On a marble base approximately six feet high stood a good-sized box made of a heavy clear plastic. This clear plastic box was a shower. It was now almost evening and we were asked if we'd like to stay. I wouldn't have missed it for the world. Other guests arrived, picked a cushion, had some wine, talked and waited. Eventually, a young wannabe model showed up and was the first to have a shower. A central spot light came on as the outer lights around the room were dimmed.

S&R was still doing well in 1960, or so it appeared. So well in fact, that if a big money paying job came in, Ernie would treat some of us. Our star salesman "Jimmy" would go out and book a double room at the old Rex Hotel. The reason for the two rooms was so that one room could hold the six or eight of us with drinks while the other adjoining room was used by the hooker. Jimmy always set this up, got the rooms, the liquor, and paid the hooker. Jimmy also thought he should be last, so he'd have more time with the girl. On this particular evening his turn came last as usual, and unfortunately, she had to run out because she had another engagement to go to. Jimmy, good salesman that he was, obviously still couldn't convince her to stay. We heard her leave, and had a glimpse of her at the elevator. We also heard Jimmy whimpering in the other room. He stayed awhile in the other room, and then came into our room and said, "Best I ever had." Boy! what a salesman.

The work that came into S&R varied a lot, some good, some not. I kept what was interesting for me, and let the other guys have the rest, of which we had more than we could handle. On occasions I had to bring in freelance people to help out. A word about art directors at most agencies: The most difficult were the new and the youngest. They got out of art school and they immediately knew everything, and of course most knew diddly-squat (polite for bullshit). In the advertising business, we had many women art directors who were wonderful. I think they realized, because you had been doing your own kind of work, whatever it was, for decades, they had more of a tendency to listen to you and what you might think. I also believe they learned more quickly because of this attitude, than the boys did. So, my hat goes off to the women. Aside from that, the girls were prettier to look at and smelled nicer. I did have one particular favourite from McCann-Erickson, who loved to come over to the studio to explain what retouching had to be done to a print. While leaning over the board table to explain, and she always wore a loose-fitting blouse with a large V in front, never a bra, and gave you a bird's eye view of her navel. There were times I had to phone her the following morning and ask what I should do.

In retouching, occasionally I'd have to airbrush a large background for a client. The client would come over to my place with a small colour sample. My job was to match the colour exactly on a large piece of blank paper. More often than not, you went a touch too dark or a little on the red side, or too blue, or whatever. After airbrushing for two or more hours, and let's say I went a touch too dark, this was easy to fix. I would airbrush the colour sample a touch darker. If it went too red, easy again, spray a little red on the sample. No one ever knew and life was beautiful. The pranks in a studio did sometimes backfire. For instance, there was the time my good friend

Bill Waldie was working at another studio on a large colour print of a Salvation Army woman, in uniform holding her folded hands to her chest and looking up to God. Above her angelic face, the ad said in bold letters: "Give." This was all very nicely done. On both collars of her uniform was a shiny, chrome letter "S." Bill Waldie added a simple line through each "S," turning them into dollar signs. It created a good laugh for the day throughout the studio and was forgotten, until it went out for printing. Nobody saw it, and hundreds were printed. Large posters of the Give poster ended up in store windows, street poles and anywhere they could be seen. Everything was quiet for a while, until someone important from the Salvation Army was waiting for a bus and saw the poster on a pole. That's when the shit hit the fan. I believe Hayhurst Advt. was the agency involved. In the studio where Bill Waldie worked, a lot of apologetic letter writing now took place, and of course all posters came down immediately.

A similar thing happened in the days when I worked at Brigden's in Toronto.. I had a big original illustration on my desk of a muscular man (no shirt) with a sledge-hammer. This was an ad to be used for a construction company. I had found a photo of a pretty little red rose, cut it out, and stuck it in the lips of this hunk of a guy. Well, after all the laughter, that too got overlooked and it was printed. For some reason no one knew I had done it and I said nothing. There were other fun jobs, sometimes done for free and referred to as "kma" jobs ("kiss my ass"), such as the one I did for General Motors. I was given a black & white photo of a well-endowed girl completely naked, standing beside a new GM car. My work was to draw a clothes line from one breast to the other, tie it around the nipples and then draw as lifelike as possible, five little towels on the clothes line held up by little clothes pins. On the towels I had to letter Pontiac on one, Oldsmobile on another, Chevrolet, Buick and finally Cadillac on the last. The public never saw this ad; it was strictly for the salesman's book. What a pity, I was proud of this one.

At another time I certainly did get a lot of heat once for a retouch I did of a Hollywood starlet. In this black & white she was seated at a round table at a fancy restaurant in Los Angeles. The table was covered with things like cigarettes, a lighter, purse, ashtray, drinks, napkins and other junk of no importance. My job was to tidy up and remove this junk and leave the candle and menu. I removed all the stuff mentioned and then, on a clear acetate overlay, I did my thing. I removed her blouse and rested her lovely breasts on the table. It all looked very real and believable. I guess I liked how it turned out, so I left the overlay on the black & white print so others could enjoy it, thinking, before it leaves the building I'll pull the overlay off. You guessed right. It left the building, was printed, and ended up in L.A. It was too late to stop it, it was gone. Days went by and I began to wonder where I could work next, and whether there would be a lawsuit. Fortunately for me, the starlet saw the humour in it and I could carry on. Bless the Hollywood starlet, I hope she does well. What a lovely girl.

Studios had a plethora of beautiful women, such as the popular Yoga Jane I mentioned previously. I figured if I could show Jane how intellectual and interesting I was, we could do okay together. So I picked a day at the coffee table and said, "How about the current economic value of money right now in Bulgaria, and should I buy a cottage in Inuvik, settle down, open a beachwear shop and do well selling thongs. She looked at me like the sun was in her eyes and said, "Wah?" I knew I'd make out okay.

I must mention Jack Hurst, a photographer at S&R. We became good friends at the studio and were both good friends with Wes Chapman, an illustrator. Wes was going to be married again soon, and it was to be his third marriage. Jack couldn't possibly make the wedding because of an earlier commitment, so he said to me, "Look, if you should be seeing Wes before I do, would you please tell him how sorry I am that I can't attend his wedding? But please tell him I will definitely make the next one." Jack had a way with words. I always wished I had said that.

Subliminal Seduction

In 1973, a fellow named Wilson Bryan Key wrote a book about advertising called "Subliminal Seduction: Ad Media's Manipulation of a Not So Innocent America." I got a phone call from The Toronto Star, because they were doing a full-page story on this clown and his book. He had also picked on an ad I had worked on; a colour ad for Gilbey's Gin. It was a lovely shot showing the frosted Gilbey's bottle covered in a cold sweat and ice particles. Next to the bottle, stood a tall Collins glass with three ice cubes in it. This glass also looked very cold, and had the usual beaded water running down the glass and onto the table. Key saw sex in everything. He saw the bottle as the male penis. The glass, I guess because of the opening, was the vagina. The cold sweat running down the glass represented to him an ejaculation. He then turned his attention to the three ice cubes in the glass. In the first cube he saw a well-retouched letter "S." In the second he saw an "E," and in the third, of course, he saw an "X." The Star reporter asked me what I thought, and also added they have to be careful what they print, but figured what I might add to this story could make good copy. I told the reporter the truth, namely, that I did absolutely nothing to the ice cubes, and for that matter, no one I have talked to since can see one letter in any of the cubes. On the subject of erotic things going on in the ice cubes, and hidden lettering, my only response was, "If it's there, the fridge must have done it."

Key also claimed that the word SEX was printed on a Ritz crackers ad. He devoted five pages of his book to the Gilbey's Gin ad, focusing mostly on the relation between the bottle, the cork and the reflection of the bottle on the table. He also claimed there are five individuals in the ad, three women and two men. And, under the label of the Gin bottle he claimed to see a stick figure with a male head. On the right of this figure he saw another, most likely to be a pregnant woman. He also saw a partial representation of a male figure complete with an erection (something to do with the arrangement of the cork and the reflection). The triangular label, reflected on the table, to him was a pair of legs. If you should be interested in seeing the ad to make your own conclusions, it's still available on the Internet. The Gilbey's Gin ad heading reads, "Break out the frosty bottle." This Gilbey's ad is now part of Advertising History, and I am very pleased I had an important part in it. As Jerry Goodis, of Goodis, Goldberg and Soren Advertising Agency, said at the time, "We've giving the sick jerk too much publicity for his book." And Jerry is absolutely right.

Another who claims the power of subliminal advertising is James Vicary. His claim to fame was made in 1957 when, as a market researcher, he claimed that over a six-week period, 45,699 people at a movie house in Fort Lee, New Jersey, were shown two advertising messages: Eat popcorn and drink Coca-Cola, while watching the film Picnic. Vicary claims the message was flashed for 3/1000 of a second once every five seconds. The duration of the messages was so short that they were never consciously perceived. Despite the fact that the people were not aware of the message, Vicary claims that over a six-week period the sales of popcorn rose 57% and Coca-Cola rose 18.1%. Although Vicary's claims are often accepted as facts, he has never released a detailed description of his study and there has never been any independent evidence to support his claims in anything. Still, in an interview with Advertising Age in 1962, Vicary confirmed that the original study was a fabrication.

Back at S&R Studios, my good friend Cec had stepped off the sidewalk in front of work and something snapped in his ankle. It looked worse that it really was, but he was uncomfortable and somewhat sore. One of the girls was very worried about Cec (I think it was Vera) and came in every day to see how he was doing. Cec was fine, but he did walk with a limp. With Cec's approval (and he certainly was enjoying the sympathy from Vera), every morning I airbrushed some greens and blues higher up on the veins around his ankle and added a little Vaseline to make it shine a bit. Dear Vera insisted Cec go to the doctor, but every morning he said, "No," and then I added a little more colour to the point where it looked like the leg should come off. This went on a little too long and we'd had enough. That night at home Cec washed everything off and he was new again. The following morning Vera was back, and couldn't believe something like that could heal overnight. Cec and Vera stayed good friends.

I enjoyed working in the evenings. The phone stopped ringing and almost everyone went home. My room was empty and quiet, so now I could have a scotch and soda while I worked. I'd also been a heavy smoker for years now, and never ever put a cigarette down--once it was in my mouth, it stayed there until I could smell the cork tip or it was out. I could talk on the phone and roll the cigarette from side to side and never drop the thing. I also had the little TV on for company. Quite often Jane would wander in from her side of the studio, bring me a coffee, and if I happened to be on the phone when she came in, I could still talk, smoke, and roll the cigarette around in my mouth, listen to the TV and still do my retouching. On this particular evening, I had to work all night. What happened earlier in the day was, "Jimmy," our star salesman, was on his way back from a meeting uptown and was now held up in traffic. What had happened was, a taxi cab had run into a courier on his bicycle. The young lad lying on the road was badly hurt and was now in a state of shock. Jimmy recognized the kid, stopped, and told the paramedics the kid's name and where he worked.

Now, lying on the road is this mangled piece of art work. Jimmy, being a good salesman had visions of picking up another client we didn't already deal with, picked up the package and without another thought in his head, left the accident and headed for the agency. And this is how we gained another agency, and I spent the night fixing a very bad and torn print of a young and pretty model holding up a jar of instant coffee.

The Art of Retouching

Retouching, when I did it in the old days, was a hell of a lot more romantic than it is now. Today nobody has any use for the people who do things by hand. Gone are the big names of illustrators, lettering people, photographers, layout and designers, retouchers, etc. The photographers that are left have mostly gone digital. All the big studios are long gone. Now, we're left with but a few small studios with computers and technical people running the show. There isn't a water bowl to be found or brushes and paint. Gone are the gifted people and personalities we worked with. The fun and play times are also gone. The agencies are doing most of the ads themselves with digital cameras, computers, and printers. Digital camera technology is so good now and fully automatic, that you don't need the big-name shooters anymore. It's all about speed today and mega pixels. The retouching I grew up with involved airbrushes, every paint on the market, tempura, watercolour, opaque, dyes, gouache, bleaches, buffers, etc. The airbrush was a beautifully made little instrument you held in one hand, as you would a pencil. As a matter a fact, to some it was known as the wind pencil. If it was well looked after you were able to airbrush a pencil line on top of the pencil line. Every product on the market, whether it was something that grew out of the ground or was put together on an assembly line, seemed to require retouching to make it more appealing to the public.

A good deal of my work was in the field of car advertising. To some, retouching photographs of cars was creative cheating. We called it creative encasing or something like that. We'd push the wheels up a little so the car looked lower, also cutting the photo print in strategic places to make the car look longer and, of course, remove unwanted reflections. We would sparkle up the chrome, make sure the doors lined up properly and that the upholstery didn't have wrinkles. On and on it went. Even the live models used standing by the car were given a better figure and a nicer look if necessary.

Everything, it seemed, was retouched back then. Cigarettes were very fussy. If you did a drawing of a cigarette and the cigarette paper had those faint lines or rings around the paper, those rings were counted, and if one was missing the whole job was garbage. From the cork tip down to the tobacco end was super important. I did have a fun retouching job once where I was given six identical black & white 8x10 inch prints of a guy who had a broken nose. My job was to give him six different noses, so he could literally pick one for his plastic surgeon. Just think, out there is someone walking around with one of my noses.

Back then every car tire had to be drawn. If you photographed a tire--be it a truck, tractor or car tire--they all looked far too thin, like bicycle tires. Today the camera can shoot just about anything you like, and make it fatter, squatter, thinner, higher, distort it, whatever appeals to you. Life was good in the '60s, except some jobs. If they involved in any way the church, women's liberation or government, you could and did go nuts. One such ad I worked on, which I still believe was one of those great ads that comes along every now and then, was, sadly shot down. I had a large dye print on my desk (20" x 24") of Michelangelo's painting The Creation of Adam, from the Sistine chapel ceiling. Beautiful, old (1508-12) and priceless, the painting shows Adam with his arm and hand outstretched to God. My work was to pull the print apart a little, to make room between Adam's hand and God's hand, so I could drop in a Cadbury chocolate bar. I also retouched in a thin yellow silk cover over Adam's private parts. This was to be a wonderful billboard. Well, the Catholic church saw the ad before printing, and it was all over.

Another job that certainly would have been an award winner for the art director was a 20" x 24" dye print of a reclining woman in a black bathing suit. What I was asked to do here was draw yellow dotted lines, running over her waist-line and hips to look like a highway that continued into a real highway and then out of sight. Now, coming over the hips I put in a motorcycle and driver, reduced of course. This was also to be a billboard but the women's lib community raised so much flack and horseshit that it, too, never saw printing. Sad as it was, this happened often. For something to do and for myself, I spent two days drawing in one exposed breast on the Mona Lisa using a sepia print as a beginning. My friend Wally suggested I use it for my Christmas card. With apologies to Leonardo Da Vinci, I had 150 printed for Christmas cards, 5 x 7 inches. It went over well, maybe too well because now people at agencies, friends, etc., began asking, "Can I have one?" I told them to phone Jerry Diachun at his dark room. It was Jerry who had printed the first 150. Then I immediately phoned Jerry and said, "Hey! It's all yours, charge what you like." Much later I heard that some outfit in Chicago was printing my Mona Lisa on T-shirts and large posters. The Toronto poster shops made money, and of course the Chicago outfit. I made nothing and couldn't do a thing about it. After all, the Mona Lisa wasn't exactly all mine, but then again, it didn't belong to the Chicago printers either.

A few words about ad agencies here: Ad firms usually have in-house copy-writers, art directors, designers and PR departments. The agencies have access to media buying, marketing, access to television time, newspapers and magazines. They can help with each step (for a price of course) from conception to implementation.

I got involved with retouching Volkswagen ads when Doyle, Dane & Bernbach got their first car account. At the beginning, in 1959, it wasn't exactly a happy time for the agency. The car didn't have any chrome, no styling to speak of, no horsepower, not even an automatic transmission. Also the worrying part was, here's an idea of Adolf Hitler's from Nazi Germany. DDB had many Jewish clients and employees. So with the creative team of Julian Koenig, Helmut Krone and the direction of Bernbach himself, the idea was to make the ads as American as possible. We've all seen those early ads, such as a black & white shot of the car with the simple heading, in large type, "Lemon." Other similar ads read "Think Small" and "We try Harder." The well-done TV commercials of the funeral or the snow plow ads were all great and fun to watch. Most of these early ads were created in the '60s. The think small ad also noted that a Buick, for example, carries 44 pounds of chrome, and that American cars averaged ten miles to a gallon of gas while the Bug gives you approximately 32 miles to a gallon.

In 1970 it would be hard to deny that Doyle Dane & Bernbach was the leading advertising agency in the United States. Aside from Volkswagen, they had Avis Rent A Car, the Jamaica Tourist Office, Colombian Coffee (Juan Valdez), Polaroid, Sony television and much more. For the beautiful VW Karmann Ghia, their ad headline read, simply: "There's a little bug in every Karmann Ghia."

In 1963 David Ogilvy, of Ogilvy Benson & Mather, wrote a best seller called "Confessions of an Advertising Man," and it's still a wonderful read today. Linda Kaplan Thaler, who I believe is still in her 50s, is compared to the Ogilvy-like reputation today. A very clever woman who co-wrote a book on marketing in 2003 and said, "Don't worry about whether the news is good or bad, Just get it covered, PR breeds PR." In 2004 more than $500-billion was spent on advertising and marketing in the United States alone--half the worldwide total. At one time, clients paid agencies 15% of each advertising dollar. By the late 1990s, some clients went against paying the flat commission, preferring to be billed by the hour. Linda Kaplan, who started the Kaplan Thaler Group in 1997, says, "I sometimes worry that clients are paying us for the hours we spend working on projects rather than the worth of the ideas."

Many of the older ad agencies have long been taken over by larger firms. One of those larger firms was Saatchi and Saatchi of New York, known to most of us as Snatch it and Snatch it. In 1971 DDB came up with "You deserve a break today" for McDonald's and it still works today. I believe in 2004 Procter & Gamble spent $2.9-billion on advertising. When last counted up by "Advertising Age" in 2003, the Kaplan Thaler Group was the second fastest growing advertising agency in the States and number one in New York. In eight years, the agency has expanded to about 140 employees and $600-million in billings. Maybe these are small numbers in the advertising world but huge for an agency of that size. The Thaler Group had six weeks to produce the "Aflac" TV commercial. Eric David becoming frustrated, and walking back from lunch began saying to himself, over and over again, "Aflac, Aflac," and then in a nasal voice again "Aflac, Aflac," more like a duck, and that was it. The Aflac sales more than doubled in the first four years. They went from an insurance company that was unknown to a well-established known brand. Part of that has come through product placement and giving away cars. On "Oprah" not long ago, General Motors' Pontiac division gave away 275 cars on the show. A 30-second commercial on Oprah costs about $75,000. It is estimated that the publicity value to Pontiac is worth at least $70-million. The Ad Agency is obviously here to stay.

Circle M Ranch

Horses and I just didn't get along. On some Saturdays many of us went riding at the Circle M ranch. Wes Chapman, one of the most talented illustrators I have ever worked with, and his wife Fran at the time lived at the Circle M. When you saw them ride, you thought they were both born on horses, they were that good. I was always put on a horse called Sleepy. Sleepy was known to follow a trail and never leave it. That is, until I came along. Frenchy, an excellent rider who worked for the Circle M, always said, "The way to get Sleepy started is to kick him in the ribs." We were all in a row on the trail like good horse people should be and ready to move out, but Sleepy would not budge. Frenchy said, "Kick him in the ribs," show him who's the boss. I kicked, and we were off like a bullet. Sleepy left the trail, and I went with him.

We headed through the forest, through the creek, up the hill and into another forest. I assumed by now we must be in another province. I was pretty much scratched up and hanging on for dear life. I figured Sleepy would probably stop before nightfall, or at least the following day. I was riding low and sideways like real cowboys do in the movies, not to go faster, but to miss a few bushes, when good old Frenchy galloped along side, grabbed my reins, and yanked hard until Sleepy stopped. I thanked Frenchy and then checked to see if I still had my testicles. Frenchy insisted I get back on or I might not ever get back on a horse again. I thought it over and said, "That's okay with me." He said, "What's okay?" I said, "To stay off forever." But I did get back on Sleepy, gave him a kick in the ribs, and Sleepy and I went on to finish our rush through the forest. I kept going to the riding festivities until I thought I was going to go through life bow-legged. Also I had trouble walking.

" SLEEPY "

There was a dark-skinned girl from one of the islands, who had just recently started working at S&R studios. She was a treat to watch on horseback, but definitely had some mental problems, and you never knew when her crazy side was going to kick in. She was here on an extended visit, and staying with a relative; that's all we knew about her. On one serious occasion, coming back from a riding evening at the Circle M ranch, Ken Craig and I had a ride in the back seat of someone's car with the girl from one of the islands sitting between us. We were moving along at a good 80 miles per hour when she decided she was going to get out of the car that very minute. She had the door only partly open, due to the fact that at that speed the wind was doing its best to close it, when Ken and I wrestled her to the floor, held her there with our feet and clenched her arms behind her back. The whole thing was very traumatic. Just as quickly, in about five to ten minutes, she was as normal as could be. Within a few days she created more problems at work, and they had to let her go. What made matters worse was the fact that Ken was sleeping with her at the time, and this gave him bigger problems at home. She would often sit on his porch in the middle of the night and ring the doorbell for attention, or sit in the yard behind the house all night. Life went on as life does until she was smitten by someone new and left town. Ken was temporarily blessed once again.

Jimmy, our star salesman at S&R, knew some interesting people, one of them being Earl Fatha Hines, a well-known and wonderful piano player who played great Jazz. We'd spend many evenings at the Savarin tavern in Toronto, listening, drinking and watching a super show. Jimmy's bad side was his drinking, and he did not like drinking alone. Thank goodness it didn't happen often, but occasionally he would phone me at home in the wee hours of the night, always drunk, wake everyone, including my kids, urging, "You have to come in and do some changes to a retouch, and it's needed at 9 a.m." I would dress, drive down to the studio and find Jimmy, booze in hand, already smashed, and no fucking art work. When I first started working here I thought I'd probably stay until it was time to retire. I initially thought it was the most exciting place I'd ever worked, but I eventually became restless and decided I'd had enough. Besides, I'd always wanted to go to Italy to paint.

Off to Europe

This seemed like the perfect time to think seriously about Italy. My sons, Gregory and Derek, hadn't started school yet, Carolyn was just as keen and eager as I was, so we decided to prepare for the trip, and go a year later. As it turned out, my good friend Bill Waldie had been planning a trip to Italy with his family for a long time. Also, his two boys were practically the same ages as our two. In a short time, the dream changed to, "Why don't we four adults and four kids go together and share expenses on house rentals, etc.?" Immediately we found an Italian tutor to come to the house once a week and give us Italian lessons. At the same time he (the tutor) was improving his English. Carolyn and I put the house up for sale, along with the car and all the furniture. Friends and neighbours thought we were nuts and irresponsible to sell everything, and also take two kids aged 9 months and 3 ½ yrs. old to Europe for such a long time.

At that time, Canadians were allowed to stay in Italy for only six months, so Bill and I went to the Italian consulate in Toronto to see if there was a way to extend that period. There were two ways to accomplish this. The first was for every one of us to leave Italy before the six months were up, then cross the border, get our passports stamped and the following day go back. That way, we wouldn't have to unpack or move. That sounded messy, so we opted for plan two. Plan two was for Bill and me to settle in Milano, Italy, and in the first six months open a retouching studio and create work for at least one Italian. It would be preferable to hire more than one, ,because we would be creating work for residents of Italy. That way, Bill and I could work and live in Italy as long as we liked. In the meantime, neighbours who thought we were a bit off in our thinking, were now starting to envy what we were about to do. To make themselves feel better, they had excuses for everything, such as, "We would do the same, but we've started to put in a patio." Another was, "John and I would be off like a shot but little Jeanette has just started ballet school." And so it went until the day of our leaving. It was tough leaving family and friends and a great job I loved, but we were still young and restless.

So in 1961 we left for Italy. Bill, Arlene, Michael and Karl Waldie, and our bunch, met in Montreal to board the Ivernia, of the Cunard Line. Also on board were other good friends, Peter and Shirley Sanderson, on their way to Italy as well. (When they arrived in Italy they bought a used Vespa for $75, and in the months that followed they saw more of Europe than we did. When it was time for Peter and Shirley to go home, they gave the Vespa to some Italian kid and sailed back to Montreal.) The plan for us was, after docking In Southampton, England, was to make our way to Wolfsburg, Germany, and pick up the two new Volkswagen Beetles that Bill and I had purchased in Toronto, and then proceed on to Italy..

I believe it was April 1961 when we boarded the Ivernia in Montreal. We were the first ship to slip out of Montreal at what was supposed to be the end of winter. Because of the ice it was slow going. This didn't matter to us, because we didn't have to arrive anywhere at a given time. Milan certainly had its retouchers, but Bill and I felt confident that we had more to offer than what they were now doing. It was a six-day trip on the Ivernia, and terribly cold weather for all of it.

The Ivernia isn't large by today's standards, but it did have three bars and a small movie theatre and ballroom. For my two boys--Derek, then 9 months old, and Greg, 3 ½--the six days did go by quickly enough. Travelling with little ones takes care of much of the time. Three meals a day plus snacks, and in between that time you've got the bar, or if you're a bit dainty and don't drink, you've got shuffleboard. You could always sit outside on a deck chair with a huge blanket up to your nose, held there with a gloved hand, and possibly a cup of Tetley's tea in the other.

During the evenings we usually all got together in the ballroom, and took turns checking on the children. By children I mean Derek in his cot and Karl, who was only 1 ½, in his cot. Greg & Michael (both exactly the same age to the day) were with us. Carolyn and Arlene would check on the boys in the separate cabins. Twenty minutes later Greg and Michael would go down and check, then Bill and I would be next, and so it went every evening. Whenever Derek woke up crying, out came the corn syrup and we would cover the end of his soother with the syrup, and stick it back into his mouth. On one occasion I went down to check after it was Greg's turn to have a look, and here was Derek in his cot covered in syrup. His face had so much syrup on him he couldn't open his eyes. They were stuck shut from the sticky goo. Fortunately he was okay with that, he was laughing. I picked him up and his blue blanket, sticking to his cheek, came with him. Now, it hit me, What do I do? I went for Carolyn.

Fifteen years later I would be crossing this same ocean, only this time it would be with two others on a 35-foot sailboat. I would reminisce a lot about the six-day cruise on the Ivernia, in which I put on weight. On the sailboat adventure I lost 27 pounds during the 29-day crossing. More on that later. The Ivernia did have all the creature comforts one needs, of course, but not like today's ships with the elevators, shopping malls, hairdressers, massage parlours, shoe repair and a lot of stuff you'll never need. We all disembarked in Southampton, stayed overnight and headed for Wolfsburg, Germany, where Bill and I would pick up our new VW Beetles at the factory. Talk about phenomenal service, that wonderful service didn't compare to the time when I picked up my brand new four-wheel drive Eagle wagon back in Toronto. I wish I could reminisce—about happier times while owning the Eagle, but now that it's over and I'm through cursing and kicking the thing, I can look back and smile at some of the adventures in the wagon. With time, I guess some things do heal.

The Eagle

The Eagle was fully loaded, top of the line, with imitation wood siding—I lost some of the moulding on the way home. I remember that day at Bob Bannerman Motors when I picked it up. The sales person who sold it to me said, "It's out in the lot somewhere, here are the keys." I found it, but couldn't move it because of all the other cars in the way. I was asked to find Henry (or whatever his name was), who looked after that sort of thing. Thanks to Henry we got the car out, but it was filthy. I went back in to complain and found Mr. Bannerman's son who said, "I'll look after you." I told him it's filthy and I don't think I should be driving home to impress my family with a brand new filthy car. He gave me a car wash voucher for the car wash in the mall.

It was getting dark when I joined the line at the car wash. Finally it was my turn to start heading through. The guy at the start of the wash hooked the chain to the undercarriage of the car, I felt it grab and began to move. I opened my power window to give him the voucher and was under way. But then, to my horror, the window wouldn't go back up and the attendant had gone. I went through the rinse, then a generous water wash. Lucky for me I had my parka on because this was winter. I held up my parka collar the best I could, then came the brushes and soap, then a good rinse, and finally the blower and I was pushed through the dancing hanging plastic door straps at the end. Once outside, my glasses froze up, the steering wheel was all shiny and slippery along with the dashboard, and I was soaked on one side only, with everything instantly turning to ice.

I was back at Bannerman Motors immediately, and stood in line now at the service counter behind other customers who were dropping off their cars. In the line in front of me was an older gentleman who every now and then turned around, gave me a good look up and down, but said nothing, Finally, he did say, "How come you're so wet on one side only and some of you is frozen?" I said, "I've been through the car wash." He said, "But you're all wet and frozen." "I know, I had the window open." He looked at me for a moment and said "OH."

Within a year and a half or so my 10,000-km. warranty was over. The rubber side mouldings hung on for a while but one by one they all got lost on the Don Valley parkway. All the door hinges (the pins) on the four doors had to be replaced because they were made of brass. If not, I was told, I could lose a door, and I may be libel if something terrible happened. Imagine, brass of all things. Then the transmission went, again at my expense, like the door hinges, and so it went on with a car with less than 24,000 km.

My reason for this little aside about the service I got from American Motors, where service obviously didn't exist, is that when Bill and I got to the Wolfsburg Volkswagen plant it was like The Pearly Gates had just opened. We were both met at the showroom door with a friendly handshake from Fritz. We pretty much spent most of the day with Fritz, We went through every page of the car manual to make sure every part of the car was familiar. The factory is one very long building. In the front of this very long building are Volkswagen buses that do nothing more than go from one end to the other all day, so wherever you come out of the building, the bus will take you where you have to go in the same building. After the car manual lesson we went for lunch on the premises with Fritz. We enjoyed a great menu with pints of beer, all with the compliments of VW. After lunch, we were taken to the accessory showroom where Bill and I bought luggage carriers with waterproof covers and tie downs. While this was being done we went for a snack and Fritz apologized for things taking so long, which certainly wasn't the case. Apparently we were supposed to have picked up our cars the previous day, so the cars were now being washed once again. The only things we had to pay for were the items we bought at the accessory showroom. How nice to arrive at and leave such a well-organized company!. We shook hands with at least five employees from the service department and a smiling Fritz, as we drove away from the factory with free road maps. My last vision and thoughts of the factory were looking into the rear-view mirror and seeing six or more employees all waving good-bye. Now that is something you never forget.

From Wolfsburg, Germany, Bill and his family, and I, with mine, went our separate ways for a while. He wanted to see some of Russia, and for me, according to the information I got from the Canadian consulate, it wasn't a good idea to go to Russia because of my Hungarian background. So we decided to see some of Europe instead. Every bit of room in the Beetle was carefully used and packed, including the ashtray (diaper pins). From Wolfsburg we drove north to Hamburg. Now Hamburg has its own waterway from the North Sea, where big shipping rigs sail in from many places around the world. We four arrived very late in Hamburg, and somehow found ourselves right in the middle of a shipping port without going through customs first.

The problem we created was, how did we get in here, and how are we going to get out of here? What little German I knew was now a big help. The two customs guys wanted to know how we got in here, when it is impossible to be there without the necessary stamped papers.

Now Derek was awake and decided to join us. He had been sleeping in the hole behind the back seat over the engine, and whenever the engine was turned off, and all went quiet, he was up like a shot. It's a perfect spot for a child because he can't fall out and the constant whining from the engine under him is soothing. On top of all this, the customs flashlights didn't help any. I told the custom man in my best German, "I drove in." They said "No, that's impossible." They also wanted the name of the ship we were on. I told them, "Cunard's Ivernia." They were now very agitated and said, "Nothing of Cunard comes in here." Finally, I guess because this was taking too long, a more important looking guy came out of the little hut and had to know everything, starting from the beginning. All was related to him. Then Derek began to cry louder and, with a full diaper, the smell became overwhelming. In German, this third guy basically said, Get the hell out of here and don't ever let us see you again. It wasn't long before we stopped at the first Gasthaus we saw. As is usually the case in Germany, the service and room couldn't have been nicer. It was far too late to shop for food, so thankfully the management sold us a sausage, sauerkraut and a rye bread. What a change from the hotel hospitality in London!

Derek's diaper was about to explode and we didn't want to be down wind from him. The smell in the VW was rank, so I left the windows open all night. Thinking back, I believe it was the diaper that got us through the Deutsche customs. I used to check into hotels first, leaving the family in the car, and left the engine running so Derek would sleep, then warmed up his milk on the small alcohol stove we had. After feeding we would load up his nutsey (pronounced newt-see), a <u>soother</u> in English, with syrup, put him to bed and hope not to see him again until morning. Greg never gave us a problem; he would go to bed without a whimper. Now it was diaper-washing time. The problem was not so much the washing, but where to hang and dry the many flannel diapers. In every village of every country the milk is quite different from the last place. No wonder the poor little guy had diarrhoea all throughout Europe (this was 1961, before Pampers or Flush-a-byes).

I can't remember exactly when we arrived in Denmark, but I certainly can't forget all the touristy things we did and saw. People-watching is wonderful wherever you are. We did do the Tivoli Gardens, a place with rides for the children and a dance floor for the older folks--and boy, do they love the Tango. (I'm told the Finns love the Tango even more.) Everything we ate at the Tivoli Gardens seemed to be on a stick. Another good thing about Europe was that we could buy Talcum powder everywhere--and a good thing too, because poor little Derek had diarrhoea that stayed with him until we finally got settled in one place. Our last stop in Denmark was to find the little statue in Copenhagen of "The Little Mermaid." You can't miss it; it's the only one covered in bird shit.

We were now on our way to Paris. Paris on a week day, or call it a work day, reminds me of New York. If you have a choice, "Don't Drive!" I love France for the people, but in the city of Paris they don't have time or the patience to give you directions for anything. You're on your own. I had been given the name and address of a wonderful place to stay in Montmartre. The kind of place Toulouse might go to for an aperitif and, if lucky, find himself a girl. I was told they played the accordion every evening and spoke like inspector Clouseau. Well, we never did find it, since not one person took the time to look at my note. Even though I was holding onto a small child and looked forlorn, nothing worked. (A bit of trivia here: Montmartre or Mont des Martyrs, known as The mountain of the martyrs, was named for three saints in the year 272 who were beheaded. One of them, called Saint Denis, picked up his head, which had rolled on the ground, washed off the blood and dirt at a nearby fountain, and walked another four miles. There, he collapsed, and on that spot they built the Basilica of Saint Denis. All the kings of France are buried there, except three. Hey ! If you don't believe this stuff, I understand. I'm just the messenger.)

I believe there are at least 12 avenues that come off from the central circle of the Arc de Triomphe. If you drive along the Champs-Elysées it would lead you to the hub in the middle, which resembles a bicycle wheel. Once you start going around this thing, do your best and just try and get off. By the time you do get off you'll need a tune up, and a washroom.

The Eiffel Tower IS Paris, just like the Statue of Liberty IS New York, Big Ben IS London and in Hungary—well, I really don't know, but in Hungary, they can do many wonderful things with a chicken. It is said Mr. Eiffel used 5,000 sheets of paper, all about a yard square, to draw up his full-scale plans, The Eiffel Tower is definitely a magical place, but don't dare sit down. I had parked the Volkswagen as close to the tower as I could, definitely within view of the tower, but then again everything is in view of the tower. Carolyn and I lifted the two-seater stroller off the roof rack, put Greg and Derek in, and took whatever would be necessary, such as diapers, baby bottles of milk, snacks and the little stove. As tourist's do, we went part way up the tower, had a good look, came down and wandered around for a time. We also took the usual pictures with the old 8-mm Bolex movie camera (no sound), under the four monstrous legs of the tower. In a park-like setting that holds this structure up, are many walking paths and benches. Carolyn and I decided on a bench well outside of the four legs, mostly to be away from the crowds. Carolyn, Greg and Derek, who was now about 10 months old, sat on the bench while I attempted to heat Derek's bottle on the alcohol stove. The milk was ready but the nipple kept getting plugged, and Derek's patience was soon over. He was crying his loudest, so I was sure all could hear him at the top of the tower. Besides of all this, Gregory had to pee, and right now. As a matter a fact, when Greg had to pee, it always had to be right now.

To make matters worse, at this very moment, a short, round and very French lady showed up with a big saddle hand bag hanging on her hip with what looked like tickets coming out from it, and said something in French about francs to sit on the bench. I pointed out that there aren't any signs about paying to sit. She made it very clear in her limited English that we pay, or she will be back with the gendarme. Derek's crying grew louder because the bottle wouldn't deliver, and Greg was now dancing because of the pee. And the round lady wanted her bloody francs. As calm as I knew how, I asked Carolyn to get off the damn bench with Derek. Greg was already off the bench and looking for a tree. I repeated to the round lady that first, I don't see any signs about sitting and paying francs to sit, and now as she can bloody well see, the god-damn bench is empty. She is now hollering she will be back with the gendarme to collect the four cents (our money) per person for sitting on an Eiffel Tower bench. She wandered off somewhere, but indeed came back with the gendarme who knew not a word of English. The squat round lady did all the interpreting for both sides. She said, he said, I have to pay the few francs and all will be okay. I said "bullshit," she said, "I can't interpret that." I said, it means "NO!"

This back and forth nonsense went on far too long. Apparently the gendarme said, according to the round lady, that they would be back with another gendarme and we would all go to the police station to sort this out. I said, "bullshit," and they were off. Derek was still crying, Carolyn was upset and figured I should pay the twelve cents, and Greg hadn't gone pee yet. I told Greg, "Go and pee on the grass. Better yet, go and pee on the bench." Far off, at one of the Eiffel Tower legs, we saw the round one with two gendarmes heading our way. I told Carolyn to start running with Derek for the car. I picked up Greg with one arm and the stroller in the other with our stuff already in it and ran for the car too. We jumped into the Volkswagen, took off and behind us could see three fists waving good-bye. Greg hadn't peed yet. I drove, and not too far along I spotted a restaurant, double parked, picked up Greg and ran into the restaurant. He didn't make it. We left a trail right through the middle of the place on the way to the toilet. When we reached the toilet, of course, he was finished. On the way out, somebody was using a mop. We left Paris in the morning.

It was time to meet up with Bill Waldie and family again in Austria. Whoever got to Innsbruck first was to check at the American Express to see if the others had arrived, and get an address. The Waldie bunch were already there. They had checked into a family home that looked similar to one of those beautifully painted cuckoo clocks. The owner's son was a policeman dressed in that wonderful forest green material, with shiny boots and a big hat. He looked seven feet tall in uniform. After a day's work he'd come home, put on sloppy pants, a t-shirt, sandals and immediately looked his true 5'10". We stayed for a week or so. Bill and I would hike the mountains behind the house and in a short time be knee deep in snow. Looking down from up there, everything looked like a postcard, spring-like and picture perfect. It was a good choice to stay here for a while.

From Innsbruck we drove to Milan, where our intention was to stay for a year or two and set up a studio. Strange, that for both families, everything changed almost instantly. We all agreed, to go sight seeing first, even though we've been doing that for a few weeks now. We did see Milan from a super highway, and never even took the time to drive in, let alone work there. After seeing a lot of Italy, we were all getting a bit travel weary, putting up with diapers and such. It was time to stay put for a while somewhere. Bill and I decided we would like to have a good look at Italy from the top to the bottom, starting with the coast on the Adriatic side, before we settled down and rented something. Next came Venice, and after a few days in Venice we figured the Mediterranean side looked better, so from Venice we went south to about Taranto, and next crossed to the west towards Salerno. At Salerno we seriously started looking for a place to live. It was about now that Bill and I decided we were going to paint every day, and the hell with retouching. From Salerno we went north and had a good look at Ravello (where the writer Gore Vidal has lived for many years). Just down the road from Ravello sits Amalfi, which we all liked very much. Positano looked good, so did Sorrento and Castellammare. We stopped looking when we got to Naples and turned back.

Ravello Italy

The Tyrrhenian seaside to us, looked more pleasing than the Adriatic seaside. We made up our minds that Amalfi had everything we wanted. And a good choice it was. We found a house for rent at the top of Amalfi. Mind you, one had to go through a maze of houses to get there. At first it seemed a puzzle each evening to find home again. First a left, another left, a short tunnel, then under one of many balconies and so on. A hand-drawn map would have solved the problem, but nobody thought of it. The Criscuolo family, who lived in the house, moved next door on the same day that we moved in. We were now two families, with two boys each in a place that had two bedrooms and a kitchen. We all lived in the kitchen because there wasn't a living room. Sadly, one had to go through one bedroom to get to the other. Another slight hindrance was the toilet. To reach the toilet you had to go outside, and we had to share with another family. This was not a big problem until I had diarrhoea for three days.

But life was good, the girls were happy and the four boys got along just great. In the mornings Bill and I took turns going to the bakery for the breakfast buns. We would get these just as they came out of the oven. You paid a few lira (less than a dollar) and walked back home with a bag full of extremely hot Italian buns. Greg and Michael got along beautifully. They played well together, except when they let out the family chicken in the courtyard, which was often. We heard the words daily, Gregorio, Micaela, cativo, cativo. Cativo, (means bad boy). Carolyn and Arlene hit it off well, and took the boys to the beach almost daily, or they took turns baby sitting-- one sat, the other went shopping or needed some free time.

A Studio in Agerola

Bill and I found ourselves a studio in nearby Agerola, about 25 minutes away. It wasn't so much a studio as a small empty room made of cement blocks with a sink. We did well in finding this because all we really needed was storage space. Vittorio, the owner's son that we dealt with, wanted four dollars (Canadian) a day for rent. In Italy the custom is to start high and try for the best price later. We got the room for 25 cents a day and both sides were happy. One of the reasons for the cheap price was the room was of no use to anyone else. The bonus for us was the large patio covered in grape vines that gave great shelter from the sun when we painted, and the view was something to die for. From this high perch we could see Capri below us. On the following day we noticed a sign Vittorio had painted himself, hanging outside the house. The English part of the sign said "Y Rent Rooms" and the French part under that had the spelling completely wrong. We told Vittoria we'd paint him a new one with the proper spelling. He was ecstatic, when at the bottom in smaller lettering, we added, "Recommended by Waldie & Karman - Artists - Canada."

Within walking distance of this perfect spot sat the charming town of Agerola. Painting that sign was our first job in Italy, and in thanks for this, Vittorio's mother made us the perfect Italian meal complete with a bottle of wine. Who could wish for more? The sun is always at its hottest at noon and of course directly over-head. At this time of day Bill and I would have our lunch daily in Agerola, where for roughly 400 hundred lira we would get one of those lovely bottles of Chianti in a basket with two mortadella sandwiches made in its own loaf of bread about 18 inches long. In 1961 one Canadian dollar got you 600 lira. I found that in some of the fancier restaurants, or for that matter any restaurant, one should always check the bill for errors. Whenever I did,, I found it was never in our favour. Many tourists will tip on the total marked at the bottom of the bill, but watch for things like Servizio incluso, which means you have been already charged for service. Another is Pane e coperto; that is a table and bread charge. Occasionally you may notice another charge should you pick up the napkin. So to tip on top of the already included tip could make for a very pricey meal. I'd say this is a good thing to keep in mind no matter where you travel.

Back in Amalfi we found a carpenter who made us two wooden easels for 600 lira each. We painted for at least a couple of months up there, and occasionally on location somewhere else. All paintings were done on canvas stretched on frames, and eventually taken off the frames and rolled up. In my case, with careful rolling, they all fit nicely under the back seat of the car. The actual underside of the seat in a Volkswagen is hollow. Without sounding like a travel agent, for me the Amalfi Coast (la Costiera Amalfitana) has got to have the nicest highway as far as looks go—and it's a voluptuous coastline. The 50-km. drive passes through mountainous terrain, starting at the Sorrento peninsula and on to Salerno. All this beauty lies just south of Naples, in the region of Campania. On the drive, you'll see picturesque villages clinging to rocky cliffs that plunge into the Mediterranean Sea. Stories have it that Hercules was in love with a nymph called Amalfi, and when she passed on, he buried her in the most beautiful place in Italy. So in her memory he gave the place her name.

When Bill and I had the studio up in Agerola, one of the highlights for us was the trip from Amalfi to Agerola. The narrow serpentine road clinging to the cliffs that plunge directly to the sea is, besides breathtaking to look at, also considered a little dangerous. In some places the road is so narrow that if two vehicles meet, such as a bus or large truck, one must back up and yield to the other. The Amalfi road being what it was didn't stop Bill and me from our ongoing contest every evening when it was time to go back to Amalfi. When in my Volks, the game was to see how far I could coast down from the studio without the engine running or applying the brakes. I would mark the spot with a stick and the following day it would be Bill's turn in his car to see if he could better that mark. Another plus about Amalfi itself was that the old paper mills, where the more famous papers of Italy were made in the past, were still operating. Bill and I bought many sheets of gorgeous papers there for whatever we were doing, some the thickness of cardboard that took to watercolour better than we've ever seen before.

I liked it up in Agerola. The towns-people, like most Italians, were warm and friendly. Lunch would always be an experience, so would a haircut. On one particular haircut occasion, Tony had just started cutting my hair when something happened outside. Tony left the barbershop and went out to investigate. I looked out of the window and apparently a donkey, towing a cart, had run into a Fiat automobile. A crowd showed up immediately; women, children, old people leaning on home-made sticks to keep from falling over, with hands waving and all talking at the same time. I'm sure if it were possible to tie all the Italians' hands together, all the talking would stop.

It seemed as though half the town was in on who did what, and to whom, including my barber, who disappeared into the front of the crowd. Meanwhile, I sat there with my tablecloth on, and half a haircut, along with one old fella I had seen in town before. A nice old gent, with no place to go, he got up and started to cut my hair. I smiled a lot and he too smiled a lot, since neither of us spoke the other's language. He had one gold tooth and many others were missing, and each sentence ended with a whistle sound. The shop didn't have a mirror in front of me, so therefore I had no idea how beautiful I would end up.

In a short time my new old friend was finished and sat down. He seemed pleased with himself until Tony came back. Tony started to berate the old man, and the Italian in him came out faster and faster. Through all this, Tony, who was standing behind me, grabbed at tufts of hair on my head and turned my head from side to side really fast, obviously in disgust at what he saw. At this point I still hadn't seen anything of the old man's work, and now didn't want to. The old fella, who believed he had done a nice thing, got up to leave, and still had not said one word. I got up to leave and didn't know whether to pay for the cut or if this one was free. I think it was free, because I just left, thinking, "How do I get home without anyone seeing me." I planned to be home after the kids were asleep, so as not to spoil their day. When I got home, I looked into the mirror, and what I saw looked like a chiappeta head that the cat was using for a litter box.

Bill and I weren't painting as much as before because of the heat. On those intensely hot days, we either drove to Naples for art supplies, or went to the big terminal building in Naples to look at the prostitutes and how they worked. This was a fascinating place. You could sit at a café table all day, drink your espresso and watch the girls parade by. The prostitutes were easy to distinguish from the other girls. The prostitutes all wore the same outfit, which was a white pleated skirt. That way, you knew one working girl from the other office working girl. Here too, you can barter for a better price. After studying the price list, the girl agreed to do a two-for-one evening. By now Bill and I had made our point about the bartering system, so, we kindly told her we weren't interested and would she join us for an espresso and a pastry, which she did. Other days we sat at our favourite Agerola outside café and drank red wine and had marvellous talks. Unfortunately this was all going to come to an end soon, when on one of those extremely hot days we thought, let's call an end to today, and go down to the Amalfi beach (where the family would be) and have a day with the girls and kids. It turned out that on this particular day, Carolyn and Arlene decided to have the Italian lady mind the boys, and spend the day alone on the beach. Bill and I parked the Volkswagen, and went to find the girls.

We saw Carolyn asleep at one end of the beach and carried on to find Arlene. After coming around a huge rock at least 30 feet high, there was Arlene, very much awake and embracing Salvatore. Bill, at first just stood there, kind of in shock. Not knowing what to do next, he picked up a few pebbles and threw them forward on the ground in front of Arlene to get her attention. Arlene looked up and her face went red. Young Salvatore pretended he wasn't there by looking out to the sea. Bill didn't say a word; he just turned and headed for his car. I saw him driving south rather quickly toward the Hotel Luna and Salerno. I too, without speaking, left Arlene on her blanket, and went to wake Carolyn and give her the news of what just took place. We assumed Bill would probably be back soon to sort things out with Arlene, so Carolyn and I sat on the beach for a few hours so they could be alone. Now it was getting dark and time to pick up the four boys from the Italian lady, and go home.

Hotel Luna in Amalfi

On the way home I picked up a bottle of Bill's favourite, Canadian Club rye whisky, which is not always available in Italy. When we got home everything was very quiet, we assumed they had sorted things out. Bill and I went outside to the toilet and sat in the empty bathtub, sideways with our legs hanging over the side, and talked while drinking the whisky out of the bottle. His decided he would leave. I tried to convince him to stay, mostly because of the kids, but Bill's answer was a flat no. This had apparently gone on before and he had now had enough. I certainly could understand and see what must have been going on in his mind. Yes, sometimes a good bottle of whisky is like drinking a truth serum and it's good to let it all out. His immediate intention was to stay at the studio for a while; at least until he could figure out what to do next. The little studio didn't have a bed; it had nothing other than the sink and block walls, so he slept in his Volkswagen. He also insisted I say nothing to Arlene, so if she were to ask, then all I know is, he has left Italy.

Carolyn and I now took the back bedroom, because there were more of us and it was our turn anyway. Each day was pretty much like it had been before, except now I was alone in the early mornings. I would tiptoe past Arlene, Michael and Karl so I could be out the door before the kids woke up. Bill did feel somewhat better now, knowing through me how things were back in Amalfi. Of course it certainly wasn't the same anymore. After a day or two, I remember saying to Bill, "What if Arlene wants a ride to Agerola to catch the bus for Naples, what should I do? She will definitely see your car and there is nowhere to hide it. There is only one road up here, and it does go past the studio".

We devised a plan that went like this. If I were indeed heading to Agerola with Arlene, I would at the beginning of the drive explain how an echo works, and with this mountain terrain being what it is, it was a perfect place for a test. Because of the Italian coastline, it is absolutely necessary for the roads to serpentine back and forth as you climb for the top, and the same applies, of course, for the trip down. Knowing that it's slow going, to get from bottom to top, when I was at the bottom, after explaining all to Arlene about the echo, I would get out of the car, and the echo word I would use is uova, Italian for "eggs." Now, Bill would hear this uova, warning him I was on my way, as it echoed up the mountain. This also gave him at least 20 minutes to take his car and hide in Agerola. I said to Bill, let's give it a try to make sure you do hear it. So tomorrow, don't leave, stay put, it's a practice run. In the morning I stopped the car, stuck my head out of the window and yelled "uova" and heard a perfect repeating echo. When I got to the studio 20 minutes later, Bill said it was perfect and we had another toast to eggs with the local wine.

The VW Beetle is a great car for travel. It's air cooled, good on gas, easy to drive, fix, park, etc. One small problem was that the senior Italians (and of course, I'm not saying all, but a few) figured us to be Tedesco (German) because of the car. On the odd occasion, driving slowly past people, things were said that included the word Tedesco so I guess some hatred was still there. It wasn't always in your favour to be American either. What helped now was that Bill and I painted small Canadian flags on the back of the cars. Wearing a Canadian pin on your clothing didn't hurt either.

In the early weeks when we all had arrived in Amalfi, when

things were better, Salvatore used to come to the house in the evenings to teach us Italian and also improve his English. Now Salvatore was not to be seen. I continued to do my daily drive up to the studio each morning, and on the way, I passed the same Italian construction worker. Some large company had just started building a new hotel up in Agerola, and he was one of the many cement workers they hired. I never did get his name, even though I gave him a ride each morning for weeks. Also, he knew not a word of English, but we got along fine with just hand movements and the odd Italian word. To show his appreciation he always wanted to buy me an expensive dinner with wine. I figured this, in a nice restaurant (which he insisted on), would cost him about 1500 lira. I politely said no, knowing that he only earned 1800 lira for a long day's work. I feel bad today having said no, because he sincerely wanted to do that. I now think I should have suggested we go somewhere some evening for a glass of wine, or an espresso. That would have pleased him, and me. When he realized the dinner wasn't going to happen he pretty much insisted, I should visit his sister in Naples and she would make me very happy. Because we both had a problem with each other's language, I didn't fully understand everything. Was the sister now going to make me dinner or what? To help explain further about his sister and me, with his left hand he put one finger together with his thumb to make what looked like a zero. With the other hand he took his index finger and put it into the zero and moved it back and forth quickly saying something about his sorella (sister) and me and no lira is involved. This was to be his treat for our friendship. I now let him buy me an espresso once or twice and that was that. I did continue to see him on the road on the way to the studio and continued to drive him to work for a while. He did continue (not often) talking about his bella sorella (beautiful sister) occasionally. Now, thinking it over, (sadly) I feel I should have included her in our espresso evening.

I did make another friend around the same time. The guy at the gas pump where I bought my gas, and who helped us find the house we were renting. He always offered me fresh snails to snack on from a folded newspaper. First he would give me a straight pin, of which he had many stuck into his lapel, and then showed me how to get the little suckers out of their shell to eat them. Being live, they'd sometimes snap right back into their little houses, so if you were indeed hungry, this process of eating took far too long. After a short time I got so good at this that nothing ever snapped back again. About this time, Peter and Shirley arrived on their Vespa for a short visit. Of course they knew nothing of Bill and Arlene's problem. When we were alone, I explained some of it, and told them Bill's up at the studio, and please not to say anything. Later, I took them up to see Bill, told them the uova story and, for the hell of it, got out of the car at the bottom and yelled "uova," so they too could witness the beautiful echo, and then drove on up to the studio. But, Bill had left. All was not lost though. I knew where to find him.

Bill decided that maybe it was time to come back to Amalfi, and settle different matters about money, and the passage home for Arlene and the boys, and this he did. He and Arlene drove to Naples to book passage on the Leonardo da Vinci liner for Arlene and the two boys. Bill left Italy for good, and headed for England where we would meet up again in roughly a month's time. Arlene was to leave Amalfi two weeks after her meeting with Bill, and I promised Bill that I'd get everybody to Naples on time for boarding. That last day in Amalfi, for me and Arlene, was bedlam. I ran around the shops looking for her so we could get going, but she was busy with her good-byes, and when she did turn up, we had to run for the luggage, get the boys, who were with Carolyn, and get in the car. We didn't waste any time sightseeing on the way to Naples. We made it to the docks with 10 minutes to spare. I said my good-byes and went for a double scotch before heading back to Amalfi.

Thinking back, Italy will always be my favourite place, and it's all to do with the people, especially if you happen to have children. You can tell immediately that Italians love children and it's not done to impress you. Now, if you're in London, England, for instance, leave your kids at home. You will immediately notice in the hotels that they're not welcome. Whenever we checked into a London hotel in the late evening, Carolyn stayed in the car with the kids while I signed in for two adults and two boys, paid in cash and then went for the luggage. I'd take Greg up first, leaving Carolyn and Derek for last. If we could get past the desk with no one noticing, we were in. But, if they saw we had a small child, even if Derek was fast asleep, we were told to go, and the money was refunded. It could be 10 p.m. and all quiet, but it was always, "You have to leave."

I had the same friction in London restaurants in the late hours. And late hours were usually when things went wrong. After a long day's drive we would get checked in somewhere and put Derek to bed after he had his milk and baby food. By then it was about 9 or 10 p.m. and the three of us were famished. I'd go to a nearby restaurant and order something like three roast beef sandwiches and three milks to go. The answer I got was, I could have it there, but not to go. They do not make sandwiches to go. I explained my problem that we can't come to the restaurant because we have a baby asleep, and because of the late hour it now was. It was still "NO." So then I politely asked if I could buy six or nine slices of beef and six slices of bread. The answer was "NO, this is not a grocery store." Fortunately we always travelled with some jam and crackers in the car, so we got by, but it was never wonderful. So forget about travelling with little ones, unless of course you're in Italy. In England, bring the dog or cat. They're allowed everywhere; hotels, pubs, especially pubs. In a pub, your dog will be given a saucer, so you can share your beer with your mutt. I should mention though, when travelling with children in England we found staying at B&B's was by far the best. They would often open the kitchen for you and your kids, no matter what the hour, and you could meet marvellous people. I could write a pretty good book about travelling with kids in England, but who in his right mind would want to read such a depressing thing? Drive a few extra miles to Scotland and have a good time, kids, dog and all, but for the time of your life, don't by-pass Italy.

Well, sad as it was, it was time for us also to leave Amalfi. I drove to Agerola for the last time to find Vittorio. As it was, I hadn't painted a damn thing since this trouble started. Vittorio was at his usual place, playing his favourite record over and over. I think it must be his only record because we heard it daily. It was rather a nice tune called "Con venti quattro mille baci," which translates "with 24,000 kisses." I've since looked for it in Canada but can't find it. I gave up the studio and now we had to break the news to the Criscuolo family in Amalfi, that we too would be leaving. The day we left they helped Carolyn and me with our luggage to the car, and yes everybody was crying. You would have thought we were family. Poor Greg and Derek, they were getting so many kisses they didn't know what the hell was going on. I like to think that after all this time, we indeed were family. It's wonderful to be able to meet such sincere people in this day and age. I miss them and will continue to miss them every time I think of Italy.

We headed along the road to Rome, heading north through Positano. Bypassing Sorrento, we had another good look at Castellamare and gave Naples a wide berth. Rome is a beautiful place with much to see, but where does one start? There's the Colosseum, Vatican city, St. Peter's Basilica, the underground catacombs, the Appian way and much more. On the first day, it's sometimes a good idea just to walk around the area close to where you're staying. One of my favourite things to do is to go eat somewhere nearby. While doing that, I sometimes noticed that some restaurants have the toilet paper that I call "waxed on one side." It's important to pay attention to what side you use. Believe me, you only make this mistake once. Another oddity is the toilets themselves. Some toilets are nothing more than a walk-in closet. Now, when you're in one of these, you find yourself standing on a piece of porcelain approximately 3 foot square. This is not a toilet as we know it. What you see are two slightly raised and ridged pieces of the porcelain for your feet. Behind you the porcelain tapers down a little, to a round six-inch hole that you should aim for. To help you with this, the builders have thoughtfully put handles on each side. Now for the last and tricky bit. When you pull the chain to flush, you're to stand on the outside of the closet. The water releases on all four sides. In one restaurant I stayed inside when I flushed. My shoes were suede with crepe bottoms. On the way back to my table, all that anyone could hear in the restaurant was the loud suction noise you get when you walk on a marble floor. I felt I should have a strong drink after this embarrassing episode, so I asked the waiter," What's a good strong drink?" He suggested a grappa. "Good, I'll have a double." Grappa is a clear brandy made with herbs. It's also a 60- to 80-proof bitter drink. In the future, I'd sooner go stand in a closet toilet and flush myself than have another grappa.

In general, Italians can be very shy with tourists. I think it's because tourists don't stay long. They're always just passing through. That's why with kids they're more relaxed around you. In restaurants on different occasions Derek was sometimes in his crying mode. This of course spoiled our meals, and annoyed the people at other tables around us. The Italian waitresses would be over to console Derek by picking him up, doing a little gentle dance with him and singing something in Italian. It always worked; they were just damn good at it. They would go even further, no matter how busy the place was. So that Carolyn and I could enjoy our lunch, they would take him to the kitchen. When we were finished eating they'd bring him back, a cookie in each hand and a face covered in jam. I often wished they could pick me up, dance a little, and take me to the kitchen for a cookie. When we lived back in Amalfi, the only question the Italians who were close to us would ask is, if we had been married now for nine years, how come we only have two bambini, and was there something wrong with mia moglie (my wife).

Driving on a super highway with flannel diapers hanging from the aerial, door handles and windows to dry is not a good idea. A cloth flying outside your car means you're in a hurry to get to a hospital. So just saying "buon giorno" (good day) to a polizia on a motorcycle isn't quite enough. A word about Venice, should you desire to visit the city on the water. Venice is a charming spot but expensive. If you sit at a café or bar, expect to pay as much for a coffee as a full lunch elsewhere. You'll also notice the Italians will stand at the bar with their birra or espresso, not sit. A real eye opener for me was just to sit (free) on a stone step in St. Mark's square and watch the tourists. Most of the tourists are Asians, followed by, I'd say, Germans. Probably the first thing you'll notice is the difference in politeness from one group to another: patience in one group and none in the other, and total confusion in both. You must keep in mind with group tours, a good 75% are old people. The bigger problem for some is having to keep up with the group, or be left behind to fend for themselves. Now to keep up with the group leader, you must learn to walk backwards. This way you can take pictures of what you've missed, to see later when you get home, putting a name to it if you can remember, because everything will go past you very quickly.

The Clock Tower, built in 1496 with two bronze figures.

The Gondola Ride: You could adopt a third-world country family cheaper than pay for a gondola ride. It can be exciting though. Occasionally, the residents will throw their garbage out the windows. The thought here is, the garbage is meant to find its way to the Adriatic sea. Venice has far too many things and places to talk about here, but one that stands out for me is, the "Torre dell'orologio," a clock tower built in 1496. This is definitely a Venetian piece of work. The clock shows the phases of the moon and signs of the zodiac. Above this, on the hour we see three kings and Jesus, plus an angel. Also you're allowed up there to see yet another mechanism that propels two bronze Moor figures who pivot and strike the bell with hammers every hour. They're known as "The Moors" because of the dark colour of the bronze. Folklore has it that when the bell was finished, it was such a wonderful thing that the guy who designed and built it was blinded, so he could never do another one. If you want to believe this, it's your choice. It makes for a good story.

I was the only one up there one morning waiting for the bell to do its thing, when a couple of tourists showed up. I recognized one to be one of the Eaton boys, and the other John Bassett Jr. They too sat and waited. We got to talking, because I had on a windbreaker that showed a hockey crest with Toronto in it. The reasons the two were travelling together was that John Bassett Jr. was to be married soon, and this was his final fling. I asked what they had seen so far, and done since they arrived. Well, for starters it's against the law to drive a power boat fast through the Grand Canal, or for that matter anywhere in the city of Venice. The wash from boats eats away the bottom portions of buildings and, sadly, Venice is and has been sinking for decades. Money does change things. Apparently by paying extra, they had the ride of their life by going flat out on the Grand Canal. So much for common sense too. We chatted for quite a long time until the bells took over. After this, I mentioned I was going to my favourite spot for a beer and told them where it was. They too said, "what a great idea" and left without me. So much again for class. If you should want to be alone, Venice is not for you. You may be lucky and find a spot for three minutes but that's about it. Venice has about 70,000 people that actually live there, but if you're looking for great art, great institutions and architecture, it's a must.

Arrivederci Venezia

Arrivederci Venezia, We now made our way to Switzerland for a short stay, and then on to England. Thanks to the American Express office we found Bill again. He looked okay, but admitted he hadn't been sober since he left Amalfi. He had made new friends (mostly journalists), so it was good for him to be moving about, instead of sitting in a room drinking alone. We did attend a couple of fun parties with Bill, and we did have a good place to stay this time. It was a B&B run by a woman who a few years earlier had lived in Canada. The big breakfast every morning would certainly carry you through to lunch. After breakfast, she would lie in her wee backyard in a bikini. The backyard lay alongside a railway line. Every time we heard the erratic blast of the train whistle we knew she was outside. Other things hadn't changed, such as the time, again late in the evening I went out to buy cookies for the boys in a grocery store. I asked for cookies and was told, "We don't sell cookies, never have and never will." But they did sell biscuits. I bought four bags of crisps and went home. I think part of the problem may have been my accent; they figured I was American. From that point on, whenever I went out to purchase anything, I was determined to sing "O Canada" and carry a beaver under one arm.

We left for Scotland in the morning, and again I left it too late to find a room. The car was running beautifully, a touch noisy and a wee bit of an odour from the nappies that didn't get washed the night before. The roads were long, dark, and quite empty, but "AHA" up ahead, well lit and four stories high stood what looked like a hotel. Over the well-lit front window on the ground floor was a big sign that said Tennants. Well, it was late and this looked perfect. Carolyn and the boys stayed in the Volkswagen and I went in to book a room. The place had the appearance of a bar and office combined. I stood in front of the long counter and said to the little man, "I would like a room please." He walked away, and when he returned he plunked down a shot glass in front of me with something in it. Now, I said to myself, "Hey, things are looking up." What a lovely and sweet greeting this is. I asked again about the room. He said, "Aye laddie, you've got yurr rhum." I was now a little embarrassed and lost for words. I drank the rum, paid and left.

We drove on and quickly found a hotel, like many others in Scotland, where kids are not a problem and Tennants happens to be a brand of beer. The following day in Edinburgh, after a wonderful sleep and a full breakfast, Carolyn, the boys and I, with the help of the stroller, were having a nice walk on one of the main streets. Coming towards us was Bill Waldie, arm in arm with a chunky pear-shaped crumpet he had picked up hitch hiking. She had this big radio on her shoulder with the volume turned up so the people on the other side of the street could also enjoy the music. She was nice enough, and polite, but seemed to say "Yah" a lot. She loved the word because it didn't interfere with her gum. Bill had a lot on his mind, and certainly did need the company.

Days later, we were finally on our way to Southampton to wait for the arrival of the Ivernia, and sail for home. Southampton is not a resort kind of place. Far from it. It's strictly for shipping. We had to give up the VW three days earlier so it could be stored for shipping on the ship. At this same time Derek came down with something serious.

We had no idea of what it was or why his temperature was climbing so rapidly. His whole body went bright red from the fever, then arched his back, went absolutely ridged and stayed that way. Next his eyes rolled back and all that was showing were the whites. From the lobby, I insisted I needed a doctor immediately. They did their best to locate someone and eventually a very old doctor finally arrived. I'm guessing he was in his 90s from the way he spoke and walked. His hearing was a problem, because whenever I spoke to him, he'd be facing in different directions to see who was talking. He looked at Derek and without touching him or checking his temperature all he said was, "Bathe him in cold water" and promptly left. The next bit of bad news was from the staff in the office who said, "We have to lock up now," and they left.

Here we were on the third floor, no telephones, no people downstairs, and now Derek was arched so far back he wasn't moving at all. To touch him felt like putting your hand on a stove. Fortunately I did get a pocketful of those big large English pennies earlier from downstairs before they locked up. I ran out of the building, down the street to look for a phone box. I found one of those red boxes and phoned a hospital, told them everything they had to know and where we were staying. Bless them. By the time it took me to run back, they were already pulling up in the ambulance. The two ambulance attendants wrapped Derek in blankets and literally ran down the three flights with him. Carolyn, of course went along in the ambulance. I asked Carolyn to phone the downstairs office when she had news, and let the damn thing ring. In the meantime I would sit outside of our room so I could hear it, even though I knew there was no way to get to the phone itself. Then, my plan was to run to the same phone box I was in before and call her. When Carolyn called, I left Greg (who was sleeping) alone, ran to the phone box, spoke to Carolyn and the wonderful news was the danger was over. At the hospital they gave Derek a penicillin shot, and the fever broke immediately. Our next problem was, would the ship's doctor allow us on board with a sick child, especially when he (the doctor) was already overworked with every crossing. The marvellous news was that the doctor said yes, and two days later I got a taxi and went to get Carolyn and Derek at the hospital. At the hospital, and on board ship, the doctor, nurses, staff, ambulance people, anyone involved since the beginning could not have been nicer. Another great plus was that with the English health plan being what it is, everything was absolutely free. You really couldn't wish for anything nicer than that.

Back in Ontario

We were back at home now in Ontario, with a Volkswagen and $500 in the bank. It was time to get back into the commercial art business. First thing in the morning I planned to start making phone calls. We were now living in my parents' basement. People asked whether Carolyn and I would do it again. "You bet, in an instant," we responded. I always thought I'd like to be a painter, but it never happened. I did submit work to galleries and managed to sell a few pictures and of course I felt most happy when some of my work was accepted into a big show like the Ontario Society of Artists, the Royal Canadian Academy, the Montreal Spring Show and the Hamilton Art Gallery. Before I left for Italy, a respected art reviewer in Toronto, Elizabeth Kilbourn, said in the Hamilton Spectator, "An artist who has excited some interest at the Art Gallery of Hamilton in recent years is a young man called Robert Karman. His austere, strongly designed landscapes have been a distinguishing feature at winter exhibitions."

So what went wrong or changed things for me? I'm not sure but I'll try to put some meaning to this, as we go on. Of course, just plain laziness has a lot to do with it, and no lazy artist, whether a writer, musician or whatever, ever succeeded at anything, except of course, being lazy. Thinking back, I guess the '60s for me was my most interesting decade. I loved the opening nights of a show. After the ribbon was cut and the speeches were over, the first thing you did was to go to see where they've hung your painting. I always liked to stand off to the side to hear what people had to say. They didn't know who you were anyway, or what the artist looked like. I remember on one occasion, two elderly ladies explaining one of my paintings to another. They wondered why I painted the cross on the outside of the fort, and not on the inside where it belonged. I don't know either, but it was fun listening to all of this.

This particular painting was my first commissioned work for a Mr. Clark at the All-State Ins. Co. Mr. Clark came to the house to discuss the painting. What medium would I work in? What size? What would I paint? And mostly, how much? I was young, nervous and didn't want to go too high because I wanted this commission. In my head I was thinking $ 180 (keep in mind this was 1959). That would have been good money, and I wasn't well known either. Finally, because I hadn't spoken yet, Mr. Clark said, "The limit for All State works of art is $ 400." I said, "I had $450 in mind but I could do it for $400." We shook hands and I painted Fort Ste Marie. That, I think was my very beginning.

When I got back from Italy, I got a phone call from a woman at the Willowdale library gallery, asking if I would consider a show at the gallery. I said yes, and that was a mistake. I didn't sell a damn thing. I think if I had painted lovely realistic flowers or kittens playing with wool in baskets or puppy dogs I might have sold something. As I said earlier, with $500 in the bank it was time to go back to retouching. Only now, there wasn't any work around. S&R, where I worked before, wasn't hiring because they were about to close up the business. It seems too much money was spent on fun and games and now it was all over.

I covered all the studios in Toronto, but all were downsizing. I left Carolyn and the boys in Toronto and drove to Montreal in the

VW. After many days, and with the help of a phone book I covered every studio one by one. It was the same story in Montreal, so feeling very rejected I headed home. It was now that I started freelancing; I had no other choice. Now, back in Toronto, three of us got together to share expenses and space. Cec Pentland, Wes Chapman and I rented a apartment at 40 Park Rd. The place was perfect. Cec took the bedroom, which was a good idea indeed. Because of his drinking problem he often passed out, so if a client came over, we could now close his door and let him sleep it off. The location for Wes couldn't be better: In the evenings he could walk up Yonge St. to the CHUM radio station. Aside from being a very talented illustrator, he had his own radio show called "Wes Chapman and the High Riders." Wes, a non-drinker and smoker, sang and played guitar. When the three of us worked evenings, which was often, Wes would always dedicate a number of hurtin' songs to his best friends. Songs with titles like—"My Dog Up't and Died Last Night" or "She Left Me For a John Deere Tractor", and my favourite, "I've Been Down So Long, It Looks Like Up." "A couple of shut-ins," he called us, "who couldn't get out anymore, named Cec and Bob." After the live show, he'd be back to work. The number on the door was 601, so after three minutes of thinking, we became known as Studio 601.

Studio 601, and Virgi

In the apartment next door to ours lived a lovely girl called Virgi. Now, Virgi did not have to work; she was fortunate enough to be born more attractive than the average girl and wasn't overly tall or curvaceous, but had a smile and personality that made her beautiful and nice to know. Virgi was being looked after by a nice rich Jewish guy, who paid all her bills, food, rent, clothes, everything. All she had to do was be home, day and night, just in case he should call. This same Jewish guy was very busy indeed, being married to a princess, running a business, and of course looking after Virgi. To keep from going stir crazy, Virgi spent much of her time in our place just for our company. Also her keeper (Mr. Big, as we called him) would drop off cases of Johnnie Walker Black Label Scotch, which she gladly shared with us. Fortunately for me, Cec hated Scotch and Wes didn't drink. She would leave her door open, and we did the same, so Virgi could hear her phone should it ring. Whenever she was out in the evenings with Mr. Big, she would leave her darling poodle "Fru-Fru" with us. Alone the thing would drive everyone nuts with its howling and Fru-Fru felt quite at home with us. For a night of doggy sitting, Virgi always gave us a bottle of Scotch.

For a short time, a girl friend of Virgi's who had nowhere to go moved in with her. I was working late one night (alone) when a knock at the door presented the new girl. I had never met the new girl, but have to admit at first appearance she looked very sensuous. She didn't have her key and Virgi wasn't home yet. She was polite and wondered if she could stay until Virgi got home. I said, "Of course. Virgi will come here first anyway, because I've got Fru-Fru." She'd had a few drinks before she got here, but asked if she could have a Scotch. I poured her a shot (straight up) of Virgi's Scotch and had one myself. After a while she pretty much spelled out what she was after. We both sat in the little den we had because it was more comfortable, with a chesterfield and coffee table. First she parted her legs just enough so I could see what I was missing. I could see she wasn't wearing underwear, and after a hug and some teasing, she finally said, "If you look after me and pay my expenses, such as an apartment somewhere, food, car payments and insurance, you could have your way with me any time you want."

"Whoa, you're out of your mind," I said. "I have enough trouble paying my third of the rent here, plus I've got plenty of other expenses." I added to this, "Obviously, you've never been with a retoucher before." She mumbled something about "That's true and I shall never make that mistake again." She put on her imitation leopard skin coat and left without closing the door. In about four days she moved out of Virgi's apartment. Possibly she found the mark she was looking for.

In the year or so that Virgi lived next door and the many talks we'd had, she did confide in me one evening about some of her past. Life hadn't always been this easy when she was growing up. Virgi had an abusive and strict stepfather. To earn a little money, she worked as a part time Nanny to a three-year-old and a baby for a wealthy working couple. Part of her day consisted of taking the baby in the carriage for fresh air in the Mount Pleasant cemetery. On one of those outings, a man jumped out from the bushes, took hold of the baby by the throat, and demanded oral sex. Another time, being in the wrong place at the wrong time, she was raped by two guys and beaten up very badly. To this day these two memories have made her very nervous, and that is why she is thankful for what she has at the present time.

S&R studios soon closed for good. Some of the staff got into the liquor cabinet and brought all the bottles to Studio 601. They were out of work and it hadn't registered yet. That was still to come. So we had a party, and a wonderful party it was, with pizza, French fries and other junk food delivered to our door. After the party when everyone was gone, Lorraine stayed behind to help me clean up. In all the years I worked with Lorraine at S&R I didn't know she had a scar that ran from her navel almost to her thigh.

Some of the artists from S&R had nowhere to go, so they also ended up freelancing like we three were doing, and rented two apartments in our building two floors below. Now we had three apartments with everyone freelancing on their own. But It wasn't such a good idea. Some of the guys in the two other units did not get along, and without going into detail something had to be done. Cec in our unit was drinking more. He had bottles hidden everywhere. In the toilet bowl was a bottle, behind the fridge on a string was another and so forth. We had to do something, the superintendent lady came up to Wes and me one day, and said, "Your other partner is out cold on the third-floor stairs, and his shoes are on the second." She also added, "Either he goes or you all go." In the three apartments I believe there were now 12 of us. After voting everyone agreed and it was decided that Cec had to leave. As luck would have it, Cec walked into the meeting when we were deciding what to do about Cec, and asked,

"What's up?" Wes told Cec about the vote and the outcome. Cec, because he and I had been the best of friends for many years, looked at me and asked if I too voted yes? "Yes," I said. With that he looked straight at me and said, "Et tu Brutus." Now, I know Cec loved Shakespeare, but in my head all I could think of was, "Boy! that's a hard act to follow." I said nothing. I remember as he turned to leave I heard him say, "Havoc, and let slip the dogs of war." I wondered, "What the hell does that mean?"

Reggie (not his real name) was another problem, very talented but with the personality of a vulgar asshole. Cec, Wes and I had worked with Reggie before at S&R studios. He was the cheapest son of a bitch I've ever met, and there was no need for this, because financially he did very well indeed. It seemed his only reason for being on this earth was to be around porn. Failing with manners didn't help him either with girls. I must admit, the one thing he had going for him was that he was a talented bastard. He was married, but was always looking for something on the side. The girls at S&R weren't interested, and for good reason. He was vulgar, so his main entertainment now became hookers. Cheap as he was, he had no choice with the hookers. You paid the set fee or you went home. One evening when the work day was over, Reggie had set it up to meet one of the regulars that he'd been with before. She met him at the studio, and off they went in his station wagon. He certainly wasn't going to spring for a motel, especially when the wagon always worked well before. So, as the story went, what we heard later was, Reggie drove for farm country out of town, where it's quieter and darker. Well, the hooker, being a working girl started early while Reggie drove. She was giving him a blow job,

Reggie came, and the car went off the road and into the ditch. The hooker bit his penis, and the front of the wagon was in bad shape. What followed, I think was pretty wonderful. The wife wanted to know how Reggie got what looked like teeth imprints on his penis, why some of the car grill was missing, and how come the front of the wagon around the bumper was full of weeds and mud when she and Reggie live in the city. Now, here he was sharing space in our building. Fortunately, at least he worked downstairs with some of the others.

Wes and I were up in our studio chatting with Virgi one evening. We three happened to be standing in the hall opposite the bathroom when Reggie came in. Now Virgi's background and lifestyle are nobody's business but her own. But Reggie, the thoughtless jerk, said to her, "Virgi, I know for enough money, I can get you to give me a blow job." Naturally the three of us looked at each other with "what the hell brought that on?" expressions. Virgi held back the best she could and answered, "A person like you would never have enough money to look at my tits, let alone anything else." This whole conversation came up as such a surprise to Wes and me that we didn't know what to say. Suddenly, Reggie pulled out a roll of bills (10s and 20s) and put it into Virgi's hand, saying, "Here, this should be more than enough to give me that blow job."

Now, there is a beautiful ending to this story. We were all standing outside our bathroom in the hallway, the bathroom light was on and the door was open. Reggie, very English, always dressed in shirt and tie with a long-sleeved sweater, stood there while Virgi took one step forward with the roll of bills, threw the money into the toilet and flushed with the little handle. The wonderful memory I have to this day is of Reggie reaching into the swirling water, sweater and all, as the money went around and around. Some of it already gone, and no blow job. Wes and I didn't speak but we sure did smile for a long time. At a later moment, I thanked and gave my compliments to Virgi for a memorable evening.

I'm not sure how long Studio 601 lasted, but it was a wonderful place to work, on the top floor, with a good view of the park below, and good surroundings too. It certainly didn't give you the feeling of being in the central part of Toronto, but like other good things it too came to an end. Once we grew beyond the original three, with all the different personalities at play, the place fell apart. Cec and I stayed friends but his drinking continued, only now, if he couldn't get his rye whisky he threatened suicide. Many evenings when he was so far gone and needed that one more drink, he'd try every trick he knew to con me out of one more, and he did know every trick and angle in the book. When he couldn't find me, he would phone my mother, crying and very upset, and would say, "Please tell Bob for me that I appreciate everything he's done for me and I love him for that, but tonight I'm going to end it all." My mother usually found me. Strangely, he always told my mother where he was. Maw always passed the message on. "Go to Cec, now, because today is his last day and he wants to say good-bye to you." Cec did always know how to get more booze or money from someone. He was good at it. After all, he'd been at it for the past 17 years.

I remember a time many years later, when I shared an apartment studio with Wally Hern at 44 Jackes Ave. I was working alone late one evening when the phone rang. It was Cec, so drunk he was difficult to understand. He was at the subway station at Carlton and Yonge St. His plan was to jump in front of the subway, but first he had to call to say good-bye. I could hear the trains in the background. I said, "Sit tight where you are, I'm coming for you." I knew how Cec's mind worked, and so he wouldn't get the better of me this time, like he usually did, I changed a few things. I had a full bottle of Seagram's rye whiskey (his favourite) and nothing to empty it into, so I poured the instant coffee into two soup dishes and placed them in the cupboard, washed the coffee bottle and filled it with whiskey. I now had about three inches of booze left in the whiskey bottle and put it away. Then I went for Cec in the Land Rover. Cec was waiting outside the Carlton station sitting on the sidewalk, and very drunk. The Land Rover is very high, and without a running board, so I had to get out, walk around and lift him in, which was not an easy task. Cec is a big man and heavy. When we got back to the studio, I figured the best thing was for me to drop him off at the entrance of the building and then go park.

The apartment Wally and I worked at had a doorman called Eddie. Well, when I pulled up, Eddie, doing what he's supposed to do, opened the door on the passenger side and Cec fell out. Eddie and I carried Cec to a lobby chair while I parked. Then Eddie helped me get him to the elevator. Before we even got to the apartment Cec started, "I've got to have a drink, look, I'm shaking, I've already peed my pants, I've really got to have a drink." But I was ready, and answer back with, "I don't have any." "Bullshit Karman, you've always got some hidden somewhere." "No, I don't, I'm going to make you a coffee." "If I have coffee, I will be sick, gimme a drink." "I don't have any." "Yes, you do." "No I don't." "you always have booze." "Well, not this time."

"Look, I've been at this all my life, so why don't you just save us both a lot of time and trouble, and get the bottle."

I went into the kitchen and got two juice glasses and the bottle. Now I split what was in the bottle in two equal parts in the juice glasses. Next, I insisted he didn't throw his drink back. "I will not take it, it's yours," I said. "I just want to plug the kettle in for us, I'll be right back, and we can talk and have a drink." It is two steps to the kitchen, and takes about three seconds to be back. When I got back both drinks were empty. In a matter of minutes Cec was also gone. He saw the booze was gone, so why stay. I'm sure he had it all thought out where he'd go next while he was with me.

When Studio 601 ended some of us went to work at a place called Studio 43. That's right, it was at 43 Edward St. How creative is that? Studio 43 had three partners. Peter Dwight, Bill Jamieson and Peter Lucas. The three partners worked quite hard to make a go of it, but later on some of the staff had other ideas. The talented bunch got together with an art salesman called Al Rubbens and, strictly on the quiet, started to plan their own studio called Rubbens, Bond & Associates at 17 Balmuto St. They had already rented the space on Balmuto St. and, not to raise too much aggravation, they quit one by one. I believe Bill Bond was the first to leave, followed by Al Rubbens. A week or two later another would go until it was all very obvious to the three partners what was happening. The studio hung on as long as it could but with most of the talent gone it was time to close. I remember Peter Dwight calling me in and saying something like, "Why don't you go and join the others, you're the only one left, and there's nothing here. You're probably next to go over there anyway." I tried to convince him I had no part in this, and I really had no plans to leave. I felt bad for the three partners, who had worked hard to get this far. But the studio was already getting ready to close its doors for good, so I didn't have a choice anyway. Before all this nonsense, and in better times, I do remember meeting an interesting guy named John Seibert at Studio 43. He had rented space in the photo studio to shoot a documentary for the Canadian Construction Safety Program, starring Buster Keaton. I believe it was Buster's last big screen shoot. Buster was a big smoker for most of his life, and it showed. He coughed constantly, so they had to shoot between coughs. I could hear him coughing through the walls in the art department. Someone on radio recently said that if you can recall the '60s, you probably weren't there. Well, I do remember the '60s, but don't ask me where, or what happened in that particular year. I, too, eventually left Studio 43. It was over. I had nowhere to go, so I rented an upstairs room from the boys at Balmuto St. and did my own thing. Others who were already there were Roy Hewitson (illustrator), Alex Dellow (photographer), Dick Marvin (illustrator) and Norm Nadalin (salesman).

Radio Days

One of the big perks of working in your own place is the radio. With radio in the '60s we had CHUM 1050 AM in Toronto. CHUM signed off in May 2000 for the last time. I remember the last song played was "All Shook Up" by Elvis Presley. It was also the first song on CHUM back in 1957. Another tune at the finish was "It's Over" by Roy Orbison. In the early '50s when I started at Brigden's my favourites were tunes like "Purple People-Eater," "Running Bear," and "My Friend the Witch Doctor." Back then I was 17 years old, and still living with my parents in Thornhill, Ont., on a street without hydro. But I had my crystal radio. It consisted of a little crystal thing smaller than an aspirin mounted on a board. It had a fine needle that touched the crystal and somewhere on this board was a coil. There were no batteries. Oh yes, the sound came out of one earphone, so therefore the volume was very low. Another way to help pull in a radio station was to hook the thing up to a farmers fence for an aerial. Gosh! Today you can buy a hand-held radio for $5.95, and they come in different flavours.

I remember from the '60s, names like Gerry & the Pacemakers, The Beatles, Dave Clark 5, Elvis, The Stones, The Mamas and the papas, The Monkees, Supremes and, one of my favourites, Creedence Clearwater revival. Big names in Toronto Maple Leafs hockey at the time included George Armstrong, Bobby Baun, Johnny Bower, King Clancy, Ron Ellis, Tim Horton, Red Kelly, Frank Mahovlich and (who can forget?) Eddie Shack. There were a couple of phone-in radio shows, hosted first by Larry Solway and next by John Gilbert. I never liked listening to Larry Solway. He had a bad habit, when people phoned in about a problem, and if he didn't agree with their point of view (which was often), he simply disconnected that person in mid-sentence. I often saw him standing in line at the waters edge at Queen's Quay and York St., waiting for the tender to go to the I.Y.C. (Island yacht club). Before the tender arrived he'd be somewhere in the back of the line. When the tender showed up, he had managed to work his way up to the front of the line.

Another person I disliked for the same reason was Gordon Sinclair. He banked where I banked at the CIBC at St. Clair and Yonge Street. Every Friday, as good bank customers we all stood quietly in the long line. That arrogant little fart would walk in and go directly to a teller. First of course, he would park his Rolls Royce illegally, directly in front of the bank doors. Why none of us ever spoke up to tell him to go to the back of the line, I'll never know.

Otherwise, Toronto was a good place to be in those golden days. We had Don Daynard at CHFI 98.1 FM. Al Boliska was around at CHUM until he died at age 40. Jungle Jay was also at CHUM. He died in 1994. There was Whipper Billy Watson, the wrestler, who fought at Maple Leaf Gardens, going back to 1940. The Whip, as he was known, became a celebrity and was great with helping at charities. He retired from the ring in 1971 after a car slid into him and nearly severed his leg, ending his career. Whipper died in 1990.

Another "hometown hero" on the wrestling circuit was Lord Athol Layton. Born in Australia, he had 25 years headlining at the Gardens. In Toronto around 1950 he had many battles with Whipper Watson. Layton used the judo chop and his 6'5" 250 lbs. helped a lot.

Layton became a tireless worker for handicapped children in the '60s. He spent five years at CFTO-TV in Toronto as a wrestling commentator. He was a true, and much-liked, gentleman till his death in 1984 at the age of 63.

A musician none of us will forget is Ronnie Hawkins, born in 1935 in Arkansas. Even though he was born in the States, he seemed more Canadian than many true Canadians. In 1958 a friend of Hawkins, "Harold Jenkins" (aka Conway Twitty), was playing in a rockabilly band called The Rock Housers. I remember Twitty used to visit Wes Chapman often when we had Studio 601. I shall always remember him as the guy with the big hair.

The Hawks, as the group was known, included Levon Helm, Robbie Robertson, Rick Danko and others. When the group broke up, Hawkins said his good-byes, wished them luck and set about to organize a peace festival with John Lennon in 1969. Lennon and Yoko Ono would be guests at Hawkins' farm for several days. Years later Hawkins did an album called "Let it Rock," which went gold and got him a Juno Award nomination. He was invited as a guest to the White House by President Bill Clinton. Ronnie Hawkins still resides here in Ontario, and what I personally miss is Toronto's New Year's eve countdown at Nathan Philips square in front of Toronto's City Hall, with Rompin' Ronnie Hawkins singing, "Bo Diddley" and "Who Do You Love?"

I did have an introduction to show biz once with the Toronto Mendelssohn Choir. Roy Raeburn and I were in a downstairs bar near Yonge St. and Rosehill Ave. when, after a concert somewhere nearby, some members of the choir dropped in. After an hour or two of drinking they stood up to sing, and sing and sing they did. Roy and I got up too, and sing and sing we did. Now my debut was over.

Somewhere along the way I found myself at A.D.S. (Art & Design Studios) at 900 Yonge St. near Davenport. This was probably the biggest art department I ever worked in. I enjoyed being there with people like Mike Skinner (he and I would become partners later on) and Fred Oakley, whom I would share the big studio fire with later on. The fire broke out on a Friday night. Fred was doing a sample for himself and I was doing some freelance work of my own, even though I was on the payroll with A.D.S. The staff had left long ago and Fred was on his way home now. It was said much later on that the fire got started on the floor below from a hot fuse panel. I was working away happily, except for a leg cast I'd been wearing for some time, thanks to a water skiing accident. I sat at my desk, shoes off, radio playing, when I started to hear sounds of breaking glass. I left my cubicle to have a look around the corner, and in Pete Dwight's room the glass in the big window was breaking and the curtains were ablaze. The fire apparently was coming up from the outside of the building. Now, I wondered, are all the floors below me on fire? Do I go down the front stairs? Or the back stairs? I knew taking the elevator could be a big mistake. Do I head for the roof? Do I stand on my window ledge? I had to make a decision because the smoke was now coming out of the air-conditioning ducts, and very heavily. Sometimes we do silly things in situations like this. I went back to shut off my radio, put my shoes on, turned off my desk lamp, and headed for the front stairs. The smoke became heavier on the next floor down. For a moment I thought I'd go back up, but firemen started passing me on my way down. When I hobbled out the front door, flashbulbs were going off. The newspaper reporters were already there. I was interviewed on the street by the Toronto Star.

The next day in the Saturday paper, I was called a hero because I notified all in the building about the fire. Not true, because I didn't know about the fire. I was alone in the building and I just wanted out. But the article was good for my young lad Derek in public school when it became show and tell time. The saddest part of this fire was the death of a young fireman. Apparently there was so much water poured into the building to control the fire that this water ended up in the basement where the photo studio was. Later, this young fireman was overcome by smoke and somehow ended up in the basement alone, passed out face down and drowned. Immediately after the fire, everyone was at loose ends as to what happens now. Fred Oakley and I went back the following day to see if there was anything salvageable of ours. Unfortunately, someone got there before us. Strange that, after a fire with high pressure water from hoses everywhere, my side table with brushes, pencils and other light items, were all still where I left them. But my Ronson lighter, my wonderful gold handled magnifying glass, brass stapler and a few other small items, all gone. Shortly after this terrible fire, things got back to normal and A.D.S. eventually moved to Merton St.

People do move around quite a bit in the art business--either to earn more money, or when it's time to learn more by moving on, or to get away from personal friction or jealousy. It can be a bit like show biz. There are too many people in the same profession with big egos, which brings on the wheeling and dealing. In this business, it seemed that everything was possible, including cheating and lying. My next move was a good one. I went to work for a small studio in the Yonge and St. Clair St. area. Yes! Dave Haughton & Assoc. was a good place. It was where I met Wally Hern, Doug Metcoff and a salesman named Gord Newsome who, after a year of selling, never brought me one retouching job, even though I was well known around town. There was one particular time with Gord when he wanted he me to join him on a trip to the Baker Lovick Ad agency to quote on something. He was quiet on the drive over, as obviously he had something important on his mind. After the elevator ride and in front of the agency front door, he said, "Ah, I'm a little embarrassed and as I'll have to introduce you, I've forgotten your name."

Bart Benson, a well-known name, worked for Haughton's for a time too. Bart was an extremely talented photographer but had a mischievous and lovable side to him, and was always restless. I wasn't living at home with my wife Doris around this time, and Bart was separated from Margo, a beautiful and successful model. Bart and I had many very memorable evenings together that I shall never forget, and of course I must mention a story or two about him. On one of those evenings we went to Tom Jones restaurant for dinner, a reputable place known for its steaks. We both had the absolutely perfect meal with wine and finished off with a double Bisquit cognac (Bart's favourite). It was nearing closing time when someone on staff went around at one point and announced, "Last call for drinks." When the opportunity was there Bart always had the urge to shock people, and tonight was no exception. When he heard this, I knew something was up, just from the smile on his face. He got up, grabbed a waiter's towel from the back of a chair, put it over his arm, dropped his penis out, and went around the tables calling out, "Last call for drinks." After covering all the tables in the room he came back and sat down. The maître d', who had known Bart for quite a long time (Bart being a regular guest), came over and whispered, "Bart, I suggest you and your friend leave immediately. The police are on their way."

I did eat at another expensive restaurant with Bart on other occasions, even though I hated the place. It was a French restaurant with a nice menu but I couldn't stand the obsequious, buttery, bootlicking, smarmy owner of the place. At the entrance, hanging on the wall, was a big reproduction of the Mona Lisa I had retouched with one breast exposed, beautifully framed in gold, with a small light over it. Bart thought the Frenchman (owner) might be interested in who did it and introduced me and mentioned it was my work. Without a word, he just walked away. So much for manners. Why Bart ate there, I'll never know.

Pranksters

Bart loved to play jokes on people, including me. Rob Bush, son of Jack Bush the painter, worked for Dave Haughton as a salesman. After a photo shoot of women's lingerie, Bart put a pair of panties and bra in one of Rob's jacket pockets. Rob was married, and you can guess the rest. It did not go over well. I was still married to Doris (my second) around this time, and we had just gotten back together once again even though we were more apart than together. Doris was extremely jealous. Bart knew this, and as of yet had never met her. I introduced Bart to Doris at the Haughton Christmas party and Bart's answer was, " Elaine, of course I know you, you've been here with Bob many times."

Doris and I separated once again. Bart and Margo got back together for a while, but it too didn't last. He felt Margo was cheating on him and seeing a male model. Bart knew where the model lived, and after finishing a shoot that Bart was on, which included a black cape with a beautiful scarlet silk lining, Bart put the cape on, headed over to the male model's flat, went up the iron fire escape at the back of the building, got to the fourth floor unseen, looked through the window, and saw that they were both indeed together and in bed. Bart had already rehearsed his next steps.. With cape and scarlet lining, he crashed through the glass window. Bart said it was the most exhilarating thing he'd ever done in his life. The guy was so terrified, he ran out of his own apartment completely naked. Whenever things went wrong for Bart and Margo, which was often, Bart would always throw Margo's clothes off the balcony. By now the police knew them both quite well and the troubles were always sorted out. I believe at one time

Bart may have spent a night in jail—again this was after a photo shoot. This shoot had to do with a bee costume. The bee costume was from the waist up only. It was beautifully made, big and round with yellow and black rings around it and see-through wings. On the head went a skull-cap with two springy things attached, and on the end of those springy things were two yellow painted ping-pong balls. After a few drinks in the studio, Bart put the outfit on and was naked from the waist down, except for the long black stockings. He left Shaftesbury St., where the studio was, and walked south on Yonge St. towards downtown. He didn't get far. The police picked him up. The problem was he wouldn't fit into the cruiser, so all waited on Yonge St. for the police wagon. Bart said, they covered his privates with a police jacket.

Of course, around this same time I wasn't exactly having a picnic at home either. Things had been getting worse for months, and naturally louder. Doris and I were living on the ground floor of a gorgeous house Wally Hern and I bought as an investment. It was situated in an expensive area and we had five renters upstairs. Doris and I had our daily asinine arguments, which were starting to escalate even further than before. There was one particularly amusing instance, thinking back. In the evening, she noticed I had my underwear on inside out. The little Stanfield label was showing. To her this meant I'd been with another woman.

Whenever these foolish arguments started, it was easier to leave for a while because these things could never be resolved. From where we lived I would walk to Fran's restaurant and usually had a western sandwich and milk, and then I'd go home again. On this occasion, while walking home, I decided to peek in the front bay window first, by pulling myself up a little on the windowsill while hiding behind the bushes. At first everything looked peaceful inside. She had her rye whisky in one hand, and the television was on. Well, from the time it took me to come in the front door, walk through the kitchen, around the corner and into the living room, the TV had been turned off, pills were scattered everywhere and she was sprawled across the floor like someone who had just committed suicide. It was a scene that we've all seen on a TV show many times, where the leg is bent just so, an arm bent in an odd position and pills all around an empty bottle. "Boy," one has to move quickly to do all this in about two minutes.

I stepped over her body to turn on the TV. Then I went to the kitchen to make myself a scotch and soda, came back and stepped over her body again to sit on the chesterfield, and stepped over her again to change channels (this was in the days before televisions had remote controls). I sat there for another minute or two thinking to myself, "This is all too silly. Why don't I draw a chalk line around her and see what happens next?"

But she was suddenly up like a shot and everything started all over again. I was off to Fran's again, only this time I took the car. Like most houses in the city, driveways in this neighbourhood were very narrow. One had to be very careful backing up because of buildings on both sides. Ours was a long and dark driveway, and looking out the little back window one had to be very careful not to hit either wall on the way out. Everything was fine as usual until I got to the street. There was Doris, barefoot and spread-eagled, on the hood holding on with both hands where the hood meets the windshield. She wouldn't get off, so I drove slowly to the first intersection, all the time wondering if any neighbours were seeing any of this. Stopping again at the corner I motioned for her to get into the car. She slid off the hood and made an attempt for the door. I took off for Fran's again for another western. This had been going on for too many years until we both woke up and saw lawyers. Thinking back, I'm sure today we both would agree how funny so many of those episodes were.

Jimmy Hill was an illustrator who did wonderful work. He won many awards for his illustrations including Playboy magazine. Still, with all this talent he never appeared to earn enough money. He lived very simply, slept on a mattress and owned one of those lovely old Volkswagen campers the hippies made popular. Fortunately, Jimmy seemed very content with his lifestyle. He had a wonderful illegal after-hours bar, where he lived and worked. It happened to be on the top floor over Isaacs Gallery on Yonge St. It wasn't a money-making bar, but with enough customers (all friends) drinking and paying, Jimmy could drink for free. Bart (photographer) and I were standing at the bar talking to some new people one evening and in about 20 minutes Bart came over to me and said, "See that stunning woman I've been talking to since we came in?" "Yes," I said. "Well, she's in the mood to blow a joint, we should be back within the hour." Son-of-a-bitch, I thought. We've only been here 20 minutes and already he's getting a blow job. I went and sat on the floor beside Jane Eastwood (the actress) and had a nice chat about show-biz, until Bart came back. My mistake was telling Bart later how I misinterpreted what he said. To Bart this was the funniest thing he'd heard in a long time, and within two days, people who knew me, and some who didn't know me, were telling the story.

CASA LOMA, TORONTO   K.

While working at Dave Haughton's, an award event was in the making. It was dreamed up by The Art Directors Club of Toronto and called The Obie Awards. This was a first time members of the Toronto Graphic Arts industry were presented with awards, for achievement in their various categories. Sounds a lot like The Academy Awards today, doesn't it? It was held at Casa Loma, a gorgeous castle in the middle of Toronto. The guests were a large and loud group from the advertising world. Of course, many nice people showed up along with the drunks and bozos. On one particular evening in 1966, the master of ceremonies deserved an award just for his night's troubles. There were problems with the PA system, and the audience wouldn't leave the bar. The MC they brought in to handle this crowd was Henry Morgan, a witty and able guy from the States. So with the lousy acoustics and the drunken bunch, Henry had a long night ahead of him and was going to earn his money the hard way.

Henry Morgan, who was a writer and TV personality, sarcastically said at the start, "Are you sure you're all in the right castle?" In spite of the boors and drunks at the back who kept shouting "Speak Louder," Henry carried on. He went on to say things about Marshall McLuhan, who had made a big contribution to Toronto's graphic arts industry. Henry said, "He's a fake, he gets a hundred grand a year to hold seminars with himself." McLuhan laughed in his Toronto home when he was later told of this, and later added, "It couldn't be better publicity for me. It's obvious he [Morgan] has difficulty understanding what I'm saying." Throughout the night Henry asked, "Don't you even respect the people in your own trade? What are you, a bunch of tourists? Have you seen your City Hall yet? Why don't you go down first thing in the morning and take a look at Lake Ontario?"

Of course, when the whole thing was over and we had more losers than winners. Then, people like Jim Donahue of MacLaren advertising said, "The whole thing's a farce, all the wrong people got the awards, it's a farce and I'm going to resign my club membership." Morgan was also quoted as saying, "if you should ever do this again, and I'm back, the price will be much higher." It was never done again. Before the nominations were read out, everybody was happy. Even in my case, the other three retouchers who were nominated besides myself were quite friendly. After I had won for retouching, only one in particular seemed to stay clear of me. Another retoucher, a little guy, had rented a tuxedo for the occasion and sadly didn't win. It's too bad they weren't filming "March of the Penguins" back in 1966. He could have gotten a job as an extra. Some of the other winners to receive an Obie were Don Murphy (best art director),.Vickers & Benson (best agency), T.D.F. artists ltd. (best art studio) and Bob Schultz (best TV director). Additional awards went to Tom McNeely for illustrator, Cy Wallace for assembly and Bert Bell for photography. I thought the Obie awards thing was a great idea; after all, I got one. I remember that John Brooke, who was on the committee, wanted to cover Casa Loma completely in aluminium foil. I believe he got the Alcan people to agree with supplying the foil free, but the people who look after the castle gave a flat No.

After the party was over a bunch of us decided to go somewhere nice for a late dinner. Besides myself there were Wally Hern, Doug Metcoff and his wife Nora, Bill Jamieson and his wife and many others. We all had a drink while looking the menu over. Finally one by one we ordered. After the waiter left with the orders, Dave Haughton said something nice to the effect of, "Because of Bob winning an Obie, which is good for the studio, the studio will treat for this evening." Immediately Bill Jamieson flagged down the waiter and he and his wife both upgraded their meal.

Freelancing Again

After working for Dave for a few years, Wally and I both went back to freelancing at 44 Jackes Ave., in a roomy apartment on the 18th floor. A good friend and illustrator joined us later on and took the bedroom for himself. Besides being a wonderful illustrator, his other talent was that he could fart the first bar of "Oh Canada." He would phone his wife daily and let rip a few. Then he'd be silent on his end of the phone because it was her turn. Around that time I was to fly to England on a Friday evening to visit my friend Bill Waldie. He said, "We live near the airport, so why not come for dinner, and after that I'll take you to the airport?" His two boys were also home, so his wife made a lovely spaghetti dinner with a salad. At the table, and in the middle of the meal, he now lifted one cheek off the chair and out came a loud BRAP. Not a soul at the table said a word. Nobody raised an eyebrow. It was as if dad were working on a new tune. And who cares? Only the basset hound, who was looking at me at the time, had a look on his face as if to say, "Please take me with you when you go." I was now anxiously waiting for the next toot from a family member. I guess the family that farts together stays together. On the way out the door, I had to smile. I don't know why, but all I could think of, was the book, "Inherit the wind." Wally and I always thought that if something should happen to either one, where could you possibly find another?

The last studio I worked in was at 5 Polson St., and it was probably the nicest I ever had. I rented this beautiful space from Oasis studio, situated across the hall. My window faced north, within feet of the waterfront. The view was of the Toronto City Harbour and shoreline with its constant traffic of ferries, water taxis and freighters from places like Libya, Norway and Hamburg. The Royal Britannia moored not far from my window when it visited Toronto (heavily guarded, of course). Geoffrey Turner, a friend for decades, shared this space and other expenses with me. Another plus was the wonderful shoreline we had for tying up Geoffrey's double ender (sailboat, all wood) in front of the studio. Besides the great view of Toronto, the studio had a small kitchen, our own bathroom with a shower, which came in handy after a weekend sail. Geoffrey did architectural renderings for a living but when the computer came along it slowly started to eat into his work, and for that matter mine too. Geoffrey went home to work and I decided to stay on. Ted Larson from Oasis put Barbara Brocklehurst (a sales person) in the other cubicle where Geoffrey had been. This cut my expenses in half.

I had already worked in this location with Geoffery for a good 10 years. One day, Barbara came running around the corner into my cubicle and said, "My God, you're the kaiser roll guy!" The story here is that, when I was 17 at my first job, and a learning apprentice at Brigden's, a lot of us would go and eat together if we had to work that evening. A favourite spot was the Horseshoe Tavern at 368 Queen St. W. near Spadina. This particular story started with me breaking my kaiser roll in half and buttering both halves. Keep in mind I was a nervous 17-year-old kid and my boss Ed Nicholls, not known for his humour or easy way, said, "You're only supposed to butter what you can put into your mouth." Why I did what I did next, I don't know. I put the whole half of the kaiser roll into my mouth and found there was no way to chew or talk. Ed Nicholls sort of just looked at the ceiling in disgust for a moment and then rolled his eyes back to me. Now, Nicholls himself had a bad habit of always having one finger busy doing something, such as pushing sugar cubes around in a sugar bowl. On this particular night he was playing with the bowl of hot chili peppers. A little later that same finger was rubbing his eye while lecturing me about the kaiser roll. Almost instantly, he was off like a shot, for the washroom to wash out the fire in his eye. He wasn't back soon, but when he did get back to our table, he had the reddest, nicely inflamed, weirdest eye I have ever seen. And here, at least 35 years later comes someone saying, "So you're the Kaiser-roll guy!"

The computer was now here for good. Manual retouching was definitely coming to an end. Not for me only, but for a lot of us. A few years previously computer technology was still in a learning cycle, but not anymore. Today it's quite magical what things can be done, and very quickly. As an example, years back if I had to add some tweed background to the side of a print, it could take me all weekend. Today, with the right technician at the computer, he may do it in 30 minutes or less, and it would be perfect. So how does one compete with that? You don't. Sadly, some technical people, although good at what they do, are not artistic. They don't know a cold shadow from a warm one or where the shadow should go in relation to the sun, etc.. The computer is here to stay and has a few flaws, but it's damn good. In the last two or three years that I did work, I made the most money ever. The computer people were still learning and there were problems along the way. I would get a call that something the computer had been working on was not acceptable, and the agency had run out of time. So I was asked if I would I take over, order the prints I needed, and do the retouching. In many cases the computer operator wasn't qualified enough and made things worse.

The last two years for me were like a light bulb before it burns out. For me, work got brighter and brighter and then it went out for good. Some retouchers got together and mortgaged their houses, spent $500,000 on computer systems and tried to compete with the large houses like Bomac, Reliance, Grip and others, which had the best that money could buy. They had no problem spending over a $1-million for a unit and changing up as it became necessary. So, after a year or so, the little guy who spent much less for a computer couldn't sell the thing, because it was already out of date and nobody wanted it. Meanwhile, he still had his payments. I stayed out of this new age and, for me, made the right decision. The fat lady sang and I listened. I have no regrets. I was there in its best years and now I was advanced enough in age to call it quits. Ted Larson of Oasis threw a great party for my finish. Many art directors that gave me work through the years showed up, while just as many didn't. I guess their reasoning was that I was now part of yesterday, and yesterday was history.

Thinking back, I've left out a hell of a lot of names here. I have also changed a few names but not many. Others I could have changed but thought it wasn't necessary. Most of the people I worked for were good about paying, but of course I had my share of a few dishonourable types who never intended to pay right from the start. One of those was Jerry Goodis, who took me twice. Another was an agency that asked me to do an interesting retouch on a colour shot by the well-known portrait photographer Yousuf Karsh. The print was 30"x40". The largest part of the work was changing a lime green background to more of a sepia colour, which had to be done in dyes, using only cotton batting to apply the colour (no airbrush). And it was a terrible shot. A portrait of an important bank official, it had to match and go on a wall with other important bank individuals. The agency asked me, when I finished, to wrap it and send it on to Yousuf Karsh, care of his wife, and informed me that she would pay the bill. I was owed $850 and did as I was asked. When Mrs. Karsh received the invoice, she immediately wrote back and said the agency was to pay the amount. This went back and forth for months and I'm still waiting. That had to be 20 years ago. To go to a lawyer might have cost me more, so I forgot the whole thing.

I've always liked Wally Hern's logic on matters like this. Wally always told me I should charge half of what a job is worth. That way, if they don't pay, I haven't lost as much. What hurts with the Karsh portrait is that I had to make a wooden box to fit the expensive portrait in for mailing, and pay postage and insurance. I tried to get that from Mrs. Karsh too. She said phone the agency and so it went (again) back and forth. Thank goodness the more reputable and larger agencies like Doyle, Dane & Bernbach always paid on time and there were never any hassles. I did work for other nice people like the singer Ann Murray, and was paid every time, usually on the same day. So there were many more good ones and only a few bad ones. Dave Haughton used freelance people and paid them on the way out the door. So did Pacesetters. This made sense. If they needed somebody right away, you came running. Thank goodness, there were many good clients.

For many years when I was fortunate to have been the

retoucher on some of Ann Murray's albums, my usual work was things like cleaning up backgrounds or facial blemishes, hair, clothing, or something as simple as fixing Ann's left eye, which is a touch smaller than the other. On one album, the late Gord Marci (photographer) took a charming shot of Ann with a group of little children around Ann's legs. The kids, too small to understand, kept wandering off the set. What the crew did was very simple. They threw cookies all around Ann's feet. The kids came back, started to pick up cookies and Gord got the shot he wanted. My work later was to retouch out the cookies and crumbs. Plus, because they were to be angels, I fixed their crooked wings and eliminated the wing straps. Finally, and this was the biggest part of the job, I drew clouds for all to stand on because they were supposed to be in heaven. As you can tell from this, every job was very different from the last. The albums were fun too, not that I did many, but mostly because they were a big change from the product stuff.

I met Ann a few times, and through this became a friend of her husband Bill Langstroth. Bill got interested in photography and occasionally I would do a small retouch for him. What I remember most about this friendship is on one occasion when I was invited to the offices of Balmur Ltd. for Ann's Christmas party. Balmur Ltd. was founded by Ann and co-owned with her first manager, Leonard Rambeau, who unfortunately died soon after of cancer. This wonderful evening was held at the agency just outside of Toronto at Yonge and Sheppard. Directly from work, without time to change and already late, I went straight to the party. At the door were two lovely Balmur girls acting as greeters, and I guess to keep out the uninvited. The party was well on its way with men in tuxedos and ladies in expensive gowns.

These people arrived from all parts of the country and all sectors of show business, all with a martini in hand or some other worldly drink, and still sober. All stood in little groups, staring at the front door to see who would arrive next. Well, I came into the spotlight, so to speak, in my work clothes. I had on a T-shirt that read, "I'm with her," and my corduroy pants no longer had any corduroy left above the knees, since I had a habit of wiping my hands on my knees whenever I used sulphuric acid and other bleaches. These pants also had the crotch an inch above the knees. To this day, I can still see the faces of the well-dressed people thinking: "Hey! Here's the guy to fix the toilet."

Bill Langstroth was the first to see the fear in my eyes. And bless him for leaving the group he was with to escort me to one of the bars. Bill suggested we take two scotch and sodas each and go and sit in Ann's office. After an hour or more, I suggested we join the party. Mostly I was thinking Ann might be upset at Bill not mingling with the guests, and by now I'd had three or four drinks and thought I should work the room. I took my position at one end of the buffet table eating shrimp the size of bananas, and noticed the guy beside me was dressed just like me. He was a favourite photographer of Ann's and, like me, came from work. Having the same taste in clothes we became fast friends. By now, thanks to the evening's libations, the whole atmosphere in the room was relaxed and we were all equals.

My friend Geoffrey, the architectural rendering artist, was doing murals for restaurants to help make ends meet. He was quick. They were good, and the money was a lot better. Some of the murals were over 20 feet long and paid upwards of $15,000. After Geoffrey had done a few for restaurants called "Filet of Sole" and "The

Whistling Oyster," the owner, a guy named Fred (who by the way owned another restaurant around the corner known as "Fred's Not Here" at 321 King St. W.), phoned Geoffrey to do one more small drawing for Filet of Sole. What was needed was a drawing of a clam for a matchbox. At this time Geoffrey and I were still sharing the waterfront studio. Fred gave Geoffrey two fresh clams from the kitchen to look at for the drawing. After the drawing was done and accepted, Geoffrey and I carefully made little round eyes for the top of the clams and gave them both legs to stand on. The waterfront studio with the small public park in front brought many people on weekends, just to relax, read a book, or look at the Toronto skyline. We put the two clams on the waterfront wall very late the night before. Geoffrey and I had to work the Saturday, so we were in early. People started to arrive and everything went well for two or three hours. The people would stare at the clams for the longest time, but the strange thing was, nobody went near them. They'd stand a good five to ten feet away and just look. This continued, until, two kids walked up right beside the clams. Not a word was spoken, and in an instant they kicked both clams into Lake Ontario.

Our studio window went from floor to ceiling and had north light. And the little park directly in front gave us great people watching. We played pranks daily in order to keep sane, usually taking 10 minutes or less away from our work. On one occasion I got the cardboard centre from a roll of paper towels, added a string to hang it from the middle, attached it to the ceiling in front of my window, and then glued a small sign on it that read, "See the Moon Free." You'd be surprised how many grown up people would look through the cardboard tube. Another time I had a cheap plaster model of a Roman soldier, left over from a retouching job I did. The agency didn't want it, we didn't want it, so to get rid of it Geoffrey and I made a rather large penis for it with plaster. Next we put it outside our window in the park bushes. On the third day, we noticed somebody had broken off the penis (which was now gone) but the soldier was still there and standing.

Geoffrey

There were many good memories at 5 Polson St., such as when Geoffrey would sail up to the wall in The Scarlet Pimpernel, tie up, come into the studio, and the two of us would be off again for the day and evening sailing around Lake Ontario. Today at 5 Polson St. there is a huge bar and dance club called "The Docks." I drove down there not long ago to reminisce and to see what they've done to the section where I sat for 10 years. Well, again so much for nostalgia and romance. It is now the men's toilet.

The problem for Geoffrey was there wasn't enough work around, and he began to drink too much. After a while he sold his beautiful Scarlet Pimpernel. As work trickled in, he did start building a new boat, a 36 ft. wooden sailboat, a double-ender named "Daydream." After at least three full years of building Daydream, preceded by about two years of planning, sending to England for drawings if available and countless hours of getting information from people in England, he started to build the dreamboat he had yearned for since his youth. I had the pleasure to sail on her on different occasions, and a beauty she was: a safe, heavy sea-going vessel built with the best material Geoffrey could find. Money was no object; the boat came first. When you were down below, the first thing that came to mind was a brothel. It had velvet maroon upholstery and matching curtains over the ports, old brass gimbaled lamps, and miniature paintings in gold frames done by Geoffrey. Aside from all this he loved varnish, and this boat had varnish.

The sad part is that Geoffrey built this boat for himself and himself only, at a cost of well over $200,000. His architectural rendering work seemed to disappear again. Then he decided to move to Montesquiou, a small village in France, and bought (in his words) a ruin for $17,000 Canadian dollars. While in France, he needed money badly, mostly because his drinking took over. He put his new boat up for sale and eventually sold it for $ 20,000.. I think what happened to Geoffrey—and mostly out of boredom, on top of not being needed anymore is—is that he stopped eating and drank his beloved rum and coke daily. He passed away in hospital soon after. What a terrible thing when there seems to be no reason for staying around anymore. I knew Geoffrey for over 30 years, and then in such a short time he was gone. Since the coming of the computer age, many good artists today have nothing to do and it's a damn shame that all this talent is now wasted. Sadly, more than a few others I've worked with have followed Geoffrey the same way.

There are many good memories of Geoffrey. Every Friday without fail, we would lock up at noon, drive over to King St. and order the same English cut prime rib at "Ed's Warehouse," with a vodka martini straight up. These drinks were doubles at a bargain price of $2.95 each. The other choice was a Manhattan, also a double at the same price. After the big Warehouse cut of Prime rib and another double, life was beautiful. Without a doubt this was the tastiest, most savoury and choicest cut that could be found anywhere on earth, along with frozen peas, mashed potatoes, kosher dill pickles, Yorkshire pudding, fresh buns baked daily and a horse radish that was freshly prepared every morning in the Mirvish kitchen. All for under $4. Very often, you would see Ed himself, together with his son David, eat here, even though they had a choice of other restaurants they owned, such as Ed's Folly, Ed's Italian, Old Ed's, Ed's Seafood and Ed's Chinese. All together the tables held about 2,600 diners and served 6,000 meals every night.

After Geoffrey and I finished our wonderful meal and capped it off with another martini, Ed always approached our table with the same question. "Boys, now tell me, please, was everything satisfactory? If not, tell me, I won't be upset." Of course, our answer was always the same. How could we lie? I must admit I did wonder what Ed would say if only once I lied about the medium rare not being medium rare, or made up some other trivial thing. As it happened, I never had to think of that ever again, because Ed Mirvish himself always said, "You know boys, If someone ever complained, I really don't have an answer, I don't know what I'd say, so how lucky can a mensch be." This happened every Friday. Today the restaurants are all closed. The last one to close, I believe, was our favourite, "Ed's Warehouse," in September 2000.

Mirvish always believed that theatres and restaurants go together, and so they did, and very well. I think, at the time, the family had too much on its plate (no pun intended) with the store (Honest Ed's) and theatres. The charm at Ed's Warehouse were the Tiffany lamps that covered the ceilings, the marble statues and hundreds of antiques and black & white glossy photos of movie stars and other famous people on every post and wall. At every lunch I wondered how I could smuggle in a black & white 8x10 print of myself, write something like, "To Anne & Ed, thank you for your hospitality, Love Bob," and attach this to a post. Of course, it would be there for an eternity without being noticed.

Honest Ed

Ed Mirvish's early years in Toronto weren't considered a good beginning. He tried working as a door-to-door salesman selling Fuller Brushes, then an encyclopaedia. And so it went, until he opened a grocery store in the Jewish area of Dundas St., and the family took up residence above the store. The grocery business didn't do well, and Ed decided to close the place and reopen as a dry-cleaner, together with his childhood and very close friend Yale Simpson as a partner. The business was known as "Simpson's." Later, the well-known Simpson's department store insisted he change the name. Ed Mirvish said, "Here is my Mr. Simpson, where is yours?" Unfortunately the dry-cleaning business didn't do well either. Next he took on a job as produce manager in a grocery store. Doing relatively well, Ed married Anne Macklin from Hamilton, Ont., in 1941. Four years later, David was born. Around 1948, they cashed in an insurance policy and opened a new business known as "Honest Ed's." well stocked with stuff from bankruptcy and fire sales, shown on orange crates. As Ed said at the time, "There is no magic in keeping the prices down. We do away with all the services, no refunds, no delivery, no credit, and no free parking. This way, we pass the savings onto the public." Very soon, "Honest Ed's" store expanded to fill a city block, bringing in millions of dollars each year. This all took place in about four years, and Ed had become a millionaire.

Honest Ed's is still located on the corner of Bloor and Bathurst Streets, running the length of a full block. The store is an interesting place to visit, even if you don't buy anything. A lot of the store's decorations consist of old posters and black & white photos of movie stars from films and stage plays. Outside are signs that read, "Come in and get lost," "Our service is rotten," Only the floors are crooked," "Honest Ed's is for the birds: cheap, cheap, cheap," "Honest Ed won't squeal, he lets his bargains do the talking." And the building is covered in many more humorous signs to read.

In 1963, Mirvish was told that the Royal Alexandra Theatre on King St. was up for sale. Being on a choice piece of property in Toronto, it was certainly something worth looking into. With it came walnut staircases and paneling, chandeliers, tapestry, marble and ducts built in for cold air blown from huge tanks of ice in the basement, to keep the audience cool in the summer months. Ed did his homework and found that in 1907 they paid $750,000 to build the theatre and he was able to buy it now for $215,000, including the land. Refurbishing the Royal Alexandra cost double the theatre's purchase price.

Miss Saigon filled the Mirvishes' new theatre, the Princess of Wales, on opening night in 1993, and ran for about two years. A $12-million production, the show took in $30-million in advance sales, the largest in Canadian history, and the Mirvish family celebrated with a million dollar party. Next came Beauty and the Beast. This too ran for a couple of years. The Princess of Wales is a 2,000 seat playhouse dream by father and son, Ed and David Mirvish, who privately own and financed the theatre.

As an interesting sideline, Ed opened Ed's Theatre Museum, located on the top floor of one of the warehouses, steps away from the Royal Alexandra. It was a museum of unusual items; some were very silly but, nevertheless, everything was for sale. The absurd items would go for 5 cents and up, but the more interesting items such as props from previous plays, beautiful costumes, furniture, china, etc., sold for top dollar. Some of the more valuable were priced in the thousands of dollars. But what a wonderful place to roam around in after a big meal downstairs.

A memorable evening my wife Beverly will never forget marked her first visit to Ed's Museum, when a well-dressed gentleman approached us on the floor wearing a horse's head. He politely asked Beverly if she found what she was looking for and whether he could be of any help. The voice was a little muffled considering the horse's head, but we had a long and interesting chat about costumes from previous plays and a general history about the pros and cons of running a theatre. After a good half hour, we said our good-byes and thanked him for the interesting talk we all enjoyed. The voice inside the horse's head was Ed himself. No wonder I ate there every Friday afternoon without fail. What a pity this is all gone now, not the theatres, but the wonderful trimmings that went with the shows. One blessing is, at least, I was here for the best of it, and the memories never leave you.

In 1982, Ed and David (known as Mirvish Productions) bought London's Old Vic for 550,000 pounds Sterling and spent even more renovating it. Under their management, the Old Vic was honoured for winning more awards for its productions than any other theatre in Britain. At the opening in 1983, Sir Laurence Olivier gave a speech, as did Her Majesty Queen Elizabeth II, and sat with the Mirvishes for the show. A year after it was re-opened, Ed was granted Freedom of the City of London, and took advantage of his right to drive a flock of sheep across London Bridge. He was also appointed CBE in 1989.

On July 11, 2007, the Mirvish family released a statement announcing the death of Ed Mirvish after midnight at St. Michael's Hospital in Toronto. The theatre impresario and much-loved businessman died just short of his 93rd birthday, as the curtain came down for the last time on Honest Ed (Edwin) Mirvish. The store was closed and the lights dimmed as the staff said good-bye. A similar gesture was made by the theatres on Broadway. They dimmed their lights for one minute at 8 p.m. on July 13. On Aug. 12, 2007, the City of Toronto granted the closure of Bloor between Bathurst and Markham Streets to allow a celebration in honour of all the good work Ed Mirvish had done for Toronto and its people.

I've enjoyed reading two books by Ed Mirvish: How to Build an Empire on an Orange Crate, or 121 Lessons I Never learned at

School, the autobiography of Edwin Mirvish (Key Porter Books, Toronto, 1993) and There's No Business Like Show Business, but I Wouldn't Ditch My Day Job (Key Porter Books, Toronto, 1997).

Grossman's and Other Hot Spots

To keep active I took a welding course for two years at George Brown College. What I had in mind was to make use of welding skills in my paintings. So for two nights a week I attended night school. It was a good class but welding in the summer is extremely hot. After classes four of us guys and Latoya, a big black girl (the only woman in the class), would go across the street to Grossman's Tavern for a nice cold beer or two. Grossman's Tavern, home of the blues at 379 Spadina Ave., was originally started in 1948 by the Grossman family and later sold in 1975 to the Louie family. We always took Latoya with us, mostly for protection. The Tavern was a tough place with pimps and hookers. It was here at Grossman's that the girls would give their share of the night's work to the pimps. It was never a problem trying to figure out who the pimps were in their yellow suits, big ties, black hats and shiny shoes. Grossman's clientele was varied, but more blacks hung out there than whites. That's why we felt secure with Latoya; she was not only a welder full-time, she looked like a welder. You'd have to be a little tetched to mess with our girl.

The tables at Grossman's were similar to long picnic tables, and always very crowded. On one evening behind me a big black pimp got up, and as he passed by behind me he tore his new threads on a nail. He was extremely unhappy and in a loud voice said, "If I don't get re-imbursed for dis outfit, I'm gonna wipe out dis fuckin' corner." Unfortunately for me, I was sitting in dis fuckin' corner. He swore on about how he spent three hundred bucks for dis outfit. With that, Latoya stood up and said, "Listen Leroy, If 'n yo don't shut yo mouth,

I'm gonna kick yo ass and take three hundred big ones outta yo. Now sit yoself down and be cool." We bought Latoya's beer for the evening.

Welding school continued as usual, but one night I brushed my hair with my hand and, still holding my arc welder in the same hand, set my hair on fire. Latoya was there first, and snuffed it out with her welding glove. I went back the following year, but the classmates were all new. Latoya had moved on. The toughest looking guy in the class looked like Wally Cox. Remember him? He was Mr. Peepers on the TV sit-com by that name. I finished the new season and never returned to school or Grossman's tavern again. If I wandered in today, I'm told I'd never recognize the place. It's all refurbished now. Also the Jewish market is not the Jewish market anymore, it's the Chinese Market. These are the same places, but with different faces. At Grossman's, the picnic tables are now gone, also gone are some of the wonderful talents like the Jeff Healey band, Burton Cummings, Allannah Myles, etc. I miss the pimp in the yellow suit. He drove one of those beautiful Excalibur cars with the chrome exhaust pipes coming out of the hood. Spadina road itself hasn't really changed all that much since then, just the people and prices. Gone are the dirt and grime, plus the odd crawly thing from the original Grossman's, but I still miss it.

Another good spot then, and popular in the '60s and '70s, was The Purple Onion at the corner of Yorkville Ave. & Avenue Rd. Bruce Cockburn played there. Buffy St. Marie wrote "Universal Soldier" in the basement of The Purple Onion. Don't confuse this Purple Onion with another called The Purple Onion on Parliament St., which is now a lesbian bar called "Pope Joan.".

Painters

When Tom Hodgson died, Toronto's Globe & Mail newspaper gave him a full page in the obituary section, and deservedly so. Tom was the last surviving member of the Canadian abstract group "Painters Eleven." Tom was 81 and had been suffering from Alzheimer's disease. His life was certainly filled with activity. He served two years in the Canadian Air Force and was a member of the Canadian Olympic Canoe Club team. With Painters Eleven, he helped push Toronto's acceptance of modernism, with colleagues like Oscar Cahen, Jack Bush, Alexandra Luke, Kazua Nakamura, William Ronald, Jock Macdonald, phenomenal Harold Town and others. I've noted some of these names before, but they're worth mentioning again. Years later, William Ronald and Ray Mead left the group, moving to New York And Montreal. Oscar Cahen had died in a car accident in 1956. As a result, Painters Eleven grew apart and was dissolved in 1960. Tom stopped painting around 2000 when his Alzheimer's took over. His last years were spent in a Toronto nursing home until his death on Feb. 27, 2006.

Some of these painters worked as commercial artists to earn a living. Harold Town was a very gifted illustrator for magazines and ad agencies. Harold was listed in the yellow pages as (Town, Harold, Advertising Artist). Oscar Cahen, the only European in the group, was also a commercial artist whose illustrations appeared in Maclean's and in ads. Cahen was only 40 when he died. I used to meet Tom Hodgson from time to time, mostly at the wonderful parties Gray Mills would have. Hodgson seemed the least intellectual of the painters, but I thought he had the most charm, especially compared to someone like Harold Town, who was always very intelligent, but an arrogant s.o.b. But you had to admire him for being possibly the most talented. I personably have always thought Harold Town's work to be far superior to that of some of the big names in New York—De Kooning, Pollock, Rothko, Lichtenstein and Frank Stella to name just a few. Don't misunderstand me, I admire the work of many of these artists, but still believe if Town had moved to the States, he would have come out on top.

Harold Town, a critic as well as an artist, was in Canada's art scene from the '50s well into the '70s. I remember him saying when his work was turned down in Italy. "It's such an honour being banned in Italy, the mother of sensuality. It's like being asked to straighten your tie in a bordello. "Any artist who doesn't think he's the best should quit," he once said. That's as clever as a prominent and well-experienced sailor saying, "I'm the best and now know everything about the sea. Shit, If I heard that from a seaman, I'd never leave shore with the guy. Since his death in 1990, Town's work has been largely forgotten, but with time I believe he will be discovered once again. The very successful Jack Bush, with his doubled breasted suits, had the most class of the bunch and did very well with sales of his work.

In the days of the Ontario Society of Artists show, put on every year by the Art Gallery of Ontario (I usually managed to get a painting accepted, bless them), I'd see most of Toronto's painters on opening night, painters I worked with in earlier years, like William Roberts and Gray Mills. Besides being a phenomenal painter, and friend I'd visit each year in Weymouth, Nova Scotia, Bill Roberts was a collector of old toys, ceramic dolls, pictures of Queen Victoria, mechanical cast iron banks and other memorabilia. This brings to mind one particular story I told at Willy's wake. (I always called him Willy, because many years back, he said he liked hearing it from me, and so it stayed all these years.) Well, on this occasion Willy was driving alone through a small town north of Toronto, when he noticed in a small lingerie shop window, what looked like a very old female mannequin with a paisley house dress on. Willy went inside and asked the owner, who was rather old himself, if he could buy the mannequin, but not the dress. Apparently, the old gentleman looked at Bill Roberts with a puzzled look, and said, "Why do you want it?" Now Willy said to himself, I know what I'd like to answer him with, but if I do, I won't get the mannequin. But I had to do it anyway. I said, "I want it because I live alone." With this, the old fella said, "I'd like it if you would leave the store." Bill Roberts never got the mannequin. In his last years, he had a house built for himself on St. Mary's Bay. It was a typical East Coast home with cedar shingle siding. The only real difference in appearance from other houses was that the upstairs was all studio, with a bank of windows and skylight.

I liked the area so much, that I bought some land nearby in Digby Nova Scotia in a place called Culloden. I purchased a piece of property with 3,200 feet of shoreline on the Bay of Fundy. I spent $20,000 for the surveying plus another $20,000 to put a road in. Things didn't quite go the way I'd hoped, so I put the land up for sale. After owning the property for nine years and paying a small sum of $9.37 a year for property tax when it was classed as forestry, everything was fine. When I made the mistake of having it surveyed into six pieces, I had become a subdivision and the taxes changed drastically. To end this tale, the beautiful land finally sold and I broke even, I think.

Bill Roberts and I often went to Frenchy's, a used clothing warehouse found all over the East Coast. Among the bargains you can find there are such items as an apricot suit with vest for $6. They will even sell you a used guitar to go with it. Shirts go for a dollar and a half. I bought a well-stitched, strong shirt, short sleeves with "manager" printed on the pocket. I had never felt this important until I bought that shirt. Bill's shirt said "Mac' on his pocket. Bill Roberts was blessed with having a great wit, even though he seemed so quiet and calm most of the time. He did, when necessary, lose his temper if it was called for. But not often. I did witness his temper on one occasion, when we were all at Bill's daughter Mary's house for dinner. After dinner, Bill's wife, Lynn (his third wife), went home early and Beverly and I stayed on with the party. Later we three headed back to Willy's house (also within walking distance from Mary's). When we rounded the corner, Lynn was sitting on the deck with a cigarette, bottle of wine and a candelabra with all the candles lit. It all looked very inviting, but to keep the candles from blowing out and with a healthy breeze blowing off St. Mary's Bay, Lynn had the candelabra hugging the wall. As I mentioned earlier, this house hugging the shoreline is covered in very dry cedar shingles. To Bill, it looked like feeding a flame to dried kindling. In reality, you couldn't wish for a better fire starter. This was also everything he owned. So, as I mentioned earlier, at times he did harden to the occasion.

Colin Clark's Wake

Colin's wish was that, after his death, he wanted Ginny (now his wife), whom he'd known as long as I'd been in the art business, or longer, to throw a big farewell party at his expense. Now, Colin never had a lot of money; matter a fact, he didn't have any. But Colin, because of his gift for babble, had more friends than anyone I know, and they all came to the church to say good-bye. The beautiful old church wasn't big enough for all, so some had to stay outside. I believe it was called the Holy Rosary Church. After the service, Roberts, Mills, Ken Arnott and I walked a short piece down the road for a drink while Colin was being cremated. Beforehand, Ginny had booked the Pier Four restaurant on the waterfront. The restaurant was closed to the public for the day, so there would be enough room for all the freeloaders in the business.

Now, instead of everyone being entitled to one drink, compliments of Colin, the bar was open to all for the night (a terrible mistake). I usually notice at these gargantuan gatherings that the bigger money earners in the business are the ones (when there's an open bar) who order doubles, be it Remy's or expensive single malts, and throw the drinks back as if someone had won the lottery. The buffet was also abused, with its large shrimp and caviar. It took only about an hour for the conversations about good old Colin to change to just drunken noise and boasting. Now, some who were ordering the expensive drinks would leave them on the nearest table unfinished and wander off to get another. In three or four hours, the room was starting to thin out. Mostly because they'd either had enough and left or had passed out. Many guests who did leave were leaving without thanking Ginny for the lovely and expensive going-away party, thanks only to Colin and Ginny. At our table with Bill Roberts, Gray Mills and Ken Arnott, no one had more than two or three drinks of the house liquor. We sat and had a great time talking about the stories of Colin's Aston Martin, the different M.G.'s he owned, car parts he collected and had stored in everybody's garage all over Toronto, and especially his restored Tiger Moth (double winger) that he kept in Maple Ont.

A word about Gray Mills. I had worked with Gray in a couple of studios but, as usually happens, people tend eventually to go their separate ways. Sometimes to further a career and sometimes not. Gray ended up teaching at the Ontario College of Art, as did Bill Roberts. One difference here was that Gray wisely stayed on until he got his pension from the college, and Bill Roberts did not. The story of Bill's leaving was that he was called onto the carpet a little too often, the reason being that he insisted on taking the class outdoors, to different locations to paint. This apparently was against school policy, so he quit in the middle of a class day. He handed in his notice and returned to the class and said, "I love you all, I hope you do well, and now I am leaving and will never be back. Good-bye." Sadly, Bill Roberts never did get his pension and had to turn to painting full time.

As for Gray, I think life was pretty good for him until, unfortunately, a few years back he was diagnosed with cancer of the throat and tongue. Like most of us, Gray was a good drinker and a big smoker. An operation followed in which the doctors removed one third of his tongue (lengthwise) and had to cut away a malignant portion inside the throat. After this came the long healing process with chemo, etc. With a piece of the tongue missing, it certainly does change your speech and it took a while at the beginning to understand Gray. Today, that is not a problem anymore; time has helped tremendously. By the way, everything Gray eats now has to go through a blender first with milk or some other substitute. The throat is raw and will stay that way. Scotch, Gray's favourite, must also go into the blender with milk, otherwise the scotch really burns. At one of his parties, he asked, "Hey Karman, would you like to have a look." "Sure," I said. With that, he went to find a flashlight.

Now, Gray has always had a great attitude toward many things, including health. His doctor gave him three years and suggested he may want to get his house and other matters in order. The first thing he did was to go out and find himself a doctor who gave him 10 years. Now, I'm not sure, but that's got to be over 20 years ago. Back then, I can still hear him saying to me, "Karman, I will outlive you." The way things are going, I believe he's right. One other sad note for Gray is that he was a guy who loved cooking and now he can't eat all those wonderful foods, only what goes into a blender. Lately vodka and milk are a little kinder on his throat.

When I think back to that wonderful home in Tullamore, Ont., where Gray and Kathy still live, I remember and miss those memorable parties that are now thinning out. So are the artists who attended. Tommy Hodgson and Bill Roberts both passed on a few years back, Colin Clark many years ago from cancer. And many more have moved on. I remember how wonderful it was just to walk around in Gray's field, an interesting place with the Land Rovers, vintage M.G.'s, Morgans, my Austin Healey, a truck or two and other relics that still got the owners to the party. Food, quite often, was a whole pig on the homemade barbeque, complete with apple in its mouth. All this was going on while guests swam in the pool, some with clothes on. One such party took place when one of Gray and Kathy's daughters was getting married. Shelagh was marrying an English fellow named Richard Rainbow Beal, whose work happened to be architectural rendering. Richard Rainbow was very English and his very English parents came from England for the wedding. In a nice touch the bride and groom came out of the church and the members of the cricket team that Richard belonged to were lined up outside with their cricket bats nicely held high, to form an archway for the bride and groom, plus the bridesmaids of course. It was quite charming to see all these big lads and Richard, for one reason or another, all wearing pink shoes. After the church ceremony all the guests went back to Gray and Kathy's for the reception. It turns out that the archway with bats was a complete surprise to Gray and, for some reason, he was not a happy man for not being told.

Much later, when all the toasts were made around the pool with champagne and everyone was feeling relaxed after this long day, the party started. With glasses in hand, some jumping into the pool, some still in tuxedos, some in gowns. Standing beside Beverly and me at the pool where Richard Rainbow's parents. I don't think I have ever seen such a bewildered look on two elderly people. There was a look on their faces of, "Where are we?" And, "Oh, my poor baby Richard." But I must admit, this was one memorable wedding and I wouldn't have missed it for anything.

When I think back to all the interesting people I've met and worked with to this day, they all, each in his or her own way, either influenced or became a teacher to me. Each helped put me where I am today, and many became good friends. When I started my first job at age 17, I met Allan Scott at Brigden's Ltd. It was Allan who introduced me to painting. My memory and vision of Allan was that he was a little man, never married and wore a long black coat that almost touched the ground. Every pocket of this black coat had newspaper clippings on the latest news about painters, living or dead. Naturally, Allan had to share all this news with you, whether you were willing to listen or not. Allan painted my portrait, for free. All he asked in return was that I would sit for him, and buy a few tubes of paint. His studio was on Queen St. on the third floor above Mesh's restaurant. Every wall in Mesh's restaurant had artwork hung up for sale: water colours, oils, charcoal sketches, line drawings, all turned out by local artists who in some cases paid their meal bills with paintings. Going to Allan's studio was like going back in time. You had to tread carefully in the dark, down a lane, past drunks, broken glass and garbage that attracted rats. You couldn't miss the place; it had the only third-floor window with the light on. With your best shot, you would throw pebbles at the window to get Allan's attention, then when he was ready, he'd come down to let you in. In the winters you kept your coat on, because there was never a trace of heat. It just didn't exist. Quite often, Allan painted with woollen gloves on or socks over his hands.

Charles Stafford (Charlie), also from Brigden's, was probably in his 60s. Charlie did watercolours in the evenings. He also invented sand painting for the hobbyist. I didn't learn much from Charlie, other than his constant chatter of, "If you want to be an artist, work at it, or bugger off."

Then there was Andy Anderson, who had some talent but preferred to work in the stock room. Andy lived alone like Allan Scott, but with Andy's free evenings he enjoyed fixing radios and old TV sets. I went to see Andy in his apartment in the Parliament and Queen Street area, curious to see what he did with his free time. Andy had every TV Guide since the first issue piled up in the hallway, the bedroom, kitchen, wherever there was an empty spot on the floor. With this weight of TV guides, I figured we'd be on the floor below at any moment. On the dining room ceiling, where a chandelier would have been at one time, hung a full-size TV antenna with all the aluminum rods extended. On the antenna was painted a big red arrow, and this huge antenna turned in all directions. Every wall had writing on it, such as Buffalo CH. 2 or Syracuse CH. 7, and sometimes with an "X" through it because that station had gone off the air. We heard later that Andy was later mugged by a gang of kids. They pulled him into the lane around where he lived; one of the boys put a rope around his neck while the others went through his pockets looking for change. Andy died in hospital that same evening. The City of Toronto buried Andy in a pine box.

There were so many faces and incidents in those first years at Brigden's that it's difficult to remember all the details. Faces like Maude Foissier. She was twice my age and I had a big crush on her during all those years working with her, but she never knew it. To me, she looked like Patricia Medina, the movie star. Maybe it's the first place one works at that starts his or her future, and that becomes the most important. I think these early days stay with you the longest in memory. What I've written here about my time in the art world is a condensed piece of it, but that's about how I saw it. Now that the commercial side of it has ended, and of course there is no pension or bonus, or even a hand shake, the question is, "Would I do it again?" Of course I would."

Since this writing, painter and sculptor Gray Mills in his 81st year has passed away in June of 2009.

Part Three: Secret Sib

I'd heard of Secret Sib for more years than I've got fingers. I was also starting to believe that the whole thing was a joke and there never was a Secret Sib. By this time, I had been working as a commercial artist for at least 25 years, and had attended many art-related opening shows, parties and so on, but there never was a Secret Sib sighting.

Things began to look up when I started sharing a great studio with my good friend Wally, who, by the way, knows everybody and everything about the art crowd. Wally was and is the Louella Parsons of the art business. Wally was another person I'd heard a lot about before I'd actually met him: He happened to be the best lettering guy around. Wally and I decided to start sharing a studio on the 18th floor at 44 Jackes Avenue in Toronto, blessed with a large balcony overlooking Rosehill Avenue. The 18th floor was certainly interesting. Wally and I were the only people who actually worked in the building. Everyone else in the large complex lived their everyday lives there. Next door, on one side, we had a young couple (just married) who, I believe, fought every other evening about some past sexual romance or, "How come you've got that pair of panties on now when you were wearing something very different this morning?" I must admit it made for an exciting evening to hear what was going on. Wally and I would put two big juice glasses to the wall, and our ears to the bottom of the glasses, to hear the latest.

Also, there was a hooker down the hall, who must have been a pricey high-class number. She never spoke to us, probably because she heard we were earning a living as artists and, therefore, probably poor.

The building itself was one of those places where pets of any kind were prohibited. Naturally, whenever there happened to be a fire alarm drill, the hall was full of old ladies, toting cats and a birdcage under each arm. Some cats were stuffed into baskets that were attached to walkers. All in a dither, they often left wondering, "Should I go to the left, or maybe go right or just stay put?"

As the months went by, little tidbits about Secret Sib would emerge. His real name was Frank Sibley. Many years back, he worked for Vickers & Benson, a large advertising agency. Frank was an art director there and, I'd been told, was apparently very talented. Fridays were paydays, and the guys usually gambled their money away playing cards or darts or on which fly would climb on the windowsill first. If they weren't doing this some of them went to The Sapphire Tavern to drink away whatever money they had left. Those early years made it a great time to be around, and to be working in a creative atmosphere. Mind you, it wasn't great if you were married. Anyway, this is where Secret Sib came into the picture for me. A lot of the guys he worked with would have spent all of their money, or lost it all gambling, and were apprehensive about going home. Frank, who had a big heart and an inability to say no, would lend money that he never saw again. This, of course, caused many problems at home between Frank and his wife. He could never say no to someone down on his luck or whatever the problem was. Frank had to hide, in order to get away from his "generosity" problem. He and his wife moved to another location in the city, got an unlisted telephone number, and didn't tell a soul where they were living. Not even his employer knew how to get hold of him. It was around that time that he got tagged with the name "Secret Sib."

Life seemed better for Frank and his wife for a long time, but, because of other problems, they finally divorced. I always thought "Secret Sib" would be a great name for a comic book, or perhaps a TV show.

Wally and I loved working in our one-bedroom unit (he in the dining room part and me in the living room). We did rent out the bedroom to other artists from time to time, but no one stayed too long. Basically, they all said, "We can't work here with all the laughing and bullshit going on." As it happened, the two of us worked best alone. The kitchen was a big plus. We had our own fridge for mix and ice, and cupboards for different bottles. There were glasses for us, and better glasses for company. I remember the day when someone gave Wally a bottle of Crown Royal Limited Edition whiskey, for doing a free lettering job. Readers who recall those days will remember that brand came in a beautiful squat bottle, slipped into a purple velvet bag with a gold pull tassel. Well, little by little, Wally and I finished the attractive bottle. Now came the beautiful part: We purchased a bottle of Four Roses whiskey, the cheapest whiskey available. It tasted a bit like a blend of gasoline and turpentine. This was poured into the "attractive" bottle, and was offered only to clients. Upon seeing the "attractive" bottle, they were hesitant to say yes to having a drink, because they felt the "attractive" bottle was too expensive. In time, Wally and I went through filling the "attractive" bottle many times until it became embarrassing. The "attractive" bottle was becoming dirty. The two of us decided that it was time to buy a new "attractive" bottle.

The rent on the studio included parking and was quite reasonable. Unfortunately, my vehicle was a very high and long–wheel-based Land Rover. It was the kind of machine you would see in those safari flicks, and because of its size it was always a problem with parking.

The houses on Rosehill Ave. were elegant, comfortable, well built and, certainly, unique in appearance to each other. With all this to their credit, the wrecking ball was on its way. As usual, it was all about money. New builders in a growing city couldn't give a tinker's damn about what kind of building came next. The bigger, the better. Whatever the city would allow. High-rise? How high? How big? Just like the average family, these houses had been around for decades. Imagine the stories they each could tell, the things they have seen and heard: the lying, the crying, the laughter. There were sad times and good times, each home with its own story, very different from the one next door.

Margaret Atwood, the writer, along with Graeme Gibson, her husband, and their children lived in one of those lovely houses. I watched Graeme on many occasions playing ball with their children on Rosehill Ave. On more than one occasion, I gave him a ride home from the liquor store at the bottom of the hill at Yonge and Summerhill. That was in the days when you had to write on a little piece of paper what you wanted, and then a government employee would walk slowly to the rear of the warehouse to get your bottle for you. This gave you all the time you needed to converse with the other regulars like Bruno Gerussi, the actor, the bunch from CHUM Radio (which was nearby), and many artists and art directors from the various studios and agencies. The liquor store was on one side of the building and the beer store was on the other side, making shopping very easy.

Before it was a liquor store, it was a train station, a beautiful train station that existed around 1880 and was rebuilt in 1916. It has again been recently restored to its original glory. The train station was built of stone and it was indestructible. One of the distinguishing marks is its grand clock tower. The train tracks were on top of the building. This lovely building is still there after these many years, and so it should be.

My friend Wally and I had a great view from our balcony on the18th floor, which faced Rosehill Ave. A delicious part of the world seemed to be right in front of us. Eventually, even the elusive Secret Sib would pass by. The neighbouring building, known as the tower, had a great many interesting people living in it. We were familiar with a handful living there, but most of them we didn't know by name. To save time, we made up names for the residents that most interested us. For instance, if I wanted Wally to check out a certain balcony, or window, I would say something like "lonely one" just came home, or "okay body" is in the bedroom, and Wally would know just where to look.

There was one, "the Italian," who was often on her balcony in her slip, a custom that is quite normal in Italy. On the balcony she would fix a table for dinner, with candles, wine and tablecloth. "The Italian" was a big, buxom woman with a seaman for a boyfriend. He seemed to arrive in town every month or so. For some reason "the Italian" would invite her girlfriend over for dinner on the same night as "the seaman." What a mistake this was. From our view, we could see "the Italian" on the balcony, preparing the wondrous evening's dinner, while "the seaman" was in the bedroom re-arranging the girlfriend's breasts. When dinner was over, and everything was put away, the girlfriend left the apartment. Then the seaman started re-arranging the Italian's breasts. Believe me, this was a great building to work in. Another one of the pluses of working there was being able to stay the night if necessary. If you drank too much, you had the choice of a sauna in the morning, after which you could go back to work feeling new again. There were always excuses to have parties. Perhaps it was a lovely day, or one of us had gotten a job, or one of us didn't get a job, or somebody we know was having a birthday. Anything was celebrated. Clients would often drop by after work for a drink, probably because they knew of our choice selection in good liquor and the "attractive" bottle.

Wanda

I always figured that someday, when I would finally meet Secret Sib, it might be where he worked, downtown in some seedy-looking building. The office would be on the ground floor. Perhaps it could be in the infamous Rex Hotel. The entrance to his office would be one of those doors with the top half in frosted glass, with black painted lettering saying SECRET SIB, PRIVATE EYE (underneath this would be a drawing of a smoking gun.) Maybe it could say SECRET SIB, GANG BUSTER, and under that it would say COME IN. Once inside, there would be a couple of chrome chairs, with faded vinyl covering on the seats. Also a side table, with magazines like *Ammo Today* and *Soldier of Fortune*, which include articles like "How to start a war and be a somebody" or "Lesbians and homos can be your friends and your mother will still love you." The walls, where there are cracks in the plaster, would be covered in calendars, some of them from this year.

Right in the middle of the room was where, I imagined, Wanda would have her desk. I saw her as Sib's secretary, and the desk an old one that The Salvation Army couldn't sell. She was eating a bowl of "Alpo" and had the gift of being able to scratch her left ear really fast with her foot. Her blond hair was a lovely shade similar to cheap beer, and just as flat, but none the less you wanted to run your toes through it. You could tell she was a class act by the way she uttered "Wha?" When she looked up and saw me, I could tell she was smitten. I knew this because of the way she chewed her gum with her mouth open. She was bathed in a cologne that gave her the scent of a wet dog. Her gams didn't know where to stop. She had on a loose-fitting blouse with a big

V in the front. When I circled around to her back and looked over her shoulder, I could see past her navel down to her pubic hair. Her breasts were fighting to get out of her blouse. I couldn't keep my eyes off her, there was just too much to look at. She had curves that couldn't be improved on and I wanted to see every one. I knew immediately that I was attracted to her, when her yellow ochre lips blurted out, "What can I do for yous?" I was about to say, "Will you have my baby, when I got a hold of myself and said, "A coffee would be nice". She said, "instant?" I replied, "Yes, right this minute would be nice." I saw her gams again when she got up to get the milk from the outside ledge of the window.

Over coffee, Wanda told me how she had given up a career in table-dancin', 'cause she had to look after her old man who was always drunk. She was also thinking about quitin' this job 'cause she hadn't been paid since she started. Finally, I got my turn to speak when I noticed it was starting to get dark outside. My stomach was making little gurgle noises because I'd been there since 10 a.m. and missed lunch. I asked when "Secret" might show up, and she said it could be anytime, but she was just guessing since she hadn't seen him in about six weeks. She mumbled, "He must be on a secret case, or somethin." I was going to leave my card with Wanda when I realized I'd never had a card. Before I had a chance to leave, she confided that she had a son, doing time in prison, for stealing an airplane. It didn't go well in court because the airplane was in the air and full of people at the time. She also told me about her drunken mother, who was in her 80s and worked for the CIA. She couldn't say more than that about her, other than, as a cover, she worked as an airline hostess on weekends.

There was such a lot of dust in the room that I felt I had a sneeze coming on. I asked Wanda if she had a tissue. She said no, but she did hand me the tea cozy to blow my nose into. I always carry a flask of brandy with me, in case of the sniffles. Wanda looked sad, so I offered her a drink. She nodded yes, and said she would prefer a Piña Colada, but please leave out the umbrella. I summoned up the courage to ask her if we could have a sleepover together. She said, "Yes" but we couldn't go to her place because she hadn't cleaned since last August. I suggested she might feel more comfortable at a Motel 6. She liked that idea but said she'd have to drop by her place first, to feed Boris, her pet goldfish. At the motel, she high-stepped out of the shower and I noticed a heart-shaped tattoo on her breast. There was tiny lettering under the heart and I couldn't read it until I got closer. It said, "Are you happy doing what you do?" I still don't know what the message meant. Coming back to reality, I wondered if I would ever meet Secret Sib, or if there really was a Secret Sib. My mind occasionally does wander . . . . Secret Sib doesn't have an office and there is no Wanda.

I had a love/hate relationship with my Land Rover, a big blue-coloured hunk of machinery. I remember the day I took possession of this 109"-wheelbase wagon (10 passenger) with a six-cylinder engine with standard equipment, including eight forward gears and two reverse. All the body panels were made of a non-corrodible light alloy and all the external fittings were heavily galvanized. Of course, the big selling feature was the four-wheel drive. The cost for this top-of-the-line model, in 1966, was $4,098. There were some extras required, such as another fender mirror for $4, a spare-wheels carrier with dished hood for $7, a hood lock for $2.60, a fuel-cap lock for $2.60, a pair of sun-visors for $5.20 and pre-delivery inspection for $25. All this was before sales tax was added. Bear in mind that around this time you could buy a nice home for about $15,000.

I had to have this vehicle. After all, people were going on safaris or off on archaeological expeditions in these things. The ads explained you could drive though water up to the windows (with alligators looking in). You could bash your way through virgin forests, knowing full well that you would find your way home again. This was the life for me: driving through murky waters and weed-infested cross-country trips. Hey, English bank robbers and guerrilla fighters all over the world were buying this machine. Why shouldn't I have one? So, I paid my money and waited for England to send me one.

I got a call from the dealer in England that my vehicle was being loaded on to a freighter in Southampton. Two weeks later it arrived in Montreal, and shortly after that, it was received at the dealer's in Toronto. It was a Saturday, and I went to look and touch it for the first time. The Rover was inside the building because it still had to be checked out. I remember sitting inside it and admiring the dashboard with its toggle switches and the wiring that went everywhere. There were big hoses that found their way to the windows for defrosting, as well as big motors at the top of the dashboard to operate the windshield wipers. Al this stuff was fully exposed and it looked great. A year later, the wipers were frozen with ice and wouldn't move. The motors for the wipers burned out and created a lot of smoke (I jumped out and waited until the smoke cleared). At least, in the Land Rover you can see everything.

SECRET SIB

In 1967, Expo came to Montreal and I decided to take my sons, Greg, 10 years old, and Derek, 7, and drive to Expo in the Rover. Sleeping accommodations were nil. Fortunately, I had a good friend living in Montreal. I phoned Bob Anderson and he allowed us to park the Rover in his back yard, where we slept in it. His wife left the back door open so we could use their toilet. Everything was falling into place very nicely considering the drive to Montreal wasn't a holiday. The Rover over-heated, so we stopped by the roadside. I lifted the heavy hood with the tire mounted in the middle, to let the motor cool down. While I went to find some water, the boys amused themselves by climbing all over the Land Rover, Including its roof (it was all indestructible, even the blue paint, so I always encouraged them to play up on top if they wished). I found some water for the Rover in a nearby creek, and soon we were off again towards Expo. I made a stop at the first garage we found, which happened to be in Quebec, and it was a French-only establishment. My French is not that good, so I used the familiar hand-gesturing method of speech. I made a lot of bubbling sounds to indicate the water boiling. It was understood that the whole system should be flushed out and new anti-freeze should be installed. It was done and once again we were on our way to Expo.

Three days at Expo was long enough and we headed for home. You must understand that at 50 miles per hour in one of these, one cannot talk and expect to be heard. The engine noise is extremely loud, so when we had a blowout no one heard it, and because of the normal rough ride, no one felt it, until there was the loud flopping sound. As we travelled along, I found it hard to believe that people were slogging through dust storms in deserts, as well as snow-covered tundras, with

243

this vehicle and I was constantly having trouble getting it to work on beautifully paved and dry roads. But, it's one of those pieces of machinery you have to have and fall in love with (sometimes).

Another thing about the Land Rover was its height. It didn't fit into the underground parking lot at the apartment building where Wally and I had our studio. I went looking for another parking spot and, as luck would have it, there was one available for rent on Rosehill Ave., just across the road from our building. The spot was next to a charming, small, two-storey house, owned by a young couple with a baby. They didn't have a car. So, besides being in a perfect location, close to where I worked, I could also see the Land Rover from our balcony. I'm mentioning all this because the little house had a porch, and on most mornings, when I parked in my spot, there was, almost always, this rather big man, all dressed in black, drinking a coffee on this porch. I remember the first time I laid eyes on him, he had this way of holding his coffee in his right hand, up high towards his left shoulder, and looked like that famous silhouette of "The Don," as he was known, found on every bottle of Sandeman port and sherry—and on billboard ads all over Spain. After many days of nodding hello, and saying good morning, he walked over to where I was standing by the Land Rover and handed me a cup of coffee and said, "Hello, I'm Frank Sibley."

Danielle

It turned out that Frank was renting the upstairs floor from the young couple, and they themselves were renting the whole house. The woman downstairs was pretty, petite and French. Frank had a crush on her. Her husband worked for a jewellery outfit as a buyer. Therefore, he was away from home a lot. The couple did have a nanny for the baby, which gave "Danielle" nothing much to do, so she was, in some respects, constantly bored.

In the coming weeks I saw a lot of "Sib," as he liked to be called. He didn't own a car so the two of us would get into the Land Rover and drive to different places to drink. We often drove over to Gerrard St. in Toronto, which through the years has changed in many ways. At the time, it stretched between Yonge St. and Bay St., and was an artistic sort of area. There were a lot of eclectic shops, bookstores and handy-craft stores like "The Fiddler's Three." In this Gerrard St. village, I think it was at the intersection of Gerrard and Bay, stood the Mary John restaurant. In earlier and better times, Sib lived over one of the bookstores, and often ate at the Mary John. We would sit outside the restaurant and order a bottle of wine and reminisce. I remember saying to Frank, when we got to know each other a little better, that he was known by another name. "Aha," he said. "So you've heard the Secret Sib story too!" "Yep," I said. Then, just to be funny I said, "Can you lend me $20 bucks?" He smiled and said, "Not a chance" or something to that effect.

Through time, he told me many things about his life: Why his marriage didn't last, how tough it is to live on the few dollars he makes now by doing caricatures at conventions for insurance companies or appliance companies, etc. He did enjoy the occasional perks, such as a free hotel room and a free brunch. Unfortunately, $2 per drawing is hard to live on. One of Sib's eyes had a fleck on the bottom of the pupil, and this same eye was a little off. It didn't appear to look in the same direction as the other one. I didn't want to embarrass myself, or him, so I tried not to look at his defective eye, but instead would look at his good eye, or his cheek, or his forehead. This didn't always work. Damn it, I'd stare at the bad eye the whole time we'd be talking. Sib was used to this reaction from people, so it didn't really bother him. I remember he once said, "I could leave my penis out and you would still look at my eye."

He kept his upstairs apartment very clean. It was rather small but had a fireplace and a good-sized front window that faced Rosehill Ave. Propped up on the window sill were five or six postcards from women. These seemed to make him comfortable and happy. On one occasion, he went to the kitchenette to make us a coffee. I couldn't resist reading the cards. They were all nicely written, but I couldn't help noticing they were all yellowish from age and badly water-stained, also 15 years old.

Around this time, Danielle's husband ran off with the nanny. And Sib, Danielle and the baby had to be out of this rented house within a couple of months because the wrecker's ball was on its way. I told Sib I'd help him move when he found a place. Working late one night and into the morning, I got a call around 4 a.m. It was Danielle. She said she saw my light on and asked, before I drive off, if I would drop in for a drink. Well, I was between marriages, and alone, so I thought, "Why not?" Now, I hadn't had anything to eat since noon. The drink turned out to be a respectable French wine, and she also offered some cheeses, crackers and a lovely paté. Her place was nicely decorated. Danielle must have lit about 30 candles. There was also incense burning in the small room where we were sitting. The place felt like a sauna and made me think that this is what a happy brothel might look like. I was invited to see the bedroom with more candles and a beautiful bottle of white wine waiting in a cooler filled with ice. The sun was coming up soon and I thought I should leave, at least before Sib was on the porch with his coffee. I did leave, but not before the wine beside the bed was empty and some of the candles were spent.

I was soon invited back for a dinner. The dinner, I remember, was very French, and prepared to perfection. Danielle obviously took some time on this gourmet meal. After a lot of wine, and feeling comfortable and mellow, I was told, in so many words, that I wouldn't be having dessert, as I did in the bedroom the last time I was there, unless I agreed to what she had written down. What a surprise this was! The letter basically stated that I should move into the new two-storey house she had rented in Leaside, and pay half the rent, half the grocery bill and half the hydro and heating bills. I wouldn't have to worry about parking for my Land Rover, since the place had a double garage and ample parking. If I agreed to the letter, I could stay and enjoy going upstairs this evening and many more to come. If not, I could go now without having my coffee with cognac and, most definitely, without dessert.

I had my coffee at Fran's Restaurant, and I was reminded of when I was a kid in Montreal. My dad was the janitor of an apartment building at the time. On most days I played ball with my best friend Jimmy. One day, Jimmy wanted something from me, and for a good reason I didn't give it to him. He then took his ball home and we never played ball again. I guess the message here (if there is a message) is that whatever age you are, there is always a give-and-take thing going on, and what a pity. I guess some things don't change. I remember thinking years back, because of Jimmy, at that time I went and bought my own ball. Today, with this Danielle nonsense and her letter, I went out and started looking for another ball.

The old houses and mansions on Spadina Rd. are in close proximity to the University of Toronto campus and the "Annex" area. This would suit Sib, since this was a youth-oriented area with record shops, cafés and junky stores. "Honest Ed's" is within walking distance and so is Casa Loma. Casa Loma stands out above all the others: a modern replica of a medieval castle, built as a home for Sir William Henry Mill Pellatt in 1911. Three hundred men worked for three years to build Casa Loma at a cost of around $3,500,000, which in the early 1900s was a lot of money. Sir Henry enjoyed his dream castle for less than 10 years before debts (mostly property taxes) forced him to give it to the city of Toronto. Located nearby is "The Spadina House," a tourist site that sat on about six acres, at 285 Spadina Rd. This was a great place to spend a day. The architecture in the area was a mixture of Victorian and Edwardian. In this house, one could watch and learn how they cooked food in 1898. From here too, it was a short walk to Casa Loma, which was also originally a private residence like The Spadina House. But Casa Loma has great rooms and passageways throughout.

It was here, on Spadina Rd., where Secret Sib found a room to live in. The big house certainly had seen better days. It was once considered a mansion but had been badly neglected. Now it was not much better than a "flop house." Sib's room was on the second floor, next to the busy toilet. Fortunately for Sib, he did have a view. His room faced Spadina Rd. Sib picked a day for moving, and we loaded the big blue Land Rover with his "stuff." He had one of those "Sea-Breeze" record players that played one record at a time, the kind with a handle for portability. The hinged lid was covered in red leatherette, and the bottom part of the case in ivory leatherette. It could play only 78s and the bigger LP records. A small cardboard box held his music: old records of Mat Monroe, Mario Lanza, Lionel Hampton, the Dorsey brothers, and a bunch of other old platters. We moved in the usual things: coffee maker, cups, dishes, wine bottle opener, and boxes of miscellaneous things that one requires to survive.

I parked in front of the building. It was a Sunday, so there wasn't a problem with traffic. Sib moved the big doorknocker up and down until, finally, the landlady arrived. She herself rented the parlour on the main floor, next to the front door. You could tell, immediately, she'd been into the cheap wine, and her breath smelled like the Don River. Sib introduced himself again, even though he'd been here the day before to pay the first and last months' rent. She asked if he knew which room was his because she had forgotten. The landlady was wearing a pink chenille housecoat that, in its first life, was probably a bedspread. The fluffy slippers probably had colour at one time, but now matched the driveway. She tried her best to make us feel welcome, with a greeting that sounded like, "Make yersefs at home, and don't let the fuckin' cat out." Then she said, "Scouse me, I'm entertaining folks from out of town." That pink housecoat was open in the front throughout the whole discussion. I must say it wasn't a pretty sight.

I could see that Sib was more than a little embarrassed about his new digs. He and I kept carrying his things upstairs. You could see that this house, in its heyday, was one gorgeous place. Once inside the front doorway, there was a huge circular staircase that wound its way to the top floor. From the staircase there was a perfect view into the parlour, where the under-nourished landlady was entertaining four gentlemen. None of them appeared to be washed, and probably had never seen water unless it rained. All five of them were on her bed. Two of the men seemed drunker than the other two, and had a great deal of trouble-making words. On one of my trips downstairs, empty-handed, the landlady was one her way up to the toilet. As she so delicately put it, "I gotta piss, and now."

I stood aside. She, very wisely, held the railing, since she had difficulty with each step. Her panties were down at her ankles. The rest of her was completely bare. I couldn't help but notice that the elastic in her panties was stretched to the point of letting go. Also, the cat was beside her all the way. I figured that if the elastic goes, so does the cat. On her way down, she was now minus the panties. She must have left them in the toilet. I was a few steps behind her, as she turned into the parlour, where the two French doors were never closed. Well, the four guys were all awake now, and saw this vision returning to the bed. They all stared like they had never seen a naked woman before, and still not one erection in the bunch.

I locked the Land Rover, because everything was now upstairs, and returned to Sib. He was staring out the front window, and seemed to have a tear in his good eye. Fortunately, I had brought up a bottle of Scotch that I had in the Rover. I always carried a bottle of Scotch in every car I've ever owned. I poured a good shot (no ice) for each of us and asked, "What's up?" Sib said, "Look out this window at the house across the road, the one with the round turret." I said, "Yes, so?" That's when he let loose, and told me about his marriage, which he clearly missed, and, in a kind of whisper, said, "That was the first place we lived in, up there in that turret." We drank a couple more shots. It was getting dark, so I left the bottle with Sib and left him alone. I was going to be seeing him the next day anyway to help him move the joy of his life, his books. We were moving them on to a little wooden boat that he kept on Ward's Island, at the other side of a small wooden bridge. This little bridge served as a walkway for the islanders, as well as the Queen City Yacht Club members. I was still a member of the Q.C.Y.C. at that time. The Club was a great place to sail out of. It was also a great place to drink and relax. Just before I left him that day, he said, "I'd appreciate it if you didn't tell anyone where I was living."

As I headed down the spiral staircase I noticed the parlour room was now empty of guests. The lady was out cold and still naked. The cat was awake, and mean. On the way out I thought, "Why not let the cat out?" I didn't have any work on my desk on Monday that couldn't wait, so I picked up Sib at Rosehill and we packed the Land Rover with books for another trip to the island. I parked as close to the ferry docks on Queen's Quay as I could, and rented one of those big plywood boxes. Unfortunately, the unit I chose had those four wobbly wheels that never go straight ahead. Again, I locked the Land Rover and we left the mainland. We put all the books into the little wooden boat and watched the waterline disappear. This little boat was Sib's last possession. It was small, but if absolutely necessary it could sleep two, plus there was very little head-room inside. After everything was all packed away, I suggested we go to the Q.C.Y.C. and have a drink. Sib loved the idea but said he was banned from the club because, years ago, he was sitting on the outside railing on the upper level of the building and fell off. Fortunately, he fell into the flower-bed below, and not on the concrete walkway. Since he was drunk, he didn't hurt himself. We went to the clubhouse anyway. Nobody remembered him. About two weeks later, for something to do, Sib and I went to the island to check on the boat. It was a sad scene. The little boat was well past the waterline, and resting on its bottom.

We went aboard and looked down below. Every book was fat and bloated, like people who have died in the water. Nothing was said. Sib didn't even lock the companionway. We walked over to the Q.C.Y.C., went upstairs, got two beers, went outside and sat on the railing.

Danielle and baby by now had moved to the newly rented house in Leaside. A lot of years have gone by since then and Sib and I have lost touch with each other. A trumpet-playing friend (Dick Park) was playing jazz at "The Selby House" at Bloor and Sherbourne St., and sitting across from the half-round bar was Sib with a new lady in his life. We talked a little and he seemed quite happy. I forgot to ask where he was living or if he had a phone. He probably wouldn't have given it to me anyway. It was likely still a secret. Through the years I've often wondered how and where Secret Sib is. I wish I knew.

Part Four: Colin and his Tiger Moth

Before I get into Colin's love affair with the Tiger Moth biplane, I think it best first to give you a little history of how this vintage double winger came to be.

Born in 1882, a shy, clever young lad, Geoffrey de Havilland, the son of an English country parson, built himself a handmade motorcycle that was so mechanically wonderful it got him a job at a motor shop. Around this time the Wright brothers had their first flight. In 1907, Geoffrey married and fortunately the new bride was also a flying enthusiast. Young Geoffrey quit his job and, together with another young mechanic, Frank Hearle, started building a plane out of wire, wood, linen and a 45-hp engine. Mrs. de Havilland did the sewing of the linen for the wings, etc. The plane was finished and with Geoffrey de Havilland at the wheel and Frank Hearle pushing it down a hill, it took off, flew about thirty-five yards and crashed. Almost immediately they started building another machine--this time stronger and a lot simpler, and it flew.

Around the 1920s and '30s the now new de Havilland Aircraft Company produced a series of light transport aircraft and private planes known as the Moth series, including the very successful Tiger Moth.

The *Toronto Daily Star* ran a headline on June 4, 1937, which read, "Tiger Moth Biplane Order Is Confirmed. Toronto plant to manufacture 20 for the R.C.A.F." On Dec. 22, 1937, the first Tiger Moth made in Canada flew over Toronto on an initial test flight. A year later in October, the *Star* reported that a $100,000 extension to the de Havilland Aircraft Plant was under construction on Sheppard Ave. in North York, Ont.

Today we get on an airplane, jump on and off without thinking or caring about how we got from here to there so fast. It's just a plane. But those few who live and breathe the romance of flying think differently than you and I. In the early days there was the open cockpit, the brown leather skullcap and goggles. Your attached parachute also acted as your seat in the cramped Tiger Moth. That was really flying, not like sitting in a 747 with a hot dinner in front of you, being served drinks while you read or watch a movie.

People did all sorts of things with the Moth, like Laura Ingalls who looped hers 344 times in succession to set some sort of record. Nobody knows why, but she did it. The boldest and best-known is Francis Chichester, who in his Gipsy Moth played a big part. A native Englishman, Chichester, who as a young lad was a bit of a problem, was sent off to the Dominions (New Zealand), where he very quickly made a lot of money in the lumber business. Financially secure, he returned to England, took flying lessons, earned his license and bought himself a Moth. After flying around Europe for a while, and with less than a hundred hours of flying time, he set off on a solo flight for Australia. Around this time (1929) only one other had flown alone to Australia.

Chichester witnessed some terrifying moments, which so excited him he next set off to be first across the Tasman Sea, the stretch between Australia and New Zealand. For this trip he had floats attached to his Moth. His navigation required him to find two tiny islands on the way across. In the lagoon of one of the islands his Moth sank, but he managed to resurface the biplane and within another year had rebuilt it. Chichester had it in mind to proceed around the world, but only managed to get to Japan where a wire stretched between two hills stopped his Moth in mid air and almost put Francis in his grave. Years later Francis Chichester chose a sail boat for his circumnavigation around the world and, faithful to his biplane, he christened the boat Gypsy Moth III. At the end of this fantastic journey, while sailing into Plymouth Harbour in 1968, flying low overhead was a Gypsy Moth airplane.

Commercial aviation died in Britain with World War II, so de Havilland switched to war production of the Tiger high-speed general purpose Mosquito aircraft. Because of the lack of steel, a twin-engine fighter-bomber was built of wood, and affectionately became known as "The Wooden Wonder." The Mosquito was the fastest plane in the war until 1944.

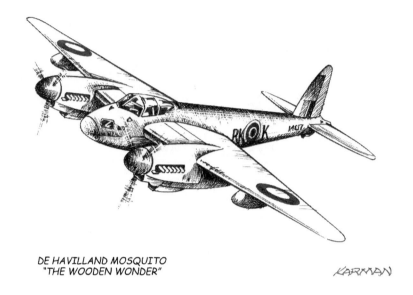

DE HAVILLAND MOSQUITO
"THE WOODEN WONDER"

KARMAN

Now—with many thanks to the Internet and magazines for this valuable information on the history of Geoffrey de Havilland and his wonderful magnificent Tiger Moth—I will do my best to tell you what I know about Colin and his first love, The Tiger Moth. I don't know how many years went by while Colin and I worked together as retouching artists at Brigden's Ltd. I also didn't know too much about Colin's early years before this, other than that he was in England and, throughout World War II, I believe flew in a Lancaster bomber. After the war, he arrived in Toronto and became a photo retoucher, and made his first love English automobiles. For transportation, his favourite was a vintage MG-TD. This was back in the '50s. At the time I drove a temperamental '56 MGA. He collected English cars and had them propped up all over Toronto in people's garages (mostly in pieces). One day on our way to lunch in the TD, Colin took an intersection far too fast. Both wheels on my side hit the curb and both tires simultaneously blew. The TD lifted on Colin's side and for a moment felt like she was going to go over on her side. The worst damage, other than embarrassment, was that the two big wire wheels on my side were bent and finished forever. As always Colin was never upset, said something like "See, I told you they never roll over," and the following morning went to a friend's garage and got his beloved Aston Martin.

Weeks later the big day arrived. I was to meet Colin at the airport in Maple, Ont. (a few short miles north of Toronto), a small airport mostly for privately owned planes. It was early on a Saturday morning and the place was already busy with owners and dreamers. Colin was easy to find, being the only owner of a Tiger Moth biplane in the field. There it was, The Holy Grail of airplanes, beautifully painted and restored by Colin himself. After a good look at the workings of the Tiger Moth, my first impression was that it reminded me of my Model A roadster. Everything about the Moth is as basic as possible, starting with the gas tank mounted overhead on the top wing—similar to the way the Model A gas tank is mounted higher than the engine, the thinking here being that the Model A does not need a fuel pump. The Model A tank also acts as the dashboard. The gas has a free fall directly into the carburetor. The Moth has the same setup, but I'm not sure how this works, because the Moth will fly upside down. When fuelling up the Moth one has to climb on top of the wing, stand on a reinforced top piece, unscrew a brass filler cap in the tank, and top up.

As I walked around the plane it became quite obvious how light

259

the Moth really is. The cables and fittings all looked to be half the diameter I thought they should be. To turn the plane around, you picked up the tail and just walked around till the nose faced your desired direction. The older model Tiger had a skid at the back. This model had the upgraded small wheel (far better). In many ways, the airplane was beautifully simple. No brakes, no heater, no adjustments for the buckets seats and too many other things to mention now. Getting in the Tiger is an uphill matter. When the Tiger sits on the tarmac (or grass) it is on a steep angle. The first time I got on the wing, I didn't know where to put my feet for fear of going through the linen. Colin told me if I couldn't reach the floor to simply step on the aluminium bucket seat. There is no cushion on the seat because your parachute is your seat cushion. Later when everything was a go, as I sat up front, I could just manage to see the top of the engine cowling. The sides of the cockpit seemed very low, even with the little flap doors up. After topping up the fuel and adding oil (often) came the pre-flight briefing, such as how the parachute works (mine came from Hercules Army Surplus, well used) and how to use the headset, which is attached to the leather hat with goggles and other minor stuff.

One of the reasons for taking this flight was to drop in at the Buttonville airport to see Henry, a good old friend of Colin's and, as Colin said, "It's very important." While Colin was busy doing the necessary checks to the Tiger Moth, other pilots were tying down their airplanes because of high winds. Some wandered over to say hello and say things like, "Hey Colin, with all this wind you're not seriously thinking of going up today, especially in a double winger, are you?"

"Well guys," said Colin, "I think we'll be fine once we're in the air. And it's important that I see Henry over in Buttonville. Also I think we should fly out of this wind once I get up high enough. Oh! And seeing how you're here, I could use three of you to hold her down when I untie her, so if one of you could each hold the bottom wings down by the handles and another at the tail, and run with me as long as you can when I take off, that would be good."

I climbed into the front seat as rehearsed. The boys held the Tiger down, Colin flipped a switch or two, went up front to the propeller, gave the propeller a good pull down a couple of times until she caught, and it sprung into life. When the smoke cleared, Colin kicked out the chocks, climbed into his seat behind me, strapped himself into the bucket, aimed the Moth into the wind, opened the throttle, got off to a brisk start and the running began. Colin had his head out to the side to see where to go for a moment, then a shove on the stick brought up the tail, enabling him and me to see ahead. We were off into the air in an instant like a child's kite tied to a string. First the wind threw us to port and just as quickly over to starboard, and so it went until we hit better weather higher up. The Tiger Moth turns a lot better in the air than it does on the ground. I'm guessing we were at an altitude of about 1,000 feet and cruising at 80 knots. I took the opportunity to have a good look at the instruments before me. Everything was pretty basic, altimeter, tachometer, fuel gauge, amp and compass. Colin had the same layout in front of him.

I've been on many jet planes but I must admit to being very impressed with how the Tiger Moth seemed to bend with the weather similar to a sailboat, and not just punch through in a straight line like jets or motorboats. As we headed for Buttonville in these wind conditions I felt the control rods move and bump against my leg as Colin adjusted for a new bearing. As we flew over Holland Marsh I could see the highway 400 that I'd driven on for years on the way to the cottage. I took out the Rolliecord camera, put the strap around my neck and took advantage by taking a few more shots. I leaned out of the cockpit as far as I could with the camera strap doing its best to draw blood with all the wind and flapping going on. I had to hold on to the camera with both hands or lose it. Autumn is a beautiful time of year, but in a convertible airplane it can be freezing. Still, the sun was shining, and in my mind only it did feel a little warmer. My headset crackled and Colin said, "Look below, that's Buttonville just ahead." And sure enough, there it was, a small building that appeared to be the size of a single-car garage.

Colin decided to circle the airport once, to show we could use a little help to set her down. On our way down it became apparent that the wind was the same as it was in Maple. As we touched down two lads ran along each side to grab a wing handle, while a third fellow took hold of the tail. We taxied slowly to the wee building. Colin shut off the engine, jumped out of the cockpit and ran into the building to see Henry. Meanwhile, the three good wise men held the plane down. In a very short few minutes, Colin was back and with one energetic turn of the propeller, the Moth engine fired into life once again. The throttle was opened, the Tiger Moth moved forward into the grass, and the three boys ran as fast as their little legs would allow until they couldn't keep up anymore. As on every flight, Colin had to stick his head out the side for a view of where to steer the Moth. We were almost into the farmer's fence when the three lads let go, Colin gave the engine a burst, the tail lifted and we were airborne once again in a kite-like climb.

The Tiger Moth reminds me a little of a kite, covered in fabric; all we're missing is the string to the ground. As the Moth lifts you towards the sky, you completely forget about the weather conditions and fall in love with the view, the sunshine, the adrenalin rush of being up there again, outside, and not a care in the world. With all those tiny cars below, the winding roads, the sparkles in the north country lakes, together with the colour of thousands of autumn trees, I turned on my headset, pushed the little switch over and through the static I asked Colin, "By the way Colin, how did you make out with your friend Henry?" There was a pause, and through the wind noise and engine I heard, "Yes! It was a boy."

After a while we saw the familiar Holland Marsh again, Colin dipped the nose and there was Maple, Ont. We flew in a bit sideways (not by choice) with three new guys running along side to catch the plane. I turned in my seat and saw Colin's head leaning out from the cockpit to get a forward view of the last few hundred yards of the best day I'd had in years.

If you should ever get the chance to experience the nostalgia of a bygone era by flying in one these remarkable things, take it. When you're done and walk away like I did, you will probably say, "I should have one of these."

Part Five: The North Atlantic
"A small boat voyage"

Society be damned!

A man comes home from work one day, gets out of his new car, steps into his warm and comfortable home, smells the cooking on the stove, pats the kids and happy dog on the head, kisses his wife and announces to all he's left his job. He has bought a boat, left some money in the bank for all, and now hugs his wife and says, "I'll be away for a while, and will write soon." He is irresistibly drawn to the sea and society be damned.

Deep down inside, I always knew that if I ever got the chance to sail the North Atlantic, I would never consider doing it single-handedly. I'm not the type to be alone for that long. If I were to try it, I'd be a gibbering idiot at the other side, if I ever got to the other side. I knew I would like to sail alone for a few days but how I would fare after that, I had no idea. Any sailing I had done at this point was mostly with friends on enjoyable holidays around Lake Ontario. Like anyone developing an interest in sailing I took the Power Squadron lessons in the evenings and joined the Queen City Yacht Club in Toronto, which opened a whole new world for me. This was in 1976.

At the Power Squadron classes, I met Al Betcke, one of the instructors on navigation. As time passed, I heard that Al was preparing for a North Atlantic crossing, and the North Atlantic had been my dream for years. Now, these days, if one expects to cross an ocean for fame, money or whatever, forget it. Everything has been done, from the smallest boat (shorter than an average man's height) to the huge maxi boats. The Atlantic and the Pacific have also both been rowed. The English Channel has been water-skied. And in many of these heroic cases, the individuals have not come back to let us know what they (almost) did. My advice: If you are determined to go to sea for a short time or a long time, at least try to get into a proven and safe boat. As many good sailors know, the sea will throw the worst at you, and when you're far out from shore, you're on your own, and there's nowhere to hide till it's over. Also, if you should believe you know everything there is to know about the sea, stay home.

I was very eager to talk to Al Betcke, and got my chance to do so one evening after class. My very first question was, "Has the crew already been picked?" "Yes, long ago," was his reply. "Damn." Now, the best I could do is somehow get involved in their ocean voyage. I was curious and had many questions, such as, When? Where to? For how long? What provisions? And the big questions, "Who's going, where is the boat, what's its length?" Al answered all my questions and ended by saying, "Why don't you go to Frenchman's Bay on Lake Ontario and introduce yourself to Leo Viljakainen, a Finn. He's always on his boat. You can't miss it, it's a 35-ft. yellow steel hull." It was on a weekday, I remember, and things were slow at work, so Woof, my dog, and I set off to find Leo.

We got to Frenchman's Bay around noon and without any trouble found the yellow boat still in the yard, sitting in its cradle. I slapped the side of the boat with the flat of my hand and up popped

Leo's head from the hatch. Now this was the first time Mr. Woof and I had met Leo. (On many occasions Mr. Woof is referred to as Mister because, I feel, he deserves the title.) I told Leo how badly I'd wanted to be crew on a trip such as this one. Leo told me that about a year previously he had to run an ad in the newspapers to find a crew. And it wasn't easy. He and Al Betcke had been friends for some time and started planning this voyage about two years ago. They'd also been getting the boat ready for the past two years. Anyway, another two were needed for crew and that's when Steve and Ruth, a young married couple, saw the ad and signed on. Steve was an Italian lad who enjoyed deep sea diving and wanted adventure, and Ruth, a lovely girl, would go anywhere Steve went. So it was a done thing. These two also decided to sail with Leo for as long as he needed them. Al Betcke had agreed to sail as far as Helsinki, Finland. Al was the owner and president of a small insurance agency and had to be back in two months if possible.

I saw a lot of Leo from that first day and helped with preparatory things. First, I painted the boat name and homeport on the boat: "TULLEN TIE" (pronounced Too-len Tee). It's a Finnish name that roughly means "to go where the wind goes." Tullen Tie was a 35-ft. ketch made of steel and built in Burlington, Ont.

A word here to those just starting to learn about sailboats and the way they can be differently rigged. A sloop can be very fast, but one thing that may bother others and me in ocean sailing is that the mast can be quite tall and carry a lot of sail for one person to handle. I'm talking here about a boat of 35 ft. or larger. So in terrible wind conditions, you could be very busy reefing in a big mainsail. Or taking down your genny. In this case, I'd probably prefer the cutter rig to the sloop. The yawl, on the other hand, has the appearance of a sloop but with the addition of a little mizzen on her aft end, where the boom hangs over the water. Try reefing or taking that down in huge following seas.

Now this brings me to Leo's boat, the ketch. I know this type of vessel won't sail to windward as well as a single-masted rig, and the mizzen does blanket the main when you're running, but windward is not so important in long-distance cruising. One nice feature of the ketch is it can very easily shift the centre of effort forward when the wind is behind you, by hauling down the mizzen. If you're short handed, changing head sails and reefing a ketch is a lot easier and safer than one very big sail. Keep in mind also that the mizzen-mast is a great thing to lean on when you're using the sextant or to lean against when you're just standing around talking.

Eventually, one gets around to talking about schooners, with very large sails and bowsprits. The bowsprits were also known as widow makers. Yes, when you fell off a bowsprit, especially in the older days of sailing, you were gone. There was no going back. What about a gaff or marconi rig? Lets not get into that. Boats also come in different materials. Fibreglass is the most popular, mostly for the weekend sailor. Like tupperware, they last and don't need much upkeep, if of course you don't bump into anything like a steel boat. Aluminium boats are worth considering: they don't rust, they're light, your compass works (no deviation), you don't have to paint it if you don't want to. If you do run into something hard like a reef, it will dent a little, but aluminium will tear, unlike steel, which will take a beating.

But, of course, steel will dent somewhat, it will rust and your compass won't know what the hell is going on. Ferro cement boats are strong, but very heavy. My favourite would be steel because of strength, and if you can afford a gyro compass everything will be wonderful. With a steel boat, the deck is welded to the hull, becoming one unit, whereas with fibreglass the deck is joined to the hull with bolts or a rivet gun.

Several problems and sinking mishaps have come about due to water coming in from the topsides, such as by a knock-down, a rollover, or, worse, a pitch-pole (somersault). Usually the mast will be torn off, taking a piece of boat with it. In many past cases the whole deck-house was ripped off when it made contact with the hard water. History has told us that a steel boat has usually fared better in a knock-down.

After a lot of money was spent and hours of preparation, Leo's boat was ready to go into the water. In the coming weeks, Mr. Woof and I sailed quite a bit with Leo and drank large quantities of Akvavit. The Finns love it, so do the Danes and the Norwegians. It's not my favourite, but if that's all there is, "It's wonderful." Woof, known as a mutt, was a wonderful sailor, from his very first day on a boat he belonged and loved every minute. He'd lean himself against a stanchion on the leeward side and watch the water flow by. No matter how far Tullen Tie healed over, Woof just leaned against the stanchion, even when the water came over the toe rail and washed over his feet. When he had enough, he would disappear down below and there you would find him on the lee side in one of the berths fast asleep. When we would come about for a different tack, Woof would smartly move to the other side. I got Woof for $9. I was told he was a black lab on the phone. I said, "I'll buy him," and went to the people to pick him up. He was sort of black, he had a white chest, a little white on the end of his tail and some paws had white on the bottom. He was a mutt and the $9 was for the papers. Oh! Yes, we lived happily ever after. Another plus for the $9 was that Woof could climb ladders, no matter how high they were. Plus he could pass you on the way up. Coming down was a problem.

My two young sons moved in with me about now, so I bought a strawberry box in Toronto's Leaside neighbourhood. Now to be a family, I figured we needed a dog, and that's how Woof came into our lives and house. I remember how nervous he was when I went to get him in my pickup truck. Thinking back, it made sense for him to be nervous: I found out later that he had four other owners before me. When we got home, Greg said, "But dad, this black lab has a white shirt on, and two white paws and some white on the end of his tail." I said, "Yeah, so? And he doesn't have any papers either and only cost $9." Three weeks went by and still no name for the so-called black lab. Greg, Derek and I were sitting in the basement watching TV one night and I asked the dog, "What did they call you at the other place where you lived?" It was like the heavens had opened up, he looked up and said, "WOOF" and Woof it was.

Oh, we had our minor problems with Woof as time went on, but nothing serious. There were times when he'd run away up the hill in front of the house. I'd stand in the driveway hollering," Woof, Woof, Woof ." Of course, my new neighbours didn't see the dog, just me. Going to the vet's was also fun. Woof and I would sit there in the waiting room with all the other owners and their thoroughbreds until one by one a name would be called. Now, some of the other pets, some with little jackets on and hair all combed (like the pampered Lady Sasha III or Hubert of High Hedges) ,were sniffing each others rear ends just like Woof would do. So much for Royalty. Then it was our turn, the vet's nurse would call out "Woof Karman," I'd stand up with Woof and everyone in the room would look at me like I had two noses. The snooty dogs now looked at Mr. Woof like they'd never seen a $9 dog before. This would happen often and eventually I grew to believe I did have two noses.

We were installing the handrails on top of the coach roof on Tullen Tie, Leo topsides drilling holes through the steel and attaching the stainless-steel grab bars (handrails) to the deck. Leo inserted the stainless-steel bolts from the top and Al was down below with the lock-washers and nuts. On one occasion, when one of the bolts was pushed through, a sliver of steel from the boat ended up in Al's eye. In less than two weeks, his eye took on a rusty look and he began to lose his sight in that eye. This was only a few weeks from the date when the Tullen Tie was scheduled to break its moorings and make its way from Toronto to the Atlantic. Al began seeing every specialist in Toronto and making trips to the States for answers and relief. Ruth, the only other crew-member on board, aside from her husband Steve, had the Tullen Tie well stocked with food for the trip across. Friends were giving going-away parties and I was invited to all. Leo's wife threw a wonderful party for Leo (even though they had separated years ago, but were still good friends). And so it went for Leo and crew until it was time to go.

The Tullen Tie left on the intended date, but Al was not on

board. The eye was getting to be a bigger problem than anticipated. A young lad, Ian Pontz, who had helped a great deal on the boat, agreed to be a temporary crew-member and sail as far as Sydney, N.S. So the four started their long trip on Lake Ontario, eventually into the St. Lawrence river, and on and on. In the interim, Al was having more operations on his eye without any luck. Meanwhile, on the Tullen Tie, Steve was seasick day and night for the entire length of the St. Lawrence river. I remember Leo telling me later on that poor Steve barfed constantly over the side, kneeling on a cock-pit cushion with his little feet pedalling up and down as fast as they could go. The upshot of all this was that Al was going to join the boat in Nova Scotia no matter what, even if he had to wear a patch. He had waited too many years now for his dream to come true, so there was no turning back.

The bigger news for me now was that I got a call from Leo when Tullen Tie had arrived and tied up in Sydney. The reason for the call was to tell me that Steve and Ruth had left the boat and would I please come. Now, I was exited (of course) but I had only two weeks to get ready, and to find someone to move into the wee house to look after Greg, Derek and Mr. Woof. Next, I had to finish whatever art work I had taken on, phone all the agency people I knew who had been good to me, and explain why I would be away for at least two months or so. Then I went to a great store on Bloor St. (Eddie Bauers) to buy the warmest socks money could buy, long underwear and a sleeping bag for $350 that turned out to be the best purchase of my life (that's 350 big ones back in 1976). My nephew Robert moved in and became warden. Al and I were now packed and ready. We got our flight tickets, made sure our passports were up to date and we both went to see our doctors and dentists. I will never forget my doctor when I got the full medical exam. I was lying on the examining table on that paper that stays with you when you leave, completely naked looking at the ceiling, when he had his hands on my testicles, and counting, "One two, one two, one two." Finally I asked, "What are you doing?" Of course, he was waiting for this, and said, "Counting, and when you get back, I will count them again." More doctors should have the sense of humour of Dr. Isaac.

I had gone through two marriages, so naturally my dear maw always worried and wondered when I would settle down. And now I was trying to explain about the cruise I was about to take. My maw, when she got a bit upset or not, would rattle off in Hungarian, then into German, a little of English and back to Hungarian all in one sentence. After all this, she'd walk away waving her hands in the air. But she did love me and knitted me a wool turtleneck sweater, which wet or dry does keep you warm. Never, ever wear dacron, nylon or some other synthetic fibre on the ocean. My sister knitted me a wool hat, another item I couldn't live without. When the waves came over the deck and me, I'd take the hat off, wring the water out of it, put it on and be completely warm again. So I do emphasize without a doubt, you will fall in love with wool in these conditions. More on clothes later.

My start came at 0630 hrs. (that's nautical talk) when Roy and Janet came by the house to deliver me to the airport for the 0800 hrs. departure for Sydney. Al Betcke and his wife Chris and three girls were already there. Janet gave me a big box of Mars bars, and what a God-send that was later on, and Al's family gave him a big box of mixed chocolate bars. On our flight Al managed to get himself invited to the cockpit (something I'm sure would be impossible today) and with the kind help of the pilot and navigator got a good picture of where the icebergs were at this time of year.

When Al and I arrived at the Northern Yacht Club in North Sydney, Steve and Ruth had already left. So now we were three unless Ian decided to join us. He didn't have any commitments or plans, so asked for a couple of days to think it over. As for the people of Cape Breton, talk about kindness and hospitality! You have yet to meet a nicer lot. At the home of one couple, Al and Dean, we were invited to dinner and learned how to eat lobster without using the necessary tools like crackers and other pointy things. Dean (the wife) first covered the table with newspapers, then dumped into the middle a huge crock full of steaming lobsters. We all washed this down with Schooner beer and left a mess on the table, that would have been an award-winning shot for Kodak.

Our last evening in Nova Scotia was spent at the Northern Yacht Club dance. I guess all the good lookers stayed home. There was a big fellow at the dance who ignored his girl from the moment he brought her in. Leo figured he should offer his condolences to the fair maiden and step in and dance with her, and dance he did, a little too much and possibly a little too close, or so it seemed to the big fellow. It now appeared as if a punch-up was about to take place, but Leo had it postponed to the following night. That was a clever move, because we were leaving in the early morning.

We're off

Sunday morning, July 6, Ian had decided he was coming with us. We had the perfect start, the sun was out, good wind and a small group on shore wishing us well. We were flying the mizzen, mainsail and the big genoa. Tullen Tie was moving nicely at a speed of about five knots. Because of the sea swells, my stomach was feeling a bit uneasy. Some of this could also have been because of too much excitement and nerves. Al appeared to have the same symptoms. Ian's complexion looked a little off too. We found out later he had an ulcer problem. It was good to have Ian on board, he being the fourth member would make the watches a lot easier. Also Ian was 23 yrs. old and had already done four years at George Brown College in Toronto, learning navigation. He had his second mate papers and had spent the last few years working on cargo ships, already as second mate on some rusty old Japanese freighters. The lad knew every bloody star in the sky, and another plus was that he was a quiet and likeable guy. As for the rest of us, I was 43, Al was 44 and Leo was 45.

Leo still had his hangover from the previous evening, and he did work hard to get it. When Leo and I took our first watch, which lasted six hours, I found I was very sleepy. I put it to the fact that I was getting far too much fresh air that I wasn't used too. The boat sailed well, perhaps a touch on the slow side because of her 11 tons, and a lot of food and gear on board. Al was still seasick and so was I. If I could only vomit I knew I'd feel better, but that wouldn't happen on cue. I once read in a seafaring book that if you can (in some cases) ride this out for three days, you'll be fine and the queasiness will be gone forever, or of course until you hit shore and stay awhile; then you'll have to start all over again. I guess it was true, because in three days Al and I felt like new and stayed that way for the complete crossing. A small yellow bird arrived on that first day and sat on my shoulder. He was worn out. I believe he had been blown off shore and was too pooped to make it back. So he stayed and we talked. He chirped that he was tired, couldn't eat, would love a drink of fresh water, mentioned things weren't great at home, but that he should go back. With that, we said our goodbyes, took a few pictures and he was off. A school of porpoise swam by and gave us entertainment for a short time, until they too had to leave.

Ian didn't look good. Aside from his stomach trouble, he simply wasn't comfortable on a sailboat. I imagine because all his sailing experience had been up on the bridge of large ships, that this, sitting so close to the water, was a problem for him. I remained hopeful that, in a few days, things would look better. Before leaving shore, Ian and I had bought a birthday cake for Al and got it on the boat without Al knowing. It was one of those cheap cakes covered in sugar icing with baby blue swirls and candy angels holding a scroll that said, Happy Birthday Al. The day of the birthday, we lit the candles, I played Happy Birthday on the harmonica, took the cake topsides, the wind blew the candles out and blew the top icing with the angels into the ocean. Boy! When you're sitting on the ocean day after day, with all that salt in the air. Does that baby-blue hard sugar taste good.

The evening shift belonged to Leo and me. It started at midnight and finished at 6 a.m. The moon sank like a stone, and it was dark and cold, and a bumpy ride. On Monday the 7th the weather was bad, with confused swells that reminded me of a washing machine in agitation mode. We had just finished a sail change and it was time for another. I took the genny down and put up a working jib. Leo was at the wheel. I took the mizzen down because we had to slow down the boat. I then reefed the main and that helped a great deal. While all this was going on, Ian decided that he wanted off. Al and Ian took the next midnight shift while Leo and I got some sleep. The weather quickened, (turned to shit.) Al went forward to take the main down. Ian apparently was doubled over the wheel with pain and frightened to death. The toe rail was under and we had water up to the ports. Al put the mizzen back up and the boat seemed to ride better with just the mizzen and working jib. That night was like being on a rocking horse with no let up. Ian's stomach became a big problem, much worse than before.

Ian wanted to be put ashore. It began to look as though it would be necessary, the following day, to drop him off at St. Pierre & Miquelon, if we could find those islands. Leo was not at all happy with this decision and I could understand why. He had his life's savings in this dream of his and we were running out of time as far as the weather was concerned: we had to make it to the other side before the worst of the storm season started. More to the point, we didn't have charts for St. Pierre & Miquelon. Now, the general knowledge of this area is that in 365 days of the year, there will be 325 days of fog. Night fell again, it began to rain and the fog persisted. As is also well known, St. Pierre has more than its share of rocks, so wisely we decide to wait for daybreak.

Tuesday was no different from Monday. Visibility in the fog was about a quarter of a mile and the fog seemed to be getting thicker.

We were under diesel power and looking for any marker available--not that that would be much help since we had no charts anyway. Ian was on the VHF to Saint-Pierre Coastal. They recommended we stay in deep water–a great help. We were proceeding at a snail's pace with the depth sounder reading 20 feet. I was on the bow staring into the fog and ready to holler if I saw rocks in front or below. Strange things happen to your eyesight when you stare into nothing for too long. For me, the water below seemed to travel uphill every now and then, so you had to look away, blink a few times to bring your vision back to normal, and then stare into nothing again. I'll swear that every time I saw a rock coming up, Leo was already throttling down, first into neutral and then reverse, full throttle up again and doing the reciprocal before I could yell "rock." I imagine all those years when Leo earned his living on a bulldozer had to be a great help now. Al and I took turns blowing the fog-horn every two minutes until we got much closer to Saint-Pierre. The bottom was now becoming very clear and with the engine off, we could hear the swells breaking on the shore. A small fishing boat came into view and was obviously heading in. This skipper had radar (as they all do) so we followed him in. The danger was over.

TULLEN TIE
IN ST. PIERRE ET MIQUELON

Saint-Pierre & Miquelon are part of a group of eight small islands in the North Atlantic, located about 15 km southwest of Newfoundland's Burin Peninsula. Miquelon is larger than Saint-Pierre, even though most of the population 7,700 (as of 2008) live on Saint-Pierre's 26 square km. The town is built on the island's east coast. Most of the island's forest cover has been cut down for fuel, leaving only low shrub growth. The people of the islands are of French origin and all speak French. Mainly Roman Catholic schools provide compulsory primary education. The islands were originally discovered by the Portuguese in the early 1500s, and at different times were occupied by the British. In 1535 Jacques Cartier claimed the islands for France and they have been in French possession since 1816. Most of the workforce here is involved in fishing and the processing of fish, such as salting, drying, canning and freezing. Unfortunately there has been a depletion of stock since the 1990s. Almost all consumer goods have to be imported. French financial aid is indispensable. All the islands are rocky, with little vegetation, cold and with a constant foggy climate.

We motored past a number of vessels—mostly draggers that fish with nets for squid, and they catch them by the thousands. Saint-Pierre, when we were there, seemed to have quite a few Japanese fishing boats moored in town. They're known as the brown boats (i.e. rusty) because they haven't seen paint since they went into the water. The Tullen Tie was allowed to tie up right in town, "free" A crowd gathered and it felt good to be among welcoming faces. On the dock, beside the customs man, was Jean Paul, a young lad and the only individual in Saint-Pierre who had a sailboat, a 35-ft. Sparkman &

Stephens that he and his girlfriend, Jacqueline, were restoring. (Jacqueline happened to be the mayor's daughter.) We visited with them often and ate in some of the better restaurants with them, had frog legs, sting ray, etc., and of course plenty of French wine. Al, who is not a big drinker but did have a few, seemed to have a little trouble putting one foot in front of the other on the way back to the boat. Jacqueline believed I was still in my 30s; what an absolutely charming, intelligent and smart girl she was.

Being in Saint-Pierre was like being in France. The currency was French francs at the time, and the shops sold baguettes, wine, croissants, pastries and so forth. Ian found a room that cost him the equivalent of $20 a day with three full meals and wine included. He ended up living there till the fog cleared, when a small plane flew him to the mainland. Our plan was to leave at 4 or 5 a.m. the next day. If you're interested in visiting Saint-Pierre, keep in mind there is not a lot of night life. If you're content with eating well and walking, good for you. The terrain is mostly barren rock, the climate is cold and wet, with a lot of mist and fog. Spring and Autumn are apparently windy. The language is French and they now have the Euro, of course. I'm told 99 percent of the residents are Roman Catholic. The coastline for both Saint-Pierre and Miquelon is about 120 km and the legal system is French law. The livelihood is pretty much fishing and servicing fishing fleets operating off the coast of Newfoundland. Railways do not exist, but I hear they have two airports now.

Our departure plans changed and we were to sail out of Saint-Pierre around 11 a.m. Before leaving, I dropped into the hardware store to say good-bye to François. While I was there, the owner went to the back of the shop to get something for me. He gave me a very large plastic container filled with fresh water and, with a waterproof marker, wrote his name and address across the front. All he wanted was a postcard from Ireland, our first landfall. We took on more diesel because we did use a lot to get in here. Al said his head really hurt more than earlier, and I believed the problem to be his eyesight. I started to help him by putting in his eye drops. We said our good-byes to Ian and other new friends and were off into a wall of fog. I've read in the past in some of my nautical literature that three people on a boat (on a long voyage) may not necessarily be a good idea. Now that we were sailing again it was time to figure out and establish a new watch system. I took two Gravols to settle my stomach. (I guess we were in port too long and I would have to start my three days all over again. Actually I was fine after one uncomfortable day.)

Al's eye looked worse and he began to have trouble reading the compass. This was really getting him down and there wasn't much Leo or I could do to help cheer him up. On top of this, the Goddamn fog won't leave; we had no wind, so the fog just lingered all around the boat. There was a three-and-a-half knot current, taking us back in more than out. Although all the sails were up, we still couldn't sail out. Visibility was about 50 feet forward of the bow. Everybody's eyes (not just Al's) were getting very tired staring into nothing. On two very serious occasions we almost put Tullen Tie on the rocks. The depth sounder read 10 feet, when out of nowhere directly on the bow was the biggest rock protruding out of the water. It wasn't just a rock because it continued on forever in both directions. I hollered "Holy shit," Leo was already in reverse with all the throttle he could give the diesel engine. The whole boat shuddered something awful and finally took hold and, in what seemed like forever, slowly reversed--but not before I was able to reach forward and actually touch this ugly menacing thing coming straight out of the water. Leo, of course, did the right thing, doing the reciprocal (backing up). If you were to steer the boat to port or starboard this could spell disaster for fear of steering into another danger. That's why it's always better to go in reverse to where you've just been, that being a known safe place.

While all this was happening we had to remember to keep blowing on the foghorn periodically, in case there was another clown out there. This last encounter was just a little too much. I noticed the three of us went quiet for a while and we didn't even talk about it until much later. It wouldn't take too much for any heavy vessel under power to hit this immovable object and put a hole in her, and of course in seconds, or less, go down. I might add to this that, in the bloody fog, we could still see the bottom in this shallow water. We motored slowly and managed to go through a few fishing nets and floats, and bump a few barrels, but thanks to a simple nylon line arrangement Leo had fastened from his keel to the skeg, we managed to plow through all this and never snagged a thing. I thought it strange to have all this excitement so early in the sail, and for some odd reason, I enjoyed it.

OH! THERE YOU ARE.

We were into Thursday the 10th and got a well-deserved beautiful day. Our new watch system of three hours on watch and six hours off seemed to work fine. It was also fair to all, because no one was going to do the same three hours as the days progressed. The three of us also seemed to stay awake in the daylight hours so at least we always ate together. The only time one might disappear for a while was if you had the three-hour watch that ended at breakfast time. Then you'd have your hot breakfast and go take a nap.

We all agreed that our breakfasts were the highlight of the day's meals, usually consisting of a hot porridge with hot milk (made from powdered milk) and beautiful brown sugar on top. How can you possibly put together something nicer than that? The cold weather was our biggest and most painful problem. Leo had one of those cheap outdoor home thermometers on a string. Occasionally we'd throw the thing in the water, which gave us a temperature of 33 degrees Fahrenheit. We also got the same temperature in the cockpit (topsides), except with the wind chill it was a hell of a lot colder. We all agreed we had never, ever been this cold in our entire lives. Day and night were always the same, and even the sun didn't help much, but psychologically, when the sun did show, we all believed it was warmer.

In the evening, with the sextant, Al took a shot of the moon and a star. We all figured that if his one good eye, and his math, were working okay, we may find out where we were. The following day around noon, we saw our first whale and then another three. I took some shots with the 35 mm Nikon but they were still too far off. What graceful mammals! They were on our windward side so when they blew and you could certainly hear it. But, talk about bad breath! I will never forget the smell.

We had very good sailing the next day, with sunny weather off Newfoundland. It looked like by the next day we would be hanging a left at Cape Race, and our last view of land for weeks to come, and finally on our way to Ireland. Friday the 11th we are definitely in the Atlantic. I began to think to myself about the number of days we had ahead of us and how things might go with just three of us, rather than four. Looking on the bright side, we had food and water for four. Yes, we were definitely in the Atlantic, with gusting winds all day and night up to 45 knots. Steep seas and the wind were giving us horses tails across the wave tops. The boat seemed to be handling very well, although it did broach to once, taking on some water through the open hatch. The strength and noise of the water can be frightening and exciting at the same time. I've read that cold water is much heavier, therefore can do more damage. It was very wise of Leo and Al to install one-inch-thick heavy-duty plastic on every port. Sort of like a storm window in your house, but a heck of a lot stronger. Plus a much thicker plastic for the companion way instead of the boards.

(By the way, a good definition of the term "broach to" is to turn the ship broadside to heavy seas, therefore losing control of steering in following seas. This can be an extremely dangerous situation because in steep seas the ship may trip on the keel and be rolled over and capsize. Either heave to or carry enough sail to give you power, and keep moving so you don't broach.)

Who said .... OH OH?

At this point we had so much noise and action going on that the three of us were taking turns at the wheel. This mayhem (can't think of a better word) had been going on day and night with no letup. Thank God we had a full moon so we could see what was going to happen next. Twice in the din I had called Al "Leo" and Leo "Al," but that was okay, they'd been calling me other things. The swells began to run higher: on the way up you see nothing but sky and on the way down into the trough you see nothing but angry water. After a while we learned that by taking on the following sea on the stern, and then with a slight angle on the way down it was definitely safer at the bottom, sooner than dig in with the bow and pitch-pole. We could have used the drogue to slow us down but it felt better to let the boat run. After tiring hours at the wheel, you could do this manoeuvre with your eyes closed.

By Saturday we were becalmed, hard to believe after the last 24 hours. I mustn't forget our fourth crew-member, by the way, nicknamed "Andy," our self-steering hydrovane system. It's made up of stainless steel rods, with mostly pulleys and lines attached to a trim tab that is somehow connected to the rudder. To this day I owe a lot to Andy for doing his work so well. A wind vane will work your boat to windward better than the best helmsman, especially at night. It will move to every wind-shift in an instant and adjust your course without getting tired, complaining, or being bored, and it doesn't mind the cold. The wind vane on Tullen Tie was designed by "Blondie Hasler" and in 1976 cost $1,500, which back then was considerable, but worth every penny. I must say that every now and then Andy does require a little tweak to stay on course. And he has a difficult time in light winds.

Water temperature was reading 40 degrees and the air 34 degrees. I had just had a Mars bar, hadn't brushed my teeth for three days or combed my hair since we left Saint-Pierre. Morale wasn't too bad at this point. Al figured we were about 160 km off shore, I was hoping it would be a lot more considering what we went through to get only this far. We still had about 3,000 km to go, and I was wishing it were the other way around! Al asked, "Where's my appendix?"

Cold all the time

Sunday the 13th. We had been on the boat one week since Sydney, N.S. The three of us were still tired from the previous lousy weather so we let Andy sail the boat. The damn fog was back. I sat in the cockpit through my night shift, flapping my arms, and my legs had been bicycling as fast as I could go for the past three hours just to keep warm. "Shit," it's cold all the time. Down below, the head is frozen and the propane cabin heater packed it in for good. On my shift, and on Leo's after me, we had waves over the bow all bloody night. I imagine salt water got into the deck exhaust and into the heater. Daylight eventually popped its greyness but we still had constant waves coming over the boat, with no let up. Down below, Al went flying across the cabin, and sounded like he broke every bone in his back. He lay there for a while and didn't want to be touched. Part of the galley unit counter broke loose from the flooring when Al went flying into it. Because of all hell going on outside, it took two of us to hold the galley counter in place, while another screwed it back to the sole of the boat. The tiller (wheel) had become loose twice now and we would need to fix it as soon as the weather held back a little. On top of all this shit going on, Al reported that we'd done only 32 km in the last 10 hours.

Cooking on this day was definitely not possible. We were doing at least three sail changes each day and repairing sails between other damage. It would also be stupid and suicidal to go on deck without your safety harness on. The boat was really bucking by now and doing its best to throw us overboard. One sail change left everyone worn out, between trying to hold onto the boat with one hand and with the other hanging onto the sail so it wouldn't end up blown into the ocean. All this kept us very busy indeed. It was also hard to hear one another in this wind, so we worked out a system for these conditions. Leo stayed at the wheel, Al made his way to the mast to handle the halyards, and I crawled to the bow on all fours to handle the sheets.

Invariably, just as one of us would finish a bloody three-hour frigid watch and climb into a wonderful sleeping bag, just about to doze off, all hell would start all over again. On one occasion, Leo had been asleep for the last three hours and I was about to drop off. Suddenly, Al (topsides) began banging on the coach roof for both of us to get out there, and fast. We could tell below that things were not good up there. Leo and I dressed as quickly as is possible, no time for underwear or socks, just slicks, boots and safety harness on and out we went. A smart addition to the boat before leaving shore turned out to be a rather simple thing. A strong thick nylon line was fastened to the aft end and run forward to the bow. With the safety harnesses Leo and I were wearing, our first plan of action when leaving from down below was to clip ourselves to this safety line. Now, in the dark, both clipped unto the line, we were on either side of the boat, Leo making his way forward to the mast and I carrying on to the bow. But my line became snagged on something, I started yanking on it and Leo began yanking back on his. All this was going on in the dark. Somehow, we were both clipped to each other. Not a good thing. How that happened didn't matter at this point, what mattered was that if one of us should go over, so would the other. I unclipped my line and we carried on. We had far too much sail up for these winds and we were heading for a knock-down at any second if nothing were done.

Leo was at the mast first and ready to drop the Genny and I was at the bow ready to pull it down, and do my best to sit on it until I bagged it. While all this was going on with screaming winds the Tullen Tie was riding down the crest of a wave and the bow dug in at the bottom of the trough. In the dark, I couldn't see much except for the phosphorescence of the furious water as I felt the cold going passed me up to my neck. Luckily I was sitting and holding onto the bow pulpit with all fours till we came up again. I managed to get the storm jib up and everything else got tied down. We had to have apparent motion in these conditions and the storm jib alone was pushing us at 8 knots. This was the fastest the boat had ever gone; the hull speed of Tullen Tie was only rated at 6 or 7 tops. Finally, when we were all back in the safety of the cockpit, Leo came out again with his wonderful philosophy of "Busy hands are happy hands."

I would be on the bow many more times on this voyage and under water, but thank goodness Tullen Tie would always lift out of harms way. Many times later on with the screaming winds and wild water, I could often just make out hearing "busy hands are happy hands."

Monday the 14th. This day was a lot worse than the previous one. Not much rest or sleep for any of us. We weren't even close to the quarter-way mark. I began to dream that when we got to the middle it would be a cake walk. Imagine once you get to the middle of this (washing machine cycle) ride, every day will be another day closer. Earlier, on our first or second day out of Sydney, Leo had found a pair of Ruth's panties stuffed into a plastic bag behind the stove. (It appears the poor girl had her period and put them there temporarily and forgot.) We hoisted the panties up the mast under the power squadron flag and after two days out to sea they were new again. Also when we were well on our way, a few days after leaving Sydney, it was time, and deservedly so, to give a toast to Ruth for she was responsible for all the stores on board. What a great job she did. She must have read everything there was on off-shore sailing.

All the tinned food had the labels removed and Ruth had applied a simple marking system, with a waterproof marker. The tops of the tins were marked S-1 for tomato soup, S-2 noodle soup, S-3 minestrone and so forth. Irish stews were M-1 (for meat), M-2 was canned ham, M-3 corned beef, etc. F was for fruit: F-1 would be pears, F-2 (my favourite) black cherries in syrup, F-3 peaches, etc. And so it went for sardines to pork and beans. All these code numbers went into a book so we knew what to look for. It's a known thing that the labels should be removed because in wet conditions they come off very easily and usually end up in the bilge, where they have a good chance of plugging up the bilge pump. Also, if you didn't do this and the labels fell off, every meal could be an unwanted surprise.

If we had known that the temperature down below (in the boat and bilge) would have been similar to the temperature of a fridge back home, we could have brought more eggs, butter and real milk (instead of powder). Speaking of powdered milk, Leo had an old suitcase filled with it. Later we figured, should we be in danger of sinking and the good coast guard people set out to look for us, the powdered milk on the water would make a fantastic marker. On board were enough Rye Krisp packages for another trip back. That stuff is practical and lasts forever. Cover it (like we did) with peanut butter and honey and still, unfortunately, it will taste like balsa wood. Leo's gourmet meal consisted of Rye Krisp with peanut butter and sardines with a little mayo, all on the same wafer.

Before leaving shore, Leo and I shared the price in two boxes of 40 oz. bottles of Scotch, and Al bought a box of rye whisky even though he was not known as a drinker. I think we were only eight days out and already running low on the Scotch, also we didn't think to buy any mix such as soda water. I drank my scotch straight up, and Leo had his with grape Tang. I guess his thinking here was, when your lips taste salty and everything around you is salty, Tang is the answer for a good mix. I believe otherwise that a good Scotch is precious, cherished, treasured and priceless and must be left alone.

Well, the damn storm just wouldn't go away. I believe it was still Monday the 14th. I went topsides again before bed, to take the storm jib down. Two bronze hanks on the forestay broke in two and were torn out of the sail and went over the side. The whole night and the following day we were running with following seas under bare poles. Leo and Al estimated the winds at nearly 100 km an hour and peaking well over that. It felt best to tie everything down and stay below until it was over, and let the boat ride, instead of tying her down with a drogue or some other means. What plays on your mind the most at these times is the howling through the rigging. We even had trouble making ourselves heard down below because of the constant screaming outside. If it would only go away for a while, we thought. A hot meal would be welcome, but with these confused seas it didn't seem like a good idea. The weather felt like it was getting worse each day (if that's possible).

Strange, I always wanted to witness the Atlantic at its worst, but I certainly didn't expect this. All my clothes were wet and had been for the last three days. My fingers had wrinkled up from the water, even my penis has shrivelled up so much it felt like it was gone. For the first time, there was no one on watch. We crawled into our bunks and fell fast asleep in minutes, thankful in the confidence that the steel-hulled Tullen Tie was well built. Al and I both had lee cloths made of sail material on our bunks. Lee cloths are like a blanket that acts as a wall so you don't fall out of bed. They're attached to the coach roof and at the bottom of your bunk with hooks and line. It is a wonderful rig that prevents you from flying from one side of the boat to the other. I could have used a few more hooks around the bottom to make up for some of the slack in the cloth, because on the second day of our storm, Leo found me wrapped around the table pedestal, sleeping bag and all, still asleep. It was starting to feel like home down here, every evening hearing the water roaring over the coach roof and filling the cockpit. With every blow, you heard a loud twang in the steel, and the sound was much like a train going by. Again, thank God for a beautiful welded steel boat. Twang or no twang, it sounded okay to me.

I began thinking that if we should get to Ireland I would then be through with adventure-- well, definitely for today anyway. I also knew I had to do this Atlantic crossing. I've heard others have done it and never changed a sail on the whole trip. I find that hard to believe and if this trip was similar to that, I would be very disappointed. Imagine, no storms, dry, no sail changes, no damage, no nothing. How depressing would that be? This is the North Atlantic, but why does it go on so long? I'm hungry, I'm wet, and I would love a Scotch without spilling it.

We were tired all the time now, and it began to show. Just getting dressed was irritating, slow and tiring. Another wall of water over the boat. The books on a shelf over my bunk, although they were well tied down, had all left the shelf and were strewn over Al's bunk on the starboard side. And Al himself had, once again, gone flying over to my side. I was always amazed he hadn't seriously hurt himself. On top of all this, it was unbearably damned cold all the time. These last few nights, I began to notice that Leo wasn't even taking his wet gear off anymore. He did remove his boots before getting into the sleeping bag, but that was all. When you get this tired it doesn't seem to matter anymore. We hadn't had anything hot now for three days, just Rye Krisp crackers with a gob of something on it. It would be a disaster to have a boiling kettle on the stove. I think Al, because he was the thinnest, was always the coldest, and now he was finally learning the odd swear word. I believe Leo was probably bearing up the best. He was kind of a bush-pilot type. For instance, I firmly believe, if you lost your compass, Leo would find land one way or another, whereas Al had to do things by the book. Obviously, both ways are good to know.

The heavy weather seemed to abate around noon on Tuesday. The wind went and was replaced by the fog again. But even with the wind gone, the confused seas stayed, which is what usually happens. We were all still asleep when the storm was over. Now it was time to go outside and check on damage. Ruth's panties survived the blow, but now were the size of a small spinnaker. The power squadron flag had frayed badly and was half its original length. It obviously should have been made of the same silk as Ruth's panties. The only real damage that could have been prevented was due to two things that we forgot to take care of. One was the fact that we didn't take down the big wind vane on Andy (the self steering mechanism). When the storm was well on its way, it was far too dangerous to attempt lifting off the unit. Anyone who tried would have left the ship and been airborne with the bloody thing. Also, we completely forgot to haul in the Walker's log-line.

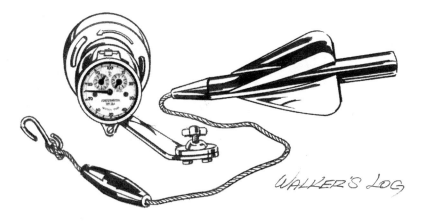

WALKER'S LOG

Thomas Walker's log-line is a mechanical log that measures a vessel's speed moving through the water. It comes with a four-bladed rotator that is towed astern. As it spins, the rotations of the towing line are registered by a wheelworks and dial mounted to the boat's railing. The line from the heavy finned rotator to the boat can be anywhere from 50 to 75 feet long. In this whole trip, one would have thought a shark would have got it, but that didn't happen. Walker's firm was a leading maker of these logs in Birmingham, England, back in the 1800s. Today, in the age of satellite navigation, these wonderful instruments are obsolete, but they do make a very attractive display item and look extremely beautiful mounted on a varnished board. If you should have a $1,000 or so, they can still be found on the Internet. As Leo said many times on the trip, "God looks after drunks and idiots," which brings me back to the Walker's log. While the storm was going on, God had thrown the heavy finned rotor and long line into the cockpit. But first, God tied everything in knots. Leo began mumbling again about "Busy hands are happy hands."

The storm abates

How nice to have the genoa and main up again. It was Tuesday or Wednesday, but does it matter? We had everything well tied, such as the life raft, dingy and most of Andy, but not the large vane, which wasn't smart. The important things did survive. Now that the storm was over and we were rested somewhat and had eaten a hot meal again, it was exciting to think back on the whole noisy, unpleasant and severe time we had just gone through together, and how good it was to witness such a thing.

The wind seemed light and the genoa kept collapsing, so the boys figured, let's take it down and put the jib up in its place with a whisker pole. That was done and working beautifully, but for a short time only because the wind began to pick up again and became very erratic. Within minutes it was blowing so much that we were surfing down the swells with the feeling that if we didn't slow Tullen Tie down, the bow would definitely bury itself in the trough. To spill some wind, I let the spinnaker pole go forward to the forestay, then standing by the mast where the spinnaker pole is attached, I took hold of the little stainless-steel thimble (a sort of u-shaped thing). This U-shape has a stainless-steel wire spliced around it and goes down the inside of the whisker pole to the other end, where a piston-type shackle is hanked to the jib. While pulling on this wire, the other end of the sail should free itself and spill the wind. All this may sound a little confusing, but it works, or is supposed to. But it wouldn't free itself at the sail end and came undone at the whisker pole, where I was working at the mast. As I held the whisker pole unattached at my end, the sail was still attached

298

at the other end full of wind, and the thimble opened up in my hand and went through my index finger. As a result, I found myself holding a full jib, my legs around the mast, and the pole and sail pulling me by my pierced finger into the water. Rather than go into the ocean, I let the U-shape thimble tear the fleshy part off of my finger to be free of it. The pole was then in the water but two of us pulled everything back on board. Time for a drink.

It's amazing how quickly some things heal in the clean salt air. The finger looked good considering that a piece of flesh had been pulled out of it. I had my safety harness to thank, and it became part of my everyday clothing. It had kept me on board twice now. We were also all feeling a little more cheerful thanks to the nicer weather. Al had been at the chart table for the last two hours and gave us the news that we were approximately one-fifth of the way. Better news came with word that it should get warmer in the Gulf stream. The 40 oz. bottle of rum was empty. I only bought the one bottle in Saint-Pierre, thinking that if it's only $4.50 it can't be very good. Naturally the rum with a picture of a parrot on the bottle was dark, thick, and the best I've ever come across. Two cases would have made more sense. Leo and I had almost finished the Scotch. The only thing left, besides Al's full box of rye whisky, was a bilge full of ice cold Coca-Cola that Ruth had put there. In this cold weather, the Coca-Cola stayed put.

Now, much earlier back home in Toronto, my friend Beverly had written me a note that I was not to read until I was far out to sea without sight of land. Beverly and I did go out occasionally, but she was still married and so was I. My wife (second marriage) and I hadn't been living together for some time, so this was not a problem. After reading Beverly's note I added a few words of my own plus my address, put it into the rum bottle, put the cork in and sent it adrift. Often a bottle will drift thousands of miles with the current, end up on a sandy beach and be found by some romantic soul who will reciprocate an answer. Or it could end up on a hostile shore and smash on the rocks. This must have happened to me, because years have since gone by without a word. What a pity when it was such a good note.

I managed to tune in CBC radio from Toronto. So far we hadn't been able to pull in anything on our expensive AM, FM, trans-oceanic shortwave, with a light for night-time (whoopee) radio. But this time it works and is wonderful. Wow!, There are other people out there, and music. Today was beautiful whatever day it happened to be and we enjoyed every hour.

But we had to be serious occasionally and think once in a while about fire and man overboard. These obviously would create a tremendous worry. Another worry is being run down by a steamer or freighter, which would probably finish us. It certainly has happened that a large ship has run down a small sailboat and kept on going. There is one sad tale of a freighter tying up in port after a crossing, and finding the rigging of a sailing ship tangled up in the ship's anchor. The heavily loaded freighter with noisy diesels running, considering the size of the tonnage, would hear nothing. It's often more than likely they're on automatic pilot and playing cards or asleep. And small boats have been known to run into whales or icebergs and open up in an instant and go down.

KARMAN

There were two specific night shifts that are worth mentioning. These are the shifts where you see the sun disappear into the ocean and immediately you're colder than you've ever been. The other shift is far better, when you see the wonderful sun come up in the east and you're warmer immediately. Of course, nothing has changed, day or night; it's all in your head. There is also a pleasant time to be alone in the evening, that is when the sea is forgiving and you sit

301

in the cockpit with a couple of porpoise swimming at arm's length beside you. A mermaid sighting would go nicely. A beautiful sight is the "fluorescence" or "phosphorescence" in the water. In zero-light conditions, the effect is amazing. The radiance coming from the hull as friction against the water upsets the algae, and you get what they call bioluminescence. where a light-producing chemical reaction occurs inside an organism. To you and me it is simply "algae." In simpler terms, this luminescence is caused by the bow wave or wake of a surface ship. Calm seas will give you a better show of this blue-green lantern dance.

If you love this stuff I suggest you click on a scientific-information website. There are websites that explain everything you need to know about fireflies and species of jellyfish. Dolphins and porpoises, which is which? There is a difference. I know they are both mammals, they breathe air to live and are warm-blooded, give birth to live babies and nurse their young. I've been told that the main difference between a dolphin and the porpoise is in the shape of the teeth. Dolphins have cone-shaped teeth whereas porpoise have spaded teeth. The largest dolphin is the orca, or killer whale. Orcas live in the oceans and are the fiercest sea predator, fearing no other in their way. In one day, a dolphin can eat an amount of food equal to nearly one-third of its own weight. Dolphins are also very streamlined in appearance and can do from 20 to 25 mph. We had daily visits from dolphins and porpoises before the bow waves of Tullen Tie but I still have no idea which I was looking at--the problem being, they didn't show me their teeth. I'm guessing "bottle-nosed dolphin," since they're known to be popular performers. Then again, the white-sided dolphin swims off the Scotian shelf of Nova Scotia, and in the North Atlantic. Porpoise are in the North Atlantic too. For that matter, Dolphins and porpoises are found in every ocean in the world.

And what's the difference between flotsam and jetsam? I used to think it had something to do with plankton, but no, not even close. Technically, flotsam is cargo or wreckage floating on the surface of the sea, while jetsam is cargo that has been thrown overboard (jettisoned) or washed up on the beach. However, occasionally the two words have been used in the newspapers in reference to homeless people. Such as: The city has done little to help the flotsam and jetsam of society.

The night temperatures seemed to hover around 40 degrees now, so we became hopeful that, by the next day, we should be in the Gulf stream. That should bring less fog and things should get warmer, we thought. I don't know why, but on this night I'd been awake for about 16 hours, which took me into the wee hours of the next morning. I was into my night watch now, and because of the darkness and fog I couldn't see beyond the next wave. This kind of visibility plays tricks with your eyesight. No moon, no stars, just the fluorescence in the water, some glowing as large as a plate. The visibility on this evening had been the worst because of the fog, so I figured I might as well go down below and make a coffee. I found some Scotch, which helped Leo get up, put some in each cup with black coffee and sat outside and saw the fog lift. A good thing too, because about a mile or two out (hard to judge) was the mother of icebergs. I couldn't take a shot with the Nikon, as it was still too dark. We woke Al so he too could have a good look. It was obviously more than two miles away because it took forever to get any closer, so to sail to it would have taken us too far off course. It was best to forget the thing, except it had a huge dark spot in it that looked monstrous. The wishful dream was that it was an ocean liner stuck in the berg, disabled, full of stuff for the taking, and we would be rich because of salvage rights and other mischievous doings. In reality it was probably a hole, where water had eaten into a section and created a large cavern. Another possibility was that it had been spotted by a ship and its position confirmed, with notifications sent out to all shipping parties. As a safety precaution an aeroplane will often go out and drop a paint bomb and mark an iceberg, making it easier to see.

From what I've read, there are times of the day when an iceberg can blend in with its surrounding atmosphere. I found that if you looked away from this one for a moment, and then looked back, it was gone and you had to find it again. This was strange because it was a big S.O.B. This is exactly why someone has to be on watch all the time. The fog closed in again. We also knew the iceberg was far away on our port side, so there was no danger. It was windward from us though, and all of a sudden the air got really cold. We knew that when we left it behind us, the air would warm up again. Icebergs are composed of fresh water, not frozen sea water. They can be white, blue or green and sometimes even black due to rock materials that were first in the glacier and ended in the sea as an iceberg. The majority of icebergs in the North Atlantic come from glaciers along the Greenland coast. It seems the glaciers of western Greenland are among the fastest moving in the world, up to 7 km per year. Icebergs can be seen on radar. We don't have radar.

In order for an iceberg to reach the North Atlantic, the

currents typically take it from Baffin Bay through the Davis Strait and the Labrador Sea. This is a long trip and most icebergs never make it. Most will melt before they enter the Atlantic Ocean. An estimate is that of the 15,000 to 30,000 icebergs produced annually by the glaciers of Greenland, only one percent, 150 to 300, will get to the Atlantic Ocean. When one does get to the Atlantic (lower down) it melts rapidly in the warmer waters. The largest known iceberg was roughly the size of the state of Rhode Island. Approximately seven-eighths of an iceberg is below the water line. We all know the story of the unsinkable Titanic, which is why I bring up the question of visibility. Lord knows we'd had our share up to now: fog, no fog, fog again and so forth. Earlier, Leo and I sat in the cockpit with our libations, the fog cleared and we saw the mother of all icebergs. The fog came back but we were out of harm's way. Leo came out with more bit of wisdom, "God does look after drunks and idiots."

Becalmed

Thursday the 17th. Becalmed, hard to believe. Sails were hanging lifeless, but the previous night was another one of those times when everybody was up and needed to take sails down or reef in. The wheel steering did take an awful beating, the strain was too much on all the moving parts. It was probably a blessing that we were becalmed, because Al and Leo were working on the steering again–and a calm sea is certainly a big help for that. The cables around the quadrant were loose again, either from the strain or possibly they stretched. While the boys were doing their best, I thought I should make one of my world-famous spaghetti dinners.

The world-famous spaghetti dinner: I start with a tin of tomatoes for the sauce, a couple of cans of tomato soup and for meat (to give it substance) I open a can of Brazil corned beef (of which we had four full boxes). This all goes into one large pot with pepper. No salt, because I use a small portion of ocean water (first time I did this I used all ocean water, and after tasting, threw the whole works into the ocean). Another pot has fresh water for the spaghetti. (This will look like the gourmet stuff you see on cooking shows, ready for a photo shoot.) I read somewhere that one cubic foot of average sea water contains 2.2 pounds of salt. I'm pleased we're not in the Red Sea, which has the saltiest water in the world. This particular day started off as a good one to spend in the galley, but I found myself making the world-famous spaghetti while a new storm had just started. Now it turned out to be a stupid idea to be in front of the stove. The pots had to be wired down to the stove (even though the stove is gimbaled beautifully) and after all the food goes into the pots, you must wire down the lids. More than once I had to jump aside to avoid getting scalded from the boiling water. While making some of those gourmet meals, I managed to get the spaghetti with sauce onto the plates when a large wave would hit broadsides, the three plates would slide and stop at the gimbaled ledge on the counter, but the spaghetti and sauce would continue to slide to the filthy indoor/outdoor carpeting covered in hair and stuff. I'd grab handfuls of the hot food, toss it back on the plates, dump some new sauce on top with a cup to cover any visible floor dirt on the plate, and hand it outside to Leo and Al. Each and every time I got back a smile and a two-thumbs-up sign. If you find you would like to go a step further with this recipe, wear one of those Italian red kerchiefs around your neck and hum something in Italian.

The rudder was fixed once again. Our progress on this day hadn't been good: five miles. I noticed the tips of my fingernails were broken and very brittle, and they hurt when I handled the sails. Leo was having the same problem. Were we lacking something, fresh vegetables, vitamin C perhaps? Of course, we'd been wet for four days, which could be the problem. I'd been in my long wet underwear for so long now that I was getting used to it, but my skin had gone funny. As long as my yellow slicks kept the wind out, everything was fine. I was also thinking more and more that I didn't want to go back to work, but of course I had no choice. The tinned goods were starting to rust up, some more than others. Now we started checking for small holes to see if any air had gotten inside to the food. As another precaution, after opening a tin we always gave what was inside a good smell. It was still cold enough that the apples and oranges we had left were holding up quite well. We should have brought more.

Friday the 19th. No wind, which was okay because Al and Leo were working on the steering quadrant once again. The quadrant is attached directly to the rudder post and was constantly slipping. Obviously, with this lousy weather we'd had, and erratic seas, there seemed to be too much outside pressure on the rudder. It is a treat to get a day now and then with nothing happening, allowing time to repair what needs fixing, or read, make a nice hot meal and deservedly, have a good sleep. What was immediately noticeable was the lack of birds on the placid windless days. But in storm conditions, bird life was very busy. They love stormy weather, because they don't have to use their wings to fly, just glide all day long.

A mesmerizing bird to watch is the northern gannet, with a wingspan of over 6 feet. Besides superb diving abilities, keen eyesight and speed, they can cover large distances in search of schooling fish, and then hit the water at 60 miles per hour without any damage to themselves, thanks to air pockets around the skull and neck. This obviously cushions the blow as the bird hits the water. The newly young leave their nesting islands in summer and may not touch land for another four or five years. Gannets are a fine example to humans for lasting relationships, for they will mate for life. Although they are migratory and will part by thousands of miles at sea during the winter, they usually return to the same partner and share the same nest each year.

Another favourite of mine is the puffin, a north Atlantic bird and a comical-looking thing with black and white plumage and a big bill. They spend most of their time in the ocean, being wonderful swimmers underwater, thanks to their large red rudder-like feet. The only time they come to shore is to breed and raise chicks. I must mention the fulmar, because it mostly resembles our sea-gull. The fulmar produces a foul-smelling, sticky, oily substance that it can shoot for a distance of up to three metres. Fulmars live at sea outside the breeding season and are graceful fliers to watch. All in all, can you think of a better place to watch birds than sitting in the cockpit of a sailboat? But if you were to ask me if I would ever consider doing this north Atlantic thing alone, my answer without hesitation would be a flat no, and six months later from today, it's still no.

On Saturday we got wind—as a matter a fact, too much wind. We were taking turns at the wheel now, mostly because Andy was doing such a perfect job of steering and keeping the boat on course, therefore, not letting up or forgiving when need be. That puts a tremendous strain on the rudder and quadrant, so with us steering we could let off a little when necessary, whereas Andy did not. The other two were sleeping until it was time for everybody up for a sail change (which happened too damned often). Before I would start my watch, I would fill my two pipes with tobacco, take my Zippo (great lighter), clip my harness to the boat and start my bloody three-hour watch. Tobacco is something we had a lot of, and it was free. Before this trip, Leo had worked for the city at the garbage dump operating a bulldozer. The tobacco firm that handled "The Four Square" line of pipe tobacco had an oversupply or possibly out-of-date tobacco at the warehouse. Whenever this happened, it had to be discarded and ended up at the dump where Leo worked. An inspector always came with the truck to make sure the vacuum packed tins were properly crushed with the bulldozer tracks. Leo, being in charge of the dump-site, would tell the driver to unload far over on the other side of the mud. Leo knew the well-dressed inspector with the shiny shoes couldn't see that far and was not going to cross over the muddy section. Now it was just a matter of going back and forth to the edge of, and not touching, the precious tins with the bulldozer. He would then signal that everything was done and the man with the shiny shoes would leave. Yes, we had a boat full of brand new Four Square pipe tobacco.

I remember Leo telling the story of the garbage trucks that came to the dump daily. A lot of those trucks came from the outskirts of Toronto. Leo's job was to tell them where to empty their trucks, but of course to get in line first with the others. Leo's work was to crush, flatten or move the garbage around. Apparently there was a trucker who would never do what he was told, and wouldn't stay in line or wait

310

his turn. He would roar in, dump his load and be off just as fast to get another load. Of course the more loads they bring in, the more money they earn. When he returned, again not listening or obeying the rules, and started to unload his dump truck, Leo was ready for him. Leo shot over there before he had time to unload and got the bulldozer blade under the side of the huge truck and flipped him over on his side. These are some of the wonderful stories we told in the cockpit in "nice weather."

A sad day on the bulldozer came when a crew of men were moving earth on a large hill on the Don Valley. Because of the huge amount of rain that fell every day for far too long, Leo told the engineer on the job site that no one should be on the hill, since it was saturated with water and it might give way. The workers were told to continue, that everything was fine. According to Leo, there was a man, apparently just home from work and still in his shirt and tie, standing in his backyard at the top of the hill, and watching the bulldozers at work, when the top of the hill including the man with his backyard broke loose and became a huge mudslide. Leo had a good idea of where he was buried and the workmen started digging. As Leo tells it, "if the guy isn't already dead, he will be now from the shovels." After the mayhem was over, Leo said, his company congratulated him for saving the bulldozer in the middle of the slide. Leo told them, "Bulldozer be damned, I needed a ride down the hill or go with the guy in his yard."

There were times when we would crawl into our sleeping bags and instantly be fast asleep. And there were other times when I just couldn't turn off the thinking. About two weeks had passed and we

311

were still not to the middle of our crossing. We cheered up for a minute after breakfast when behind our stern came a most beautiful sight. A German cargo ship from Bremen named "Log" appeared on the horizon, and seemed to proceed closer to have a look (we thought). No one was on deck and we couldn't see a sole on the bridge either. The only thing alive about the big black ship was the sound of the diesel engines. While Al was trying to communicate with someone on the VHF, without luck, I was busy taking photographs (without telephoto lens) of the Log. This sighting lasted only a few minutes and they were gone. As big as the oceans are, this shows how easy and possible it is to be run down.

Sunday, the sun came out for a few minutes in the morning and then we had overcast skies for the rest of the day. Finally Al announced, "We are at the halfway point." Fantastic, the best news we'd had since we left Sydney. A wonderful thought helped ease the mind, knowing that each day was a day closer, or a day minus from the middle. Sometimes I would look at the water and think, What if I were on a raft out here with no food or water, wet, cold? A frightening thought. Without food a person can last a while, but without water, you are in big trouble after three days. An aeroplane flew by a short time ago, and I was thinking, imagine in two or three hours they'll be landing! But probably at this moment, the people are eating hot food with wine while watching a movie, and later having a martini before taking a blanket for a wee nap, then waking and going to the toilet to enjoy dry cloth towels.

Instead of the usual wooden boards that cover the companionway (to go down below) Leo had installed thick clear plastic panels. The thinking here was that when someone is on watch alone, cold, wet and in the dark, being tossed around, he will feel better being able to see down below (through the plastic), knowing there are people down there. On the night watch we'd also have a gimbaled anchor light hanging from the top of the coach roof ceiling. This too gave the added feature of getting rid of some dampness. The anchor light, by the way, takes fuel oil, and the plastic boards were always in, so water couldn't get down below in the event of a knockdown. I really recommend this to any sailor contemplating a crossing. The light is also wonderful for the crew down below, should you have to put your boots on in a hurry. In a blow if the lamp is hitting the coach roof, of course, common sense will tell you to blow the thing out. As I said earlier, you sure don't want a fire on board.

After a lovely breakfast of cream of wheat washed down with a rum and coke, everyone seemed a bit quiet, probably because we'd only managed to do 100 miles a day on two occasions. Al had just been thrown into the companionway steps and broke them. A rudder bolt broke while I was asleep and now it was snowing. Ireland, where the bloody hell are you? It was Tuesday and we came across another discovery, this one at the sink. With every roll of the ship, a drop of our precious fresh water ran out of the faucet. This was priceless water, and not knowing how long this had been going on, we decided it was imperative we start paying attention on the water we were using. All face washing and tooth brushing was now to be done with sea water. We were short of wind on this day, and thinking it sure would be nice to see Ireland by the end of the month. But that did not look likely.

Leo had been a little too quiet for some time now. He didn't have the drive he had earlier on the trip. I think a number of things had been piling up, such as the fact that we were not making enough mileage on the water or that he was concerned about the damage to the boat--most seriously the steering problem. This dream of Leo's had been and still was a financially costly undertaking for him, and being skipper, everything rested on his shoulders. I was the fortunate one. I could just crawl into my bunk and close my eyes and be asleep in an instant. But for Leo, I started to notice that when he crawled into his quarter berth, worn out and still in his slicker, he would sort of wake in a dream calling out things like, "Nobody's at the wheel. Who's watching for icebergs? We have too much sail up." From my bunk, I hollered over and assured him that everything was fine, indicating "Al's is out there" and so forth. In minutes he would be fast asleep until the next time. He was worn out. Even when he slept, it wasn't a good sleep.

When we first started out on this trip, the sail changes, being on watch, cooking, and all the other things that one has to do and share, were all part of the sailing. Now that we were fed up and tired, all that stuff was putting us all on edge and irritable. The wind could howl as loud as it wanted and as long as it wanted, it didn't matter one little bit anymore. After a while it just became a way of life. Of course, this attitude was not good for the safety of the boat, or us for that matter.

But things started to look up one day, and I believe it started with a bright sun and became nicer when the highlight of the day was the arrival of a very big Russian fishing and canning boat. We could see through the binoculars that the vessel altered course just to see if we were okay. The huge ship came along side on our leeward side, as it should, our being a sailboat and dependant on the wind for steerage. These ships are known as floating factory ships. Everything that is caught is cleaned, gutted, washed and canned aboard the factory ship. So this big crew, many on deck, male and female, all waving frantically, came at a good time for us. It did cheer us up tremendously, but not so much for Leo. It seems Leo didn't have any affection for the Russians, an attitude that went back to his boyhood. The Viljakainen family (Leo) all lived in a small town on the borders of Finland and Russia. Because of the war between these two countries, many bombs were dropped on the small town with much damage and death. This Russian ship stayed out far enough so our rigging wouldn't be destroyed with this erratic sea around us. Al now made contact with the Russian radio operator on the VHF. In the meantime Leo had his back to the Russians and stayed that way. Now, this part I found quite humorous. Picture two boats in the middle of the Atlantic Ocean, not another living thing in sight, your VHF is only good for about 25 miles in the best of conditions, and the communication went something like this.

First Al would start with, "This is the sailing vessel Tullen Tie on your starboard side, call letters VE 930681724, V as in Veronica, E as in Edward, over." Then with this wonderful Russian accent, we heard, "Hallo Boyz. Hover." Now back to Al with, "This is the sailing vessel Tullen Tie on your starboard side, call letters VE 930681724, V as in Veronica, E as in Edward, Hello fishing boat, over." The Russians answered back, "You boyz hokay? Hover." Al replied again,, "This is the sailing vessel Tullen Tie on your starboard . . ." I think by now you have an idea of how it went. But a summary of the conversation between the two ships went like this: Al: "We're fine thank you, over." They: "Yu boyz want fud, vodka, bread? Hover." Leo now told Al, Tell them no. Al said, "You're very kind, but no, we are okay. But could you please give us our latitude and longitude?" After having our position confirmed we, I mean Al and I, waved goodbye and were on our way again.

The Russians seemed to be heading home. It certainly would have been a treat to get some of that free vodka, but in these sloppy seas it would have been damaging to Tullen Tie's rigging if they came along side. But if it were necessary we would have put the little blue-bottomed boat in the water and with a long painter, let it drift over to the sides of the Russian ship and they could have lowered the treasure.

In any event, the distraction came at a good time. The sun was still out, the seas calmed down, so out came every wet item we had and we draped the stuff wherever possible. Tullen Tie looked like a rag ship heading to market. Somehow I became cook on this boat. How that happened, I have no idea. I don't cook and never knew how, but now I was going to be self-taught, and I was going to do it the easy way. Whenever possible everything would be done in one large pot. For one of my favourites, I would first throw into the pot one can of stewed tomatoes, add a soup that works with tomatoes such as minestrone, then a couple of handfuls of rice, open another tin of that Brazilian corned beef, break it into little bits with my fingers and toss it in. I would then let the whole mess cook until done. If it was a little watery, I would throw in a bunch of those Rye Krisp crackers to thicken the stuff. Oh! Season with something if necessary and you have another gourmet dinner.

I started reading Zorba the Greek again. Leo was sitting aft fishing. Some fisherman back in Sydney gave him a fishing lure that looked like it came off a 1939 Buick, all chrome and swivels. Leo had been trolling this thing since Cape Race, without a nibble. I thought for sure a shark would have taken the thing before now. Al was doing dishes. I wondered what Woof was doing back home, or for that matter anybody. We'd had too much excitement here to think about anything else. We didn't even ask the Russians if they needed anything. I really don't think it was necessary to ask. Their ship, the size of a building, I'm sure had everything, but it would have been fun to ask.

I hadn't washed since Toronto and I had just changed into my third pair of underwear. The other two went over the side. Leo insists the ocean threw them back. Thursday, Friday, Saturday were all good sailing days. I'd been eating Mars bars for energy and not one pimple. Funny thing, out here in the ocean, you learn things like, How come no one has caught a cold, considering the wind, and being wet for days plus the damnable cold weather we've been in? Here's another silly thing: None of us has been picking our noses or ears. They have never been so clean. Is it the salt air or is it just pollution free out here? Your lips constantly taste of salt, which is everywhere. My Nikon and Al's camera have both seized up from the salt air. To fix this problem I prepared two plastic bags with rice, put the cameras into the bags and in a couple of days all was new again.

Ah Yes! This is the life.
Just think, back home they're probably having the usual prime
rib dinner with Yorkshire pudding, hot gravy, peas, mashed
potatoes, cheese cake, and a brandy with coffee.

Not one of us had one evening where we got into our sleeping
bag and were allowed to stay there without interruption until next
watch. Just as you nicely nodded off, it was time for everybody to get
up, change sail or reef in. Sometimes there were three changes in one
night. We would be up, down, up, down, up, down.

Al reported, "I think Ireland may be four days away." I hoped
he was right, since we were getting low on fresh water and Scotch.
What a lazy bunch we were, just eating, sleeping and scratching. I
started thinking a bath would be pretty nice. We figured we could be in
Ireland in two-and-a-half days. Al took a sun shot with the sextant
using his good eye, while I took a shot of the Scotch. Al's bad eye had

worsened, and he couldn't see through it at all now. I was still putting his eye drops in for him because it was easier for me to do. A very large school of dolphins put on a show for us around noon. There must have been a hundred or more. They seemed to enjoy swimming two or three abreast of each other, and on both sides of the bow, then crossing in front of each other. This went on and on, and as quickly as it started, all of a sudden it was over and they were gone. We usually did get a repeat matinee show around seven.

I seem to have made a mess again with the spaghetti dinner. It was on the floor. But it wasn't a problem. I added a quarter cup of Al's whisky to it and it was instantly world-famous again.

The temperatures had been in the high 50s. Life aboard the Tullen Tie was happier and Leo and I toasted the Queen once again–something to drink to. We were doing six knots, which is pretty much the hull speed of the boat. Our best distance was the previous day: 130 nautical miles. Our slowest in a 24-hour run was 22 miles. Our course should have been 077 degrees, but because of the boat's deviation and the earth's variation we were steering 120 degrees for Ireland. I asked Leo, "What if all of this math is wrong and we're not where we think we think we are? What happens then?" Leo said, "No problem. If we should happen to be too far down below Ireland, and as we approach shore we see that all the faces are black, we turn left."

We were becalmed and doing 0 knots, also not sure of our position. The compass was doing strange things again, and I imagined it had a lot to do with the steel boat. Things looked promising though. We had three Russian fishing boats around us but unfortunately we didn't speak Russian and they didn't speak English. We made our way into Tuesday and more sail changes. A new problem: The boom had pulled itself out from the stainless-steel unit that kept it attached to the mast. All the pop rivets had worn through and fell out, causing the boom to completely come out of its circular housing. The only thing that kept the boom from falling out onto the deck was the main sail itself. Fortunately, Leo carried a complete tool chest for this repair. A hand drill, a pop rivet gun and more than the 15 stainless-steel rivets were needed.

Landfall!

Wednesday the 30th. Landfall! A happy day, indeed. After 2,195 nautical miles from Sydney, we sighted land again. Strange thing about land, after smelling nothing but salt air for weeks, once you get within a hundred miles of actual earth and foliage you can sure smell it before you see it. Another telltale sight is all the plastic garbage passed along the way in. One big clue for us was a group of pigeons that appeared to be standing on the surface of the water, but in reality when we got closer they were all perched atop a wooden picnic table. I was at the wheel and we had just passed through the early morning mist when, exactly where it should be, I spied Slyne Head with the two towers in silhouette, one being a light. What a welcome sight after three weeks or so! Al and Leo were awake now, so we got out the bottle of Mumms Champagne to celebrate our first sighting of land. Now, it's a fact that champagne doesn't travel well, especially on this roller coaster ride. To us it tasted damned good anyway. We poured a shot glass full on Andy too; with all the work he did, he deserved it. Slyne Head is just north of Galway Bay. We agreed to carry on for Scotland and not put into Ireland after all, mostly because of all the time lost going into Saint-Pierre--and we still did have a long way to go.

A lovely sunny day with a temperature around 69 degrees, but no wind. We were, without a doubt off Ireland, unfortunately too low down, so now we had to work our way up without wind and very little fuel. There was just enough fuel to charge the batteries so we agreed not to waste it in motoring. Fresh water for drinking and cooking was pretty much gone, and there was no bread, no veggies and no rum. I said to the boys, "I heard a choo-choo." But no one else heard it. I didn't care, I heard it.

Our plan was to head north to the Caledonian canal in Scotland and hope to put in around Oban at the Firth of Lorn. Still off the northern end of Ireland, we had just passed Inishbofin, which lies next to Inishshark. The word Inish means Island and bofin means white cow. Inishbofin did have more grass than some of the other Inish places. A small distance off, it appeared as if a small fishing boat might be having some sort of trouble, but as we got closer we found there were three fishermen hauling in their nets. I hollered over and asked, "Could you please tell us where we are?" The reply across the gap of water was, "Aye dinna know wat yer sayin?" I asked again, louder and slower, and what came back was, "Aye still dinna know what yer wantin?" We went on our way thinking, Does anybody here speak English?

Later that afternoon another ship came into view. This time it was a big trawler, and very close she was. She came along side of us to within 20 ft. and the crew gave us a friendly wave. I would imagine they saw we were flying the Canadian flag, and the stern of the Tullen Tie indicated our home port, Toronto, Ont. Canada.. The trawler's name was Captain Cook. What a beautiful sight. The railings around the length and stern of the trawler were shoulder-to-shoulder pigeons. It seemed as if all were enjoying the ride and waiting for the next load of the trawler's nets to be brought on board. We should have taken advantage of the VHF to ask where we could purchase diesel fuel. But with all the excitement of the birds, we forgot. Today was and would have been the perfect day for motoring, definitely not sailing. It's a terrible thing when you peel off your socks, throw them in the water and they don't sink.

I'm guessing we sailed across two or three nets on that day without damage to any. I explained earlier what Leo had done to prevent us snagging a fishing line or net; obviously it worked again. While the boat was still in its cradle back in Frenchman's Bay (Toronto), Leo had welded a u-shaped piece of steel to the aft end of the keel at the very bottom, and likewise welded another u-shape at the bottom of the skeg. We then attached a three-quarter-inch nylon line from one u-shape to the other. The engine prop is, of course, between these two points and higher up, so anything the boat glances over just slides by and out the stern. Believe me, it works every time and saved us a potentially bad time with some Irishman.

On one occasion, we had a nice fellow come along side in his dingy and ask if we would mind following him around his nets. Like most of the smaller boats fishing there (what we would call inland), they were fishing for salmon. One fisherman held up a beauty. I really believed he was going to throw us a fish, but no. So I treated the boys and made a pudding. Next day there wasn't a hint of wind and I started to feel as though I were going to be facing Ireland for the rest of my days. Damn, the damned pudding didn't pudd or whatever puddings do. I jettisoned the pudding. Gosh darn, wouldn't it just be the greatest thing to go ashore in one of these little fishing villages and find a pub, drink a pint of Guinness or Murphys and look at a woman for a change, instead of Al or Leo. I'll bet they smell nicer too, all soft and pink and washed. A decent meal, a few songs and "crack" (craic) as it's known in Ireland. (The word crack is a Scot's language word meaning talk, chat, news, boast, brag, and so forth. In recent years in Ireland the spelling craic has been adopted. This spelling craic causes serious nausea among intelligent people.) Unfortunately, we had to keep going, as we were running late. The booze was all gone so it was time to wait for Al to go to sleep so we could look at his untouched boxful. We were south of "Bloody Foreland." I just love these names. If nothing else, it was really great just reading the places we were leaving in our wake. Names like "Whore's Cove." Wouldn't you just love to visit the place?

We are still eating those Rye Krisp things from Sweden. The tinned goods continued to rust, so when I opened one I put my ear to the can to listen for that air-sucking sound you get when the can opener does its thing. If the smell was even a bit iffy, over the side it went. Some sailors before a trip are known to varnish the cans; this may help but everything rolls around so much in a boat, you're bound to get some chipping. In hot climates, the crew or skipper will dip the eggs in wax a few times to make them last longer. We, of course, had a different problem with eggs: how to keep them from freezing.

I thought back to when I had my medical with Dr. Geoffrey

Isaac back in Toronto. He had said that he and his wife (also a doctor) would be in Dublin for a seminar when we would be somewhere in Ireland, and he urged us to call him at this hotel number saying that he would love to treat us to a wonderful dinner with drinks. Wow! But instead, I opened another rusty tin of beans to throw on the Rye Krisp crackers. For dessert we indulged in a Mars bar each. We were hove to for the night and I began thinking about the fact that the nasty stuff must be behind us, for a while anyway. It's somewhat uncomfortable when you sit in front of the wheel and behind you are 25-ft. or higher waves trying their best to get on board. Someone once said to me, "Don't look behind you, the crew is doing that for you, just look at their faces. But when they look up they probably know something, so just hold on." A sailor named Hugo Vilhen asked, "Why do they name them swells? There's nothing swell about them, they should call them awfuls."

I believe it was Friday the 9th when we thought we could very well be in the Firth of Lorn, which would take us into Oban. After not seeing land for a few days and now sighting land on our port side, it seemed like a good idea to find out what land this was. Looking through the binoculars we could see what appeared to be a mother and two little ones on the beach. Now, I realize it isn't exactly good seamanship to ask where we are; one is supposed to know this at all times. But all is forgiven, because similar to Saint-Pierre, we didn't have coastal charts for Scotland either. We had a pretty map but the pretty map didn't tell us where the rocks were, or the times of low tide and high tide, or the entrance to a port or cove and all the other nautical niceties that could help make our day. So, I volunteered to row the baby blue-bottomed play boat ashore and ask the nice lady, "Where the hell might we be?"

We dropped anchor and lowered the wee boat into the water. With the help of the one paddle, I made for shore. I should mention, this boat has a flat bottom, no keel, and goes pretty much where it wants to go. A strong current was running and I just rowed past a basking shark about 12 ft. long. What I do know is they love basking in the sun and it was longer than my play boat. The basking shark is the second largest fish in the world. They can be up to 11 metres long and weight up to seven tons. I was concentrating on going in on a straight line (sort of) towards the people on shore. Later Leo asked, "Why did you go through the rocks where all the walrus were sun bathing and not go around?" The truth is, I was busy with the current and didn't see the 30odd walrus. On top of all this, I know nothing about the habits of walrus and whether they ever maimed people or more importantly, if angry, whether they ever sunk their tusks into a wee boat.

I beached the boat beside the nice lady. This was to be my first landfall. As I stepped out of the boat and into the water it only took a minute to realize how wobbly I was. I had to hold onto one of the children's heads to stop from falling over. Also, I had a pencil in my teeth and the pretty map tucked into my belt. The nice lady's first words were, "Welcome to Scotland, and you're lost." Apparently she too had been looking through the binoculars and saw our Canadian flag. Elizabeth, her husband Andrew and the two wee-uns were on holiday. This nice couple marked on the chart that we were between Tiree and Coll in the Inner Hebrides and the way we were going would soon be in the Sea of the Hebrides, obviously going the wrong way.

This was my first actual landfall and I couldn't believe how unsteady I was on my feet. Here I was on non-moving land, swaying from side to side. More than once I had to reach down for the beach to keep from falling over. Elizabeth seemed to know a lot about the sea, especially this area. Having six brothers (all seamen) there wasn't much she didn't know. She suggested because we've bypassed Oban, why not just head north and watch for the first big opening, turn starboard (hang a right) go in a short way and stop at Tobermory? There is no prettier port in the west of Scotland than Tobermory, Mull's main village.

I was about to thank Elizabeth and Andrew for all this needed advice and say goodbye when she asked, "Where did you think you were?" I showed her on our map the little penciled in X. I can still see that smile as she blew wind out of her cheeks, and said, "Well, thank the Lord you and your friends are not there, that's Corryvreckan, an evil place." We found out later that this evil place is situated between the islands of Jura and Scarba. The Royal Navy says it's unnavigable and if you're 10 to 12 miles away you can still hear it. Twice a day the ocean tidal surge of water is funnelled between the long coast of Kintyre and the just-as-long isle of Jura. This bulge of water is squished through a shallow and narrow channel between the north coast of Jura and the island of Scarba at nine knots. An eddy is formed that would swallow up the largest ship. That is roughly how a whirlpool works. "Maelstrom" would be a better word.

If you would love to be entertained in the comfort of your living room about Corryvreckan without all the above worries, try and rent a movie if you can find it, called *"I Know Where I'm Going,"* starring Wendy Hiller and Roger Livesey. It's a romantic story of Hiller stranded in a Scottish seacoast town for a week because of bad weather, where she falls in love with Livesey. It's a quiet gem of a film, made in 1945, with the added bonus of Corryvreckan thrown in. The actual shooting of the Corryvreckan itself was far too risky so the film company decided to shoot the scenes between the islands of Scarba and Lunga. Apparently The Corryvreckan whirlpool is one of the largest permanent whirlpools on earth and the most dangerous stretch of water around the British Isles.

Apparently minke whales and porpoises swim in the fast-moving waters of this region. George Orwell wrote his novel "1984" while living on Jura near Corryvreckan. When on his boat in the gulf of Corryvreckan, he was drawn into the whirlpool and his boat capsized. Luckily, he and his crew escaped death. Many others have not been this lucky. A lot has been written about "Corryvreckan." Folklore has it that near this channel the local villagers were attacked by Norsemen and their homes were looted. The locals lured the marauders back into their boats and led them into these dangerous waters. Using their local knowledge of the tides and eddies, the local mariners were able to row ashore at the very last minute, while their attackers were swept into the jaws of the gulf of Corryvreckan and were sucked to their death in the whirlpool.

I now said goodbye to Elizabeth and family for all this interesting Corryvreckan news and rowed myself back to the Tullen Tie with the big news. Before actually arriving in Tobermory, Al got on the VHF and spoke with the customs man about mooring.

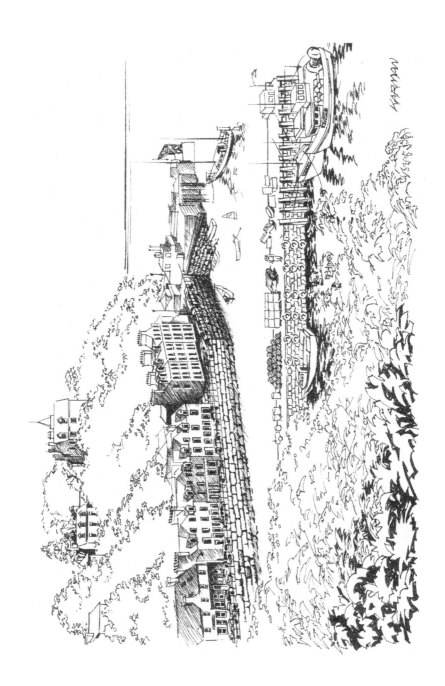

Dee and Joyce

On the dock, in uniform, was the customs official, a charming red-faced little man who was as round as he was high. He took us in tow and we three followed him home. But first, after having a few pleasantries on the dock with Dee and Joyce (two Scottish girls on holidays; we made arrangements to see them later), we went to Bill Heath's home. "Before we do any of the customs paperwork," he said, "you lads must have a wee dram of single malt Scotch. Bill filled four juice glasses to the brim with single malt. Al. not being a connoisseur of a good Scotch, didn't touch his, and Leo and I being gentlemen obliged to help. The paperwork consisted of the usual: How long is the sailboat, is it wood, fibreglass? What is the engine, horsepower, serial number? Now we did know the engine was a Farymann diesel and the horsepower was no problem. But for the serial number, one of us had to go back to the boat. Bill, our new friend with the single malt, said it's a long way back to the boat, and it would take the same time as having two more wee drams. With that wise statement, he said, "I believe the engine number I need is F for Farymann and 2791643, plus I'll add another 4 to that." Now everything was signed, stamped and finished.

Bill's home was a comfortable place, very much as you'd expect to find in a British home. The big heavy chesterfield with a flower pattern, doilies on the arms, pillows on every blank space, every wall covered in busy wallpaper, heavy drapes that were probably used in the last war when there were still blackouts. The fireplace with the red bulb and the silver paper that turned slowly, to give one the impression of heat, had on its mantle all the family photos (mostly

330

sepia prints of past kin in uniform). Bill lived here with his wife, the children long gone and working in the big cities. You could tell they were very frugal and never threw anything away. We made arrangements to meet Bill later at the pub in the Mishnish Hotel, where the drinks would be our treat.

The population here was about 900, and everybody knew everybody. The Mishnish Hotel is on the sea front of Tobermory's busy fishing harbour and had been in the family for over 100 years. It is now run by Robert MacLeod, but when we were there it was still run by Robbie MacLeod (the father). Robbie played the accordion, so well apparently that he had played at Massey Hall in Toronto many years earlier (he knew Toronto very well). The Mishnish is unmistakable in the red, yellow and blue building near the main pier of Tobermory. Tobermory isn't very big by any means, but has everything one might need. The laundromat, post office, grocery store, hotel, pub and a lot more, all within walking distance of each other. Bill stayed with us drinking his favourite, pints of beer until it was time for him to go home.

For the three of us Tobermory was our first landfall. Of course, for me it was earlier on Tiree. The greeting and welcome at Tobermory and the same again at the Mishnish Hotel, (pub) were overwhelming. Robbie MacLeod started with a free round of drinks for us and announced he wouldn't be closing this evening. On top of this, another nice coincidence for us was that another six sailboats were there on holiday from England. The six skippers all had their dads with them for crew, and there was no way we could pay for a drink. Every time you'd reach into your pocket for a schilling, some lad or his dad had already paid. Also Dee and Joyce (the girls from the pier) had arrived. Al was in his glory explaining how the crossing went to a small group of sailors while Leo was busy getting acquainted with Joyce. I was now seated with Dee at a booth with my head buried in her hair. I had never smelled anything so clean and fresh since Nova Scotia. As a matter a fact, I still hadn't combed my hair since Nova Scotia.

All was going wonderfully, the drinks kept coming, the girls looked good, and the hours were slipping by nicely, until something happened. In all this noise, Leo, I'm sure misunderstood and thought he heard Al telling this little group of sailors about how he brought the boat across. Leo being very tired, as we all were, and Leo being skipper would have a lot more to worry about than Al or I would, plus the anxious times when the storm hit, plus damage and so forth. Well, now it was about to be said, and there would no taking it back. Leo was up like a shot and in a loud voice said something like, "You son-of-a-bitch, if it was up to you, we'd all be at the bottom. And who was down below making instant soup instead of watching for icebergs?" Sure, Al was down below every now and then--he was a lot thinner than we two, and colder--but now, what's more important is how do we patch this up? Al was, apparently referring to his navigation. It's unfortunate, but at a time like this, I guess they were ill-chosen words. Embarrassing, but it happened. The room went quiet. Al headed for the door and was gone.

Leo and I now had another drink or two with the girls while I convinced him that we had to go and find Al, and apologize to him, if indeed he would even listen to Leo. We told Dee and Joyce we'd be back if things went well. Now, here we were in the wee hours,

Tobermory fast asleep and where is Al? We checked the boat first. No Al. We walked around Tobermory for a while. Not a soul around. Tobermory is sleeping, everything is very quiet. Now Leo starts with, and at first not too loud, "Al, I'm sorry." Then a little louder, "AL, you son-of-a-bitch, where are you?" And so it went.

We did finally find Al propped up behind a small shed. The apologies were accepted and all was forgiven (sort of). They both shook hands and Al went back to the boat to sleep. Leo and I headed back to the Mishnish, one reason being that the girls said we could shower in their room. The sun was coming up when we walked into the Mishnish and found the girls had left for their room. Leo and I went up and the girls were awake and sitting on the bed. The unit they were in consisted of one room, no toilet (it was down the hall), but it did have one of those metal boxes for a shower standing in the corner. Leo and I undressed (now completely naked) and took our turns in the shower box. Meanwhile, Dee and Joyce had a book each and pretended to read, never once flipping a page.

The next day (still today), having missed sleep because of last night, I took my filthy clothes in a garbage bag to the laundry place. Now, the custom here was for the Laundromat to do your wash, fold it, pack it and have you pick it up when done. I was quite embarrassed about my laundry, so I told the girl it was Leo's and that if he didn't come for it, I'd be back. That day we also had to move the Tullen Tie because the fishing boats were returning and this was where they'd unload their catch. We were now anchored out, so it did create a small problem getting to shore, since we had only the one baby-blue play boat. If one wanted to go ashore, everybody went ashore. Or if not, you stayed on the boat.

That evening Al decided to stay on the boat, so Leo and I took the play boat and went ashore to see the girls. Dee and I walked around town in one direction and Leo with Joyce in the other direction. It was getting quite dark when Dee and I were approached by two young Scottish lads from out of town. They were coming towards us and had been celebrating, so they were very drunk--one more so then the other. The drunker of the two wanted to fight because, as he put it, "You foreign arseholes aren't going to take our girls away." Dee and I and his buddy got him calmed down and the two of them staggered off. Apparently about an hour later, these two came across Leo and Joyce, only this time the belligerent one had a big wrench and was thinking of using it on Leo. Well, Leo had a habit of carrying a big knife in its case, tucked into his belt at the small part of his back. When he put this blade under the guy's nose and said, "Think about it for a minute," that's when they both ran away.

It was late now and the later it got, the colder it got. Dee and I headed back to the Mishnish and went up to the girls' room to warm up a little before I went looking for Leo and Joyce. Since we only had the one boat, I waited for Leo at the wee boat, but being cold I decided to walk to keep warm. All of Tobermory was fast asleep again, as the previous night, and extremely quiet. All the lights were out except for a bright moon. I came around a small shack in the dark, and there in the wild grass were Leo and Joyce going at it like they'd both been in prison for years. I sat quietly with my back to the shack and, with the help of the moonlight, saw Joyce's legs going up and down, up and down with every thrust of Leo. I wanted to yell out, "For Christ sake

Leo, she still has her panty-hose on." To this day, I haven't told him about my being there. I didn't stay too long anyway, because the damned midges (pronounced midgees) will eat you alive if you sit still. Possibly Joyce's legs were going up and down so fast because of the midges. The midge is a no-see-um fly that bites anything and everything exposed. On Monday Dee took me shopping in her M.G. for groceries. We also filled up with diesel, fresh water and did some general repairs..

We were moored to the dock, waiting for the diesel truck. It was low tide and the boat was aground when the diesel man arrived. I opened the filler cap on the deck plate, and Leo, who was a good 20 feet up above me on the dock, lowered the hose. Being a simple free fall from the truck to the boat, everything seemed to be working nicely and quietly until Leo asked the diesel man, "About how much has gone in?" He said, "Exactly 122 gallons." "Whoa, shut it down, we only hold 100 gallons," said Leo. I went below and sure enough, the hose under the filler cap had blown off, and the diesel wasn't going into the tank at all but straight into the bilge —and the diesel was now above the carpeting. I was wearing my Hush Puppy shoes with the crepe soles and the soles immediately went soft and gummy from the diesel. Talk about sticky! I was now capable of walking up walls. We pumped out what we could in Tobermory, the law being you are not allowed to empty into any waterway, which of course makes sense.

We were all prepared to leave Tobermory in the morning when a fellow showed up at the boat and said, "The Police would like to have a word with you." It had something to do with the two drunks we met the previous night. The following morning, early, we were given the story of the two and they had just been arrested. They were now in a police car parked on the main street of town, and Leo and I were asked if we would casually walk past the police car without stopping, and have a good look and then verify that, yes, they were the two from last night. Apparently, they had stolen some old gentleman's Morris Oxford and pushed it over a cliff. We were very concerned that we might have to stay for the trial, but we were free to go. The other evening when this nonsense was going on, I had asked Dee if I could keep her frilly black panties to put up on the halyard next to Ruth's, which were ready to come down anyway. She said, "Yes, under one condition, I don't want you to put them up while you're still here."

We were without charts to get out of here and we were in a place with tides and currents, plus I was sure there would be other surprises. Good old Robbie MacLeod came to our rescue. He didn't have charts but he did have a very old book with drawings of the Caledonian Canal. Tattered as it was, we borrowed this bit of treasure and I promised to mail it back when I got home. Which I did, only first I restored it the best I could and added a nice thank-you note in the opening pages of the book.

We left Tobermory between 4 and 5 a.m. to take advantage of the ebb and flood tides. In the meantime, we had the possibility of a litre or two of diesel still in the bilge. Fortunately, we could motor safely, even though there was a small amount of diesel around the engine. The plan was, when we got to the North Sea, to add small amounts of kitchen detergent to the bilge, plus water, so the swells would give us a washing machine effect. Then, little by little, we would pump some out of the bilge without leaving a trail of bubbles. I was very tired and hung over, and thought it a blessing to get away from shore for a while.

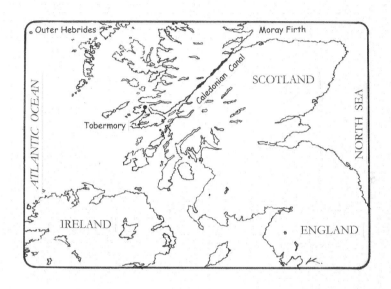

The Caledonian Canal is approximately 97 km long and cuts diagonally across Scotland from Loch Linnhe on the southwest to Moray Firth on the northeast. Opened in 1882, with the intention of linking the Atlantic to the North Sea for the shipping trade, it is today used mainly by pleasure craft. Construction of the canal, which began in 1803, cost around 840,000 pounds. But when it opened, it turned out to be too shallow for the larger boats. This 180-year-old-plus waterway bisects the northern chunk of Scotland through the Great Glen, Loch Ness, and some of the most beautiful scenery I've ever seen. The Caledonian Canal has approximately 26 locks to go through, some say 29 locks and nine bridges. Also along its 60-mile length, the whole thing was in bad need of repair when we went through. A beautiful part of the canal is Loch Ness, and probably the most popular, being 23 miles long and the largest lake in Britain. All locks seem to be operated by keepers, but it's up to each vessel to open and close the lock gates, except for a few.

Britain's highest mountain is at the Great Glen, and Inverness has its imposing castles, so there is certainly a lot to see on the way. There are many piers, jetties and mooring places along Loch Ness and the Great Glen. There are also pubs and well-stocked shops in the villages. The great midge was here in the canal too. From Tobermory we sailed along the sound of Mull, then up Lynn of Morven, next Loch Lynne to Corpach, which is the start of the Caledonian Canal. Leo and Al were still not talking since we left the Mishnish Hotel (pub) incident. Naturally, this made things very awkward and uncomfortable on board, for all of us. The boat was only so long, so there was no place to go and be alone.

Finally, to break the tension, I'd say, "If you two don't start talking to each other, I'm getting off when we reach the North Sea." A day or two later Al tried first with, "Leo, I think we should be in Corpach within the hour." Leo then looked at me and said, "Tell Al I know." I came back with, "Shit Bugger Damn." About two days later, Al tried again with, "Bob and Leo, would you two like a cup of tea?" And Leo responded, "Al, I'd love a cup of tea." Well, the Heavens opened and everything was fine again. (For now anyway.)

After climbing the first three locks we had to dock for the night because the next six were closed until the next day and wouldn't open before 8 a.m. The canal charge for the whole works from one end to the other was 18 pounds. I think that's a bargain when you consider your only other choice is a passage round Scotland's notoriously rough northern coast. We were motoring for quite some time now, behind a touring canal boat, going through lock after lock with "Sarnda," owned by Alan and his wife Pat. Sarnda had one crew, a young girl who looked to be about 18 or so, named Lorna. The cruise boat itself held another eight paying passengers. These four elderly couples were all on holidays. One couple, I chatted with later happened to come from Woodbridge, Ont. This group all ate and slept on board for the length of the canal to Inverness, the end of the trip. Sarnda (the boat) wasn't big enough for refrigeration, so Alan and Pat slept somewhere on shore each evening and shopped very early for the breakfast stuff. Then Pat dropped Alan off with the food at the boat. Pat would then follow the boat along the shoreline and shop for the rest of the day's food.

And so it went, day after day till everyone got to Inverness, only to do it again on the way back with a bunch of new faces. I spent my evenings with Lorna, who certainly knew this water and shoreline as well as any guide would. The locks all seemed to close early, so you had no choice but to stay put, and enjoy your evening, or go exploring. Sadly, many of the locks were in bad condition at that time, and in need of instant repair, but there wasn't any money. So the locks tended to break constantly, one way or another. Mostly there was a problem with silt build-up, which got higher and higher each year. When we went through it was at a point where the doors wouldn't open or close properly anymore.

We heard from another boat, two locks behind us, that the doors had collapsed and sank, so now nobody could get through, for a while anyway. Luckily we had just nicely escaped that disaster. So far with this trip in the canal, we were motoring more than sailing. We had done quite a few locks, so it was getting easier to open and close them than at the beginning.. Through trial and error I think Al and I have it all figured out now. It's Friday. Last evening we were tied up at Fort Augustus. A group of young lads came around and played guitar and sang till their curfew, which was 9 p.m. for one group and 10 p.m. for the other. I believe they hung around as long as they could because of Lorna. Can't say that I blame them, she was a pretty wee lass.

Times have changed since our trip. The new, revamped Caledonian Canal can now take cargo, so congestion on the A82 could be eased by freight being transported on the Caledonian Canal. This completion of restoration on the waterway took about 10 years and 20 million pounds. I believe this work started around 1996. The repairs and refurbishment work were carried out on most of the 29 locks between the sea locks at Clachnaharry and Corpach. Of course, when we went through, there was none of this.

Loch Ness, which opens into Moray Firth and the North Sea, itself is at least one-third the length of the canal. We've all heard of "Nessie" the Loch Ness monster, also known as a cryptozoological creature of the world. The earliest recorded sighting of the Loch Ness monster was in 565 AD. The monster apparently attacked and killed a man who was swimming in the River Ness. The monster didn't make headlines again until Aug. 27,1930, when three fishermen saw something in the water. What they saw was a creature 20 feet long approach their boat, throwing water into the air, and then it was gone. In 1962 The Loch Ness Investigation Bureau was formed, and in 1964

340

they established camera stations all over the place. Searches were conducted using infrared night scanners, hot air balloons, sonar and submarines.

BOB, AL AND LEO WITNESS ANOTHER
SIGHTING OF THE LOCH NESS MONSTER

Loch Ness is one of a series of interlinked Lochs (lakes) that run along the Great Glen. The Great Glen is more than 700 feet (213 m) deep and ice free year round. It is fed by the Oich and other streams drained by the Ness to the Moray Firth. By volume, Loch Ness is the largest freshwater lake in Great Britain. In 1933 (the year of my birth, obviously an important year) there were published accounts of sightings of a monster 40 to 50 feet long. Many people believe that the size and great depth of the Loch, together with potential underwater caves, give the monster many hiding places. There is a list as long as your arm of sightings. But today the Tullen Tie is in Loch Ness with five eyes on the watch. The cameras are loaded with film and everything is a go. Hours have passed and nothing. We throw Rye Krisp crackers in the water, some stale beer, still nothing. I play the harmonica, which should bring everything to the surface, I have a whiz in the water. Our experiment is almost over. We decide, there is no F'n Nessie.

I'd been seeing Lorna every evening since we met at the beginning of the Caledonia canal, and I was getting ready to see her again this evening, probably our last night together. I borrowed Leo's black nylon ski jacket again so I could look presentable, even though Leo did say something like, "It would be nice if maybe this time you didn't bring it back with all the grass stains." It's one of those thin lightweight nylon pullover things with a zipper in front. Everything of my own would be fine if I were going out to look after a flock of sheep for the winter. I knew the next day would be busy with shopping and some work on the boat, so it seems best to say our good-byes.

I waited until I figured most of the guests on Sarnda had gone to sleep. (Lorna told me they were always in bed early because the fresh air knocked them out.) Also to make sure Alan and Pat have left the boat, Lorna was to meet me on shore, and I didn't know which cabin was hers anyway. It seemed late enough so I made my way over to where Sarnda was moored on the other side of a small inlet. Lorna was outside and explained we must be very quiet because some of them were elderly and didn't sleep that well, and that when we got to her wee room we were to whisper. Whispering was a good idea, especially when we could hear people breathing in their sleep through the thin wall. The other adjoining wall had a snorer. And a very wee room it was, with a bunk and dresser, nothing more. I stayed the night and we whispered a lot, and tried not to breathe too loudly.

At the first sign of daybreak I was dressed and gone before the group of eight were up. I sure didn't want to meet Alan on the way in. Halfway back to the Tullen Tie I realized I'd left Leo's jacket in the wee room, but I wasn't going back, and it was probably too late anyway. I was sure Lorna would bring it later when we went shopping. With Lorna's help we both went shopping in Inverness. She knew where the best foods were sold. One can't say a bad word about the Highland people. Wherever we went, they were friendly and helpful. Inverness carried everything one might need plus treats like Haggis (I think). Another nice thing about Inverness is you can walk for 15 minutes out of town and find yourself up in the hills. I thought of it for a minute or two, but then figured, better not, there is too much of the grass up there.

The North Sea

This was the day we were to start for the North Sea, and I hoped Leo and Al would be talking again. Lorna joined us for coffee on the Tullen Tie, and after our good-byes to all we were off into the Moray Firth. Sailing was slow along the coast of Scotland. The Moray Firth is well south of the Orkney Islands (another place I would love to visit in the future). I took the evening shift along this beautiful coastline. The towns and villages were all lit with orange street lamps. It is very attractive and peaceful looking, compared to the harsh white lights of other shorelines. You've got to pay attention here and watch for the skerries. The skerries are a rock mass that protrude out from shore and at times are difficult to see. As morning came we had a full moon on the starboard and the sun on the port side. (We were out far enough by now that it became necessary to watch for the oil rigs. A sea captain in Inverness told us there are more than 85 rigs out there.) Another beautiful day had arrived but we were doing only two to three knots. When we did the grocery shopping, Lorna insisted I buy a big haggis, and that when I cooked the thing I should put a hole in it and fill it with whisky, or we may have trouble swallowing the innards.

It was the perfect day to eat a haggis. The sea was calm and the wind was almost non-existent. Haggis is, of course, the national dish of Scotland. The most haggis eaten in a single day is usually on Robbie Burns' birthday, Jan. 25, served with tatties and neeps (potatoes and turnips). And, it goes without saying, a wee dram of single malt scotch. Very few people make haggis from scratch. Most would rather buy a finished haggis from the butcher's, which I feel is wise. But if you must, you must. First, you go out and buy one sheep's lung (illegal in the U.S.A.). Then one sheep's stomach, one sheep's heart, one sheep's liver, 3/4 cup oatmeal and onions and spices (because you're gonna need it). Wash lungs and stomach well, rub with salt and rinse. Remove membranes and excess fat. Now soak the thing in salted water for hours, turn the stomach inside out for the stuff to go in. Bring to a boil, cover and simmer for another 30 minutes. Chop the heart and grate the liver. Toast the oatmeal, pack it all into the stomach loosely (oatmeal expands) press the air out of the stomach and tie the bugger up and throw the whole works over the side. I'm only kidding. You are now finished.

Do what we did. Buy a haggis, put cheap whisky inside and drink more good whisky in a glass. That's my recipe. Oh, I was recently told that if you can't find a sheep's stomach, you can use a cow's bladder.

Well into the North Sea, we started seeing more oil rigs, mostly in the evenings when they were all lit up like a Christmas tree. Far off at the horizon (when it's dark) the drilling rigs look their best, or were we possibly looking at a village? But there were no villages on the chart, so that answers that. Most of the rigs we saw had a three- or four-story building mounted on the platform, for the sleeping quarters. They also all require a tender of some kind. It can be anything from a tug with a flat stern to carry supplies, pipe, etc., or a ship that resembles a small freighter. These tenders are anchored close to the drilling rig for any emergency. We thought, now that we're here, let's sail in closer to have a better look at this monstrous thing on legs, take a few pictures and be off. As we were on our sail toward the rig, we could see through the binoculars they were pulling up anchor and bringing the freighter around in position between us and the oil rig. The obvious message being, if we proceed to come any closer they will probably ram us out of the water. When you think of it, if you have an oil rig worth something in the many millions of dollars, and some clown sails in with a boat weighing a few tons and has a good possibility of colliding with one of the legs, then there is a decent chance of the whole works going over. After we were out of harm's way, the freighter went back to its original position and dropped anchor.

What a day! The atmosphere on board stunk. These two were still not talking, and I was in the middle as interpreter. Another day of this, I thought, and we'll all be crazy. But the following day the sun came out and we had wind and, wisely, libations again, even though the libations didn't matter to Al. The mood seemed a lot better than the previous day. It is amazing what sunshine can do. We did the North Atlantic, we'd finished with the Caledonian Canal and now the North Sea. It's odd and good at the same time, how quickly you can forget the nasty stuff and move on. I was starting to realize and think how difficult it was going to be to leave the boat and go back to work.

Leo asked me to consider staying on after Finland, to do the Rhine and go through France. Then on to the Mediterranean and once in the Mediterranean we would have Italy with Rome, Naples, Salerno, Palermo, Malta and on and on. What could be nicer? But I did have to go home, since I had two mortgages on the strawberry box (my house), ongoing bills to pay, my two boys at home, my studio rent and work to attend to. And my mother thinks I've lost my mind. If only there were some sensible answer to this, but there's none and that's that. Years later, I knew I'd be kicking myself for missing this opportunity, but it couldn't be helped.

It happened to me once before, when I turned down "George of the Jungle." I had my studio in an apartment building at the time when I met George. I never did know or find out his last name, but it didn't matter. What mattered was that George, who was retired, wealthy, and a white hunter in Africa, lived down the hall from me. To condense some of this story, George wanted me to go with him into the heart of Africa. We were to be away for two or three months on a safari hunt. He had done this numerous times before, and he had photographs to prove it—plus, his large apartment down the hall was full of wild animal heads and other memorabilia. My first true words to George were that is was completely impossible for me to come up with this sort of money, but thanks very much. George of the Jungle insisted he would look after all the money necessary, and he himself was to be the guide. He already owned three of the necessary four-wheel-drive vehicles, plus he had eight or ten porters who already worked for him, so the rest would not be a problem. Because of my personal life and expenses at home, I didn't go.

Looking back, I probably could have gone and definitely should have gone. These opportunities don't happen often, if ever, and this offer never came up again. It may have been a blessing that I stayed home, because when George did come back from his safari I saw him in the hall. He was very ill and was on his way to the hospital. After a week or so he was back home because the hospital (St. Michael's in Toronto) couldn't help and had no idea how to treat him.

It turns out, something had bitten him in the eye and the poison went through his system. George of the Jungle passed away soon after, all alone in his bathroom.

We had been in the North Sea now at least four days, with one full day and all night of constant pounding. Wind and sea right on the beam. Two days back we did a total of 22 miles in 24 hrs. We all agreed we should find a port in Norway, especially since we were running short of diesel fuel. The Norwegian coastline has to be one of the most threatening shorelines to be seen. The pilot book says, and I quote, "Entrance for local knowledge only." Looking at the rusted wrecks and holed boats lying on their sides, I'd say it looks pretty true (the local knowledge part). We put into a place called Tjorve, which is almost at the very bottom of Norway near Lindesness at the entrance to the Skagerrak Sea. Tjorve is a small fishing village. Most here fish for mackerel. We got permission to tie up alongside a good-sized shrimp boat with three people on board: Gul Brand, 22 years old, owner and skipper, his girlfriend Ingrid, 19, pretty, with a very healthy looking complexion thanks to the ocean air, and the forever smiling crew member Ourvind (Irwin), 28. They happen to be temporarily finished with shrimp fishing and on a three-week holiday heading across the Skagerrak to Denmark. Wonderful people, they invited us on board for dinner. We ate fish cakes that looked and tasted very much like our hamburger. We enjoyed their Norwegian beer and they enjoyed our Scottish canned beer. Our beer cans had gorgeous pictures of women on the cans. Ourvind (Irwin) had one of each of the lovely girls. We also took with us a bottle of Scotch. Apparently Scotch in Norway is very expensive so it went down rather quickly.

We learned that these personally owned shrimp boats are all extremely clean, when you consider they are working vessels. Gul Brand's boat had no fish smell whatsoever. The outside hull of a shrimp boat is all varnish, and it will put your pride and joy coffee table to shame. These people fish for shrimp day and night, without sleep if necessary, as long as the shrimp are running. When they've got a good catch and the hole is full, they boil the shrimp. After boiling a batch, somebody has to taste one shrimp to see if they're well cooked. They will have a taste and immediately spit it out. None of them enjoy shrimp. On the return trip home, they set the automated steering to the compass and go to sleep. As Gul said, "It has happened where one tired crew has hit another tired crew and somebody would go down." In the morning we all had coffee together, shook hands, a hug and said good-bye.

Friday the16th. Thank God for a full tank of diesel. We'd been motoring all day and night and the Skagerrak looked like it had the life of Jello. This is very unusual, considering this is mostly a stormy country. Before leaving Norway's shores forever, we did tuck in a little to have a look at the Fiords. They most definitely are worth looking at. Fiords were formed by glaciers a long time ago. The glaciers began to melt and recede, the ocean moved in to fill the void, and left us with this beautiful sight. On Saturday while motoring we saw four absolutely huge fishing floats, each the size of a small fridge. These were those bright orange day-glow balls that fishermen use for markers. The four were all tied together as one and had a heavy chain attached, going straight down into the sea. While Leo manoeuvred the boat under power, I got the boat hook out to salvage the markers. We were miles out from any shore. Each time we got close enough to grapple onto the chain, the whole works would pull away faster than we could keep up. Then the balls would stop and we'd go after it again, and again off it would go. Meanwhile, Al was getting a bit nervous, saying, "Why don't you leave it alone, you don't know what's down there." He was probably right, so we decided to carry on. There had been a storm through the night and more than likely the whole works had broken away from the side of a trawler. We never did find out what was down below, but we had no choice. I did have the hook on it for a moment though, but I couldn't lift it and then, whatever it was, it was off again. This time it didn't stop.

Where the hell is Sweden? A plus thing about sailing is, when you sit for hours in a small cockpit of a sailboat, there are many things to talk about. Leo and I, lately, seemed to chat more than Al and I. The reason for this, I think, is that Al is worried about his eye. It is a big worry, and with this weather he's colder than we are. That unfortunate incident In Tobermory didn't help either. I never thought of it before, but I must thank Al sometime soon. Now, Al is in the insurance business, owns his own agency, has had me in his grasp these many weeks, and never, not once, tried to sell me insurance. That deserves recognition and a thank-you.

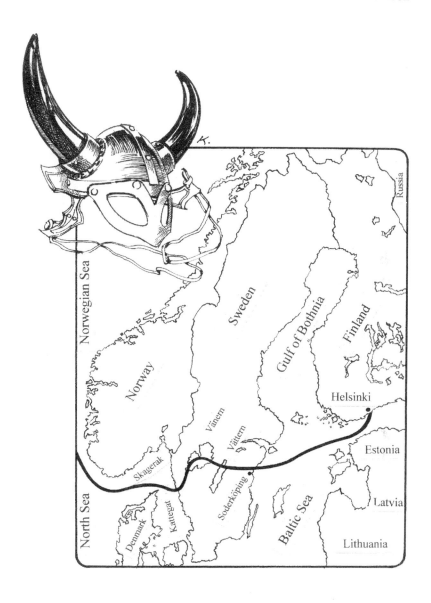

Sweden

On a very black evening (no moon) we found our way into the entrance of Göteborg, Sweden, by following the big passenger liners. We soon realized we would be there for some time because of the length of the Göta canal, some 300 miles (485 km). This long canal crosses through the country, linking the North Sea to the Baltic Sea via rivers and lakes (including Lake Vänern and Lake Vättern), with more than 60 locks between Göteborg and Stockholm. Göteborg (locally pronounced yot-e-burr) has a population of 800,000 plus, and a great many of these people cross over to Denmark for the weekend. Here we were in Sweden, among the people who invented dynamite, the freezer, the computer mouse, the propeller, the match, the Nobel prize, the pacemaker, Volvo, Ikea furniture and, of course, the wonderful Absolut Vodka. Sweden, per capita, consumes more coffee than any nation in the world. Swedes also have the highest divorce rate in the world (more than 50% of all marriages fail in less than 10 years) and the highest income tax in the world--up to 55 percent of one's salary.

Göteborg, called Gothenburg in English and German, is Sweden's second largest city. It was here that most of the very big shipbuilding took place, but from around the 1970s many operations have closed down. Hundreds of ships were built just across from the city on an island. It is said that only two shipbuilding companies survive today, and they do mostly repair work. When we sailed through there in 1976, we still did see many of these monstrous ships being put together. The north side of the Göta River has changed dramatically in recent years now that the ship building has moved on. Now it's populated with expensive fashionable condos and high-tech companies. If you ever visit and have the time, do spend some time on "the avenue" (Kungsportsavenyn) shopping, and taking in the restaurants and hotels.

The sailors we met on the Göteborg canal didn't seem to mind the high taxes because most people live very well here, and the big salaries are enough to cover all expenses and still have money left over. Most Swedes are tall, with fair or brown hair and blue eyes. They're very well dressed and at first may seem a little cold, but given time that all changes. The first lock we put into didn't go well. Everywhere I've been in the past, sailors will always jump up and grab your mooring line, or help fend you off, or whatever is appropriate. The Swedes will just sit on their boat and watch. Naturally, we did meet a few other thoughtful sailors who couldn't do enough for you. The Swedish standard of living is one of the highest in the world. Sweden ranks among the leading European nations in the number of cars, telephones and televisions it has in relation to its population. Swedes will spend more money per person on holidays than any other person in Europe. Of interest here, too, is the Swedish government operates one of the most far-reaching social security systems in the world. The government provides the education and largely free medical service. It pays pensions to the elderly, widows and orphans. After most Swedes retire, they receive annual pensions of about 60 percent of their average earnings during their 15 highest-paid years. The government also provides health insurance and financial aid for housing.

AFTER SAILING ACROSS THE NORTH ATLANTIC,
AL, BOB AND LEO GO TO THE LIBRARY

DO YOU HAVE ANYTHING ON RAPE AND PILLAGE?

We three were soon off to locate a big book store to find something to read in English. We would be tied up in a marina for the next two days, so we could shower, buy groceries, more diesel and maybe a treat or two. During our first evening here it was decided we deserved a good restaurant meal. Earlier we had met a lovely girl who suggested a certain restaurant she figured we'd find interesting. Thanks to her directions, we found the place without any trouble (actually she took us to the front door, and then she headed back to where she started from about 15 minutes back). For her kindness we mentioned she should have dinner with us, but she had to be elsewhere. What greeted us first inside the restaurant was an absolutely monster of a pool in the middle of a large room, but only about 15 inches deep. Decorated inside the pool were a couple of lighthouses, some rocks, sand dunes, markers, a small island, buoys, a reef or two, and other stuff. The restaurant tables were all around the pool's edge. The kitchen door was at the far end of the pool where all the model boats were moored to the wharf. The boats were all operated with a hand-held remote, and every table had its own remote for your boat, be it a freighter, a shrimp boat, coast guard, whatever. All were different but all had a flat deck. Just before your order was ready, they would start you off by practising (learning) how to bring the salt and pepper across the water to your table. Then you'd send the boat over for your drinks. Some of the patrons would go up on the rocks or run aground. That's when the cook, with a very long telescopic pole, would pull you off.

Now, this is the good part. Whenever the food order was ready for a table, the cook would put a tape into the machine that played ocean sounds, starting with a big diesel engine, then seagulls, a foghorn in the distance and more seagulls, while the diesel seemed to get louder as it approached your table. The menu was all seafood. The evening was a first for us, and a complete success. By the way, much later on during the trip we were in thick fog somewhere in the Baltic sea, and we heard a deep-throated sound of a diesel engine getting closer and closer and louder and louder. Leo chimed in, "It's about time, here come the salt and pepper."

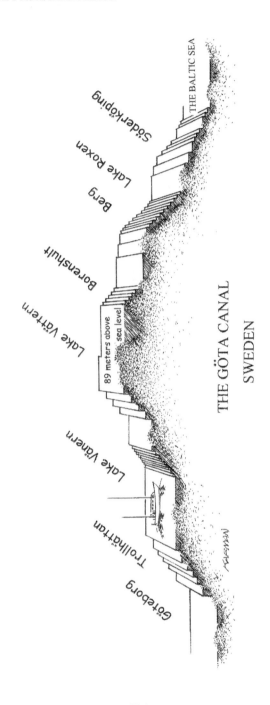

THE BALTIC SEA

Söderköping

Lake Roxen

Berg

Borenshult

Lake Vättern

89 meters above
sea level

Lake Vänern

Trollhättan

Göteborg

THE GÖTA CANAL

SWEDEN

I believe the first lock we went through was at Lilla Edet, the first lock to be built in Sweden. The Trollhattan canal locks that came along next were the most impressive, consisting of four locks covering a distance of 32 meters in water level. This is a commercial affair, set up for large ships. It is wide and it's deep. When comparing this to the locks in the Caledonian canal in Scotland, it is clear the Swedish locks are well looked after (money doesn't seem to be a problem). Everything is operated remotely, supervised by TV cameras, and controlled by lights. You soon get used to the traffic lights on the locks, bridges and the canal itself. You really have no other choice but to learn, and quickly. In the locks, a different technique is used compared to the Caledonian canal. Here they have bollards (a steel rod) set into the wall at about five-foot vertical intervals, and you must get a rope onto these. As you rise or fall you put a second rope on the next bollard going up or down, releasing the previous rope. The drop is too great to leave ropes in place to retrieve later. There is also the odd ladder (if you can find one) where you can use the rungs. Best thing if you have a choice is to aim for a ladder and put the stern rope on a rung and bow rope on a bollard.

Believe me, when that water is let in or out, it is done in a hurry, so there is no time for mistakes. I prefer the water going out; it feels a little more gentle. When they let the water come in, they will quite often let it in too quickly, thereby giving you a whirlpool effect. So do your best not to drop a line. If you did, I promise you, you and other boaters would not be happy.

Most locks are open from 8 a.m. to 8 p.m., with one hour for lunch. We anchored one night in the Vänern, where we met up with, not one, but two of the most beautiful home-made boats I'd seen in a long time. Each boat had two men on board, who were on a little holiday. You could tell immediately they were professional people, successful at whatever they did. What is more important, they invited us aboard one of the boats for dinner with the best of drinks and gourmet food. An interesting part of the evening was listening to their side about taxes and government. In Sweden, the basic outcome of all this was, that they can afford it and life is wonderful. In the following days we were out of the Vänern and into our way to the Vättern (another big lake), 89 metres above sea level.

The Vättern is Sweden's second largest lake., Though there was much to look at, we kept on moving to make up time. Along the way, not too sure where it happened, we were heading for one of the locks up ahead under power, when Leo put the Tullen Tie into reverse to slow down, but nothing happened. Leo, thinking quickly, rather than running into the lock gate (door), ran the Tullen Tie into the mud. The universal joint broke in half. The universal is similar to a large grapefruit in size, only made of a very hard rubber with a steel plate on either side. On the one side, the steel plate is bolted to the drive shaft that the propeller is attached to. The other side is bolted to the engine transmission. This very hard rubber ball had broken in half. It looked the same as if you had taken an apple, and with two hands broke it in two. This bit of bad luck happened in the canal where (of course) there wasn't a dealer around for hundreds of miles. We now put the two halves together and, with the help of a lot of thin boat line, tied the works into a big ball. On top of that went a makeshift clamp. We carried on, but all too often had to stop and re-tie the whole works.

This was okay for a short time, but it definitely had be repaired properly.

At Borensberg is a manually operated lock. After all the experience in the Caledonian canal this was not a problem. At Berg we encountered a 15-lock system, like huge steps in a row. Lake Roxen is 33 metres above sea level, whereas Lake Vättern holds the title at 89 metres. Finally, a set of nine locks took us into Söderköping, a good-sized town dating back to the 13th century. Söderköping is a beautiful and picturesque small town that can be found just south of Norrköping. If you were to look at a map of Sweden you'd notice many Swedish cities end in köping; another is Linköping. Evidently, a "köping" is an old Swedish saying for a market town. The term market town is no longer used and most köpings have since grown to a larger city status. The name Söderköping comes from the word "söder," meaning south, and "köping" from the word market town.

Being a Sunday, with most shops closed, we had no choice but to sit in the cockpit and have a look at the marina. On another boat nearby (talk about luck) we met Ingmar Johannson (not the boxer). Ingmar joined us on the Tullen Tie for drinks and assured us to not worry about the universal joint because he'd help find someone to repair it. On this same day, we were surprised to see, walking across the boat yard in a baby-blue summer suit, a squat little figure carrying two large paper bags full of bottles. Leo looked up first and immediately said, "God dammit, it looks like the kangaroo! Son-of-a-bitch, it is, it's Ronnie MacDonald." It wasn't the hamburger clown. This Ronnie MacDonald, an Australian, was Leo's friend from Toronto. Ronnie, in his lifetime, has never really worked hard at anything, but he has a gift.

He is sort of a wheeler-dealer and his expertise was moving money. If someone had money to invest, he helped move it to someone who needed money, and as it went by, took a piece. I had met Ronnie before, just briefly in Toronto at one of the going-away parties for Leo. You couldn't miss him, He was short, drove up in a white Cadillac and had a baby-blue suit on. And here he was in the Göteborg canal in the same baby-blue suit.

Our first question: "How the hell did you ever find us?" First he phoned almost all the customs people in Ireland with the same question: "Has a yellow sailboat from Canada called Tullen Tie gone through the locks here?" Of course not. We never went into Ireland. Then he guessed we must be headed for Scotland, and would possibly go through the Caledonian canal. He finally got an answer from the lock keeper in Inverness, saying that the Tullen Tie had been there and gone, reporting on the time we left, Ronnie figured by this time we must be somewhere in Sweden on the Göteborg canal. He flew to Sweden and got himself an interpreter to phone lock after lock to hear if we've gone through yet, or not. Eventually he heard we were in Söderköping, and were still there because of motor trouble. He hired a car, went to the liquor store and here he was.

I had never had a drink of Calvados before. In those two brown paper bags with many bottles were two bottles of a brandy called Calvados. Ronnie, of course, gave me the history of these two French bottles from Normandy. We tasted, and I've been sold ever since. Like anything wonderful, it's not cheap. Sweden is lovely, but you do need money to make it lovely. Eating and drinking out is rather expensive. With Ingmar on the boat now, I decided to make my world-famous spaghetti dinner. And I wouldn't have to wire down pots or lids. The boys would love it (sans hair this time).

On Monday, Ingmar drove Leo and me in his old Volvo to different boat people, for the Farymann engine part. No luck today, but maybe tomorrow will be better. In the evening, Ingmar mentioned a good place for a sauna not far from here, and the woman who owned the sauna also owed the four-story hotel and the pub. The five of us got into the Volvo feeling very mellow (mellow is a polite word). We arrived at the pub (Ronnie still in his blue suit, that's all he came with). We sat at a round table, away from the live music (a group of Swedes singing Elvis Presley songs). Ronnie was at the bar at his charming best, introducing himself to the lady owner. (To put a face to Ronnie MacDonald, he's about 5'1" in socks, nice smile, round face, fair hair and looks good in baby blue. The blue matches his eyes.) In an hour or so, Ronnie was back with good news: the sauna will be free and Ronnie is going to help the nice lady move a lot of Krona to Canada as a tax break. She smiles our way and sends over a large platter of Smorgasbord (an assortment of hot and cold foods). Ah yes! Life is good when you run with royalty. Leo and I drank to the Queen.

In the morning we found Ingmar on his own boat. Apparently, his wife had locked him out (something to do with him making new friends and arriving home in the morning). The damned universal part still wasn't available anywhere, and to order it from Germany would have taken weeks. So Ingmar took Leo to a machine shop where they made one (all steel) similar to the kind you'd find in an automobile. It worked well but it was very noisy. Because Ingmar had been such a fantastic help that we couldn't do without, and he wouldn't take anything in return, we bought a big bunch of flowers for his wife to take home, plus a nice toy for his son. Later Ingmar did say, "Things at home okay now, and she happy again." With that good news, Leo and I drank to the Queen. We drank to the Queen a lot.

Ronnie MacDonald was now with us. We had just gone through the Södertälje lock, which I think is the last and largest before Stockholm. The following morning we were in the Baltic sea, the last leg of the trip to the Gulf of Finland (and the end of the sail for Al and me). The first thing I did on this day was to give Ronnie, who was topside, a pair of my pants because he was shivering from the cold, and the blue suit needed a rest. We rolled up the pant legs and he was presentable. Unfortunately the kangaroo was very sea-sick for the next two days.

Wednesday the 28th. I had just scalded my arm with boiling water. I was going to throw some of my world-famous spaghetti in the pot when a freak wave hit. So I made pea soup instead; it's quicker. Ronnie was sitting on the port side bunk (my bunk) drinking his pea soup out of a cup when the next wave hit, sending him, the pea soup and crackers over to the starboard and splattering it on everything that Al owned and slept in. While this was going on down below, Al was topsides with Leo's sextant taking a noon shot with the good eye, when the boom came around (on the side of Al's blind eye) and gave him the biggest crack across the side of his head. The sextant went flying into the cockpit and Al went down. I heard the noise from down below and went topside to see, where I found Leo checking over his sextant to see if the mirrors and other moving parts were damaged. Meanwhile, Al was lying in the cockpit sole holding the side of his head. After getting Al back up and on his feet, Ronnie and I got him below and helped him into his pea soup bunk. Al wanted to sleep, but we had to keep him awake for fear of concussion. Our medical book said, keep the patient walking. "On a sailboat," they must be kidding. Another recommendation in the book is to keep waking the patient and keep him or her talking. Ask their name, address and so forth. In reply, Al said, "My name is Maxine," and another time "Che Guevara." I tell him "Fuck You" and go topsides; he's fine.

Because of the constant strain on the rudder in the Atlantic, the magnesium quadrant (part of the steering) finally had enough and snapped. One of the magnesium spokes had broken in two. The whole quadrant consists of four spokes. It now had to be fixed or the whole works would let go, and then it would be too late to fix anything. Fortunately, on board among all the bits and pieces we found two steel rods to use as a splint, and enough cheap u-bolts from Canadian Tire. In the meantime, we thought, a Scotch would help. Ronnie leaned over the side again. Why did I bother making pea soup?

Finland

Al was still hurting, so I took the night shift. It had been raining very hard for the past two hours and the seas were building up. Visibility was non-existent, and wearing glasses (as I do) in the rain makes matters worse. We couldn't have Andy working in these conditions because of the busy shipping lanes, traffic with fishing boats, etc. So since it was my watch, I sailed on. We figured earlier that we must be in the Gulf of Finland. At one point in the night, I started to get a little uncomfortable. For a half hour or so, I'd had a large vessel on my stern. When I changed position to port, so did he, then I changed to starboard, so did he. Now, I knew we were a tad close to the shores of Estonia, and Estonia at that time was still part of Russia. So here we were in this nightmare weather, lousy visibility, with Finland on the port side, and Russia on the starboard. Now I could see, through the rain, a silhouette of the guy in the wheel house, smoking a pipe, When I saw that, I knew the son-of-a-bitch was too close. I immediately started banging on the coach roof to wake somebody up, anybody. Ronnie MacDonald opened the hatch. I asked him to plug into the cigarette lighter the big spotlight and hand it to me and quickly. I shone the big torch on the sails to show the jerk in the wheel house that I was under sail and couldn't manoeuvre as well as he could. I also put the light on our Canadian flag. In less than a minute, he waved and altered course for Estonia. I now had a side view of him, and it definitely looked like a patrol boat.

It's not a well-known thing, and few people know this, but Finland is possibly the only country in the world to have stood up to the might of the Soviet Army, and won. In late 1939, Leo would have been 8 or 9 years old, and while the eyes of the world were elsewhere, Stalin thought it an opportune time to invade Finland's Baltic Sea ports, making them militarily useful. The Russians also believed it would be a cakewalk, but they never even reached the gates of Helsinki. Massively outnumbered, short of artillery, tanks and aircraft, the Finns fought with ingenuity and determination under the leadership of General Mannerheim, who later became president of Finland. By the time the Russians concluded a peace accord in late 1944, so they could then focus their efforts on the push to Berlin, they had lost three million men, all dead in the Finnish forest. The Finns lost just 300,000. Today, Finland's independence day is Dec. 6, the day the mighty ski soldiers known as the "white death" defeated the soldiers of mother Russia. After our episode with the patrol boat (which Leo and Al slept through), I told Leo about it and how it went. His reply, "Busy hands are happy hands."

Leo began to talk more and more about the crayfish feast we would have when we got to his mother's. The gastronomic peak of the summer is the start of the crayfish season on July 21. A neighbour of Leo's mother, a teenaged girl, was all excited because of our imminent arrival, and the young girl insisted on getting pails of crayfish. Crayfish are a fresh-water crustacean. One problem we thought we might have was getting into Helsinki at night. Apparently it is not a good idea unless you have local knowledge of the water and a safe way in. There are more than enough rocks and islands to watch for, plus the usual currents. We thought if we went in at night, we'd just follow the Silva Line in (passenger cruise ships). We didn't think we'd have a problem because they ride so deep in the water. Well, here we were going in at night following a Silva ship, but the problem is they're too fast and disappear quickly. Next, we tried to stay exactly where we were left, while we waited for another Silva Line to show. But the current had other ideas. Al kept finding an opening to go through (with his good eye) that always turned into one big long rock without an opening. Thanks to many Silva Line boats we finally motored into the downtown harbour very late. We moored for a short time at the city harbour, long enough to open the other bottle of champagne. This one was saved for the Helsinki arrival. Sadly, this too didn't travel well. We now moved Tullen Tie to an island yacht club and we enjoyed a well-deserved sleep.

In the morning, after showering and a big breakfast, Leo phoned the family. And a big family it is. They all arrived from the mainland by way of water taxi around noon. There were brothers and sisters and the many children who had never met their uncle Leo. Leo had left home about 17 years ago and had never been back. I have never seen so many people on one boat at the same time; the water line on the Tullen Tie disappeared. Not knowing the language, Ronnie, again dressed in his blues, and I stood back and watched. Putting a bit of a damper on everything, Al had all his stuff already packed two days before, and before Leo's family arrived, Al had already left the boat without a whisper. I never saw him again while I was in Helsinki.

Little by little the families started to leave, all but brother Abel. Now, we three were off to Abel's house for dinner, and what a dinner. One thing I love about travelling is the different foods and customs that people have. It's wonderful, so unlike ours. After this perfect meal with Abel and his family, the men sat, smoked and drink Aquavit. Next, and always next in a Finnish house, came the sauna. Nearly every Finn has a sauna and uses the sauna at least once a day. Men, women, boys and girls will go into the sauna together, and almost always will be naked. The sauna room is heated to 120-plus (Fahrenheit). The oven is usually filled with red-hot stones that are heated with firewood. Some of Leo's family lived in apartment buildings, where they had electric sauna ovens. It is a fact that almost every Finnish house has a sauna, and it is not considered a luxury. Typically there are three levels of sitting. The higher you sit, the hotter it is. Water is poured on the stones, creating more steam. The sauna itself doesn't get any hotter, but with the steam it feels hotter. Now came the fun part. The vihta or vasta, which is a bunch of birch twigs, with the leaves, usually warmed first with hot water before the hitting starts. We men went down to Abel's sauna with a bottle of Aquavit, everybody naked. Water was thrown on the hot rocks, we'd throw back a shot of Aquavit, lie down on a bench and let the whipping begin.

That night we didn't go back to the boat. We three (Leo, Ronnie and I) slept in a row under a big picture window in Abel's living room. At some hour in the night, Leo must have thought he was still on the boat, because he was talking very loudly in his sleep, saying things like, "There's no one at the wheel, no one's outside." I shook him a little and said, "It's okay, Al's out there," and he'd roll over and go back to sleep. It took more than a few days for all of us to adjust one way or another. Even Ronnie MacDonald, who hadn't been with us for long, soon had enough, and he certainly will never have pea soup again.

After a hot breakfast that Abel's wife put together, Leo's brother, Olli, drove up in his pride and joy, a Saab automobile, and drove us to Leo's 86-year-old mother's farm. Just as we drove in, she was on her way into the sauna. The farm needed work. Since she lived there alone and the farming stopped years ago, things had deteriorated and stayed that way. The house itself was exceptionally clean and well looked after by Leo's mother. Leo's mother had already prepared a bed for Ronnie and me in the wood shed. She made a mattress on the ground with straw and put new white sheets on top with big pillows. I must say, I hadn't had a better sleep in a long time. As for Ronnie MacDonald, he was awake the whole night. Being strictly a big city boy, he felt uncomfortable on the ground. He believed mice would try to get into the bed. I did my best to convince him this wouldn't happen, because they don't like you. I don't think I convinced him, because the following evening he wore his blue pants to bed, after tucking them into his socks first.

The next day was crayfish day. Neighbours came from all over to see Leo and, of course, to eat crayfish. Naturally, everybody brought Aquavit. The Finns have a thing about keeping the bottle on the floor beside a table leg. It's never on the table.

Olli was a little guy, but wiry and tough. In the war with the Russians, he was shot in the throat on a battlefield and left for dead. He lay unconscious for nobody knows how long. His fellow soldiers went back to their lines, leaving Olli where he dropped. Later on, six Russian soldiers arrived back to this spot where the many bodies lay. Assuming everybody to be dead, they made a fire to warm themselves. Later Olli came to, lying on top of his gun, got up and shot the six. His next problem was getting himself back to his people. When he got close enough to his lines, the Finns started shooting. He couldn't make himself heard because his throat was shot away, so he did the next best thing. He struggled all the way around the rear of the camp and came in the back, and spent the rest of the war in hospital. Now, these many years later, Olli does speak (in English too) but has difficulty vocalizing and making himself understood. Like many of us when we get older, Olli's eyesight isn't what it once was. He does drive too fast, and when a car in front comes into view, for Olli, it comes a little too late. All of a sudden the car would be in front, Olli would apply the brakes and we'd all stand up. Then it would be back with the gas peddle to the floor and we'd sit down again until another car came into view, the brakes again and we'd all stand up again. We did this all the way to the farm.

The day after the farm visit, we visited three different relatives' homes in the same day. And had to have a sauna in each. I have never in my life had three saunas on the same day. Even my eyes were shiny and sparkling. The following day I was back on the boat and packed my things. I intended to fly out the next morning if I could arrange a flight. I planned on spending the evening just sitting in the cockpit and reminiscing about everything that went by these last two months. But as it happened, Ronnie MacDonald said, "I'm going to put on my blue suit and buy you a drink or two at The Klippan (island) next door." To get to The Klippan, you had to go by tender to the mainland first, then change to another tender to go to The Klippan. I'm not sure if it was a weekend or what day it was, but it was a dance night. Ronnie and I got a good table and watched the pretty girls starting to come in. The music got going and so did Ronnie. He was already dancing with a girl a little shorter than he was, and a bit rounder. He never did make it back to our table. Every now and then, though, I would see them twirl by.

I sat alone for a short time and then moved myself to another table with two Finnish girls. One was named Rhitta and the other's name I don't remember. I heard their stories, how they went to Mikonos every year for the holidays, and about a Greek drink called Raki. The only drink I enjoyed from Greece was Retsina, and some of their white wines. The talk got around to other drinks including red wines. Then the other girl (I shall call her the big girl) ordered a red wine for each of us and said, "I want to show you something I learned in Mikonos." She drank her wine, and then taking the goblet in her right hand, crushed it. I do mean crushed it; it literally blew itself into little glass pieces. Not one scratch or sign of blood, nothing. The waiter came running over with a worried look. The big girl paid for two more empty glasses after explaining what she did. In the palm of her hand, while staring me right in the eye and with a smile, another glass was gone. I thought, "Boy!" Do I know how to pick a table? Thank goodness, Rhitta, the one I preferred over the two, was the more delicate. Later in the evening, Ronnie came over to the table and said that he and "her roundness" were going to the boat. I told him, I'd whistle a tune from the *Nutcracker* suite before I stepped on board. And not to worry, I'd be quite late.

As it turned out, it was getting quite late. The dance people announced on the PA system that the last tender for the night would be leaving for the mainland in 15 minutes. On the ride to the mainland,

Rhitta and I agreed to see each other the next evening. My immediate problem, though, was how to get to the other island where Tullen Tie was moored, since that tender had stopped running two hours ago. I thought maybe I could swim across, but in this current I realized that would be stupid, plus I could end up heading for the Baltic. On top of that, I am not a strong swimmer. I did have a lot of Raki in me, and stupidly that told me I could do it. While I was contemplating my dilemma, Rhitta was up front talking to the tender driver, and I noticed she very secretly slipped him some money. When everyone got off the tender, Rhitta told me to stay put because he would take me back to my island.

I was whistling "I've Got A Lovely Bunch Of Coconuts" when I climbed back on the Tullen Tie. Ronnie still had his company; they were both in my bed. With the table lowered in my bunk it became a larger bed for two. Now, at this hour, there was no way for anyone to get off the island. Since Leo was staying with family, I crawled into his quarter berth. I pretended I was asleep, and they pretended they were on their honeymoon. The only English Ronnie's date knew was, "I Luf You, Ron" and she also repeated over and over, "More Ron, please more Ron." Ronnie was now pleading, "I can't, go to sleep, please, go to sleep." To save embarrassment for everybody, I pretended to snore. God knows, there was no way to sleep. I gather when Ronnie couldn't deliver anymore, she started to cry and wanted to go home. Ron began to call over to me for help, but I just snored louder. He was trying to tell his date that the tender was not running and she couldn't get off the island. Of course she didn't understand a word and this went on for most of the night.

Ron's lady-friend was to come over the next night again, so I got a room at the Hotel Hispanola for the next two nights. I phoned Rhitta at work and explained why I decided to check in there, and suggested we stay in that evening and possibly send out for a pizza or Chinese food. Not knowing what was available in Helsinki I figured we could sort that out later. She agreed and I went to the liquor store for a bottle of wine. All they had was Henkell Trocken, the German sparkling wine on special. If you purchased the 1.5 litre bottle, it came with a candle in a crystal base, which gave a lovely atmosphere to the evening. The next evening, our last together, I bought another candle in the crystal base with the bottle. I said my good-byes to Rhitta, and the first thing in the morning I got on an Air Canada flight at 9:10 a.m. for a flight to London and on to Toronto.

Flying home

Sitting on the plane gives you plenty of time to think. You have mixed thoughts about everything; what you should do now, or shouldn't do now, what you just went through, was it long enough? What would you do differently? Would you do it again? What do you miss the most about what just happened? The truth was that I wouldn't change it for the world, except next time I definitely would bring more wool clothing. None of this trip could have taken place without Leo; his dream, his boat, his trip and, most important, it included me.

The trip from Sydney, N.S., where I got on the Tullen Tie to Tobermory, Scotland, took 29 days, in which I lost 27 pounds. It certainly wasn't from dieting, because we ate very well. It probably was because of a lack of sleep, too much exercise with the sails, storms and everything else that goes with getting across the North Atlantic Ocean. I had never felt better and more fit in my life. When I got back to Toronto, It was only a matter of a few days before I started to feel like I'd never been away, and I didn't like that. I went back to my little studio and phoned clients at the agencies. Some said, "It's nice to have you back." Others said, "Oh, were you away?" What I couldn't hide from was the fact that I had, like everybody, expenses and obligations to keep. Little by little I got back to work and life went on, until Leo phoned again.

This time he was taking it slowly in the Mediterranean Sea. He phoned, either from Ibiza (an island of Spain), a favourite place of mine, or from Majorca, wanting me to join him for the sail home in the spring. I've been unhappy with myself ever since, for having to say no.

But looking back, I had no choice. These opportunities don't happen very often, if at all. There was just no possible way I could go. When Leo finally did get back to Toronto, someone threw a party for him, and at the party his exact words to me were, "Sailing back in the lower latitudes was the icing on the cake! never once changed sail in the crossing, sat in my underwear and put on sunblock every day."

Leo did add that the new crew he found (from an ad he put on the yacht club bulletin board) wasn't exactly what he was hoping for, as he found out later. An Englishman and a Dutchman. The Tullen Tie had pulled in somewhere for supplies, and Leo went ashore alone. He didn't get too far from the boat when he realized he didn't have his pipe (and he doesn't go anywhere without his pipe). When he got back the boys weren't on deck. He went below for the pipe and found the crew busy pulling their pants up really quickly. Leo and the gay crew were in the Straits of Gibraltar, with the next landfall to be St. Thomas in the Caribbean, and after that a northerly direction and home. Now, a big mistake on Leo's part (being skipper) was that he hadn't checked to see if his crew had passports, and if they were still valid.

The Tullen Tie arrived and tied up in St. Thomas. The custom is that only the skipper of a vessel goes ashore first, with his and the passports of the crew. Usually after that, a customs person will come to the ship and do an inspection. You guessed right, Tom, the Englishman didn't have a passport. Leo had to make an appointment to see the magistrate of the island. An appointed date was made, and in the meantime, no one was allowed off the boat. On the appointed day, Leo and Tom went to the government building for the interview. The hall was packed with people waiting in line, all with their own serious problems—real estate, child support, divorce—all there to see one magistrate. After only a few minutes in line, Tom hollered out to the room, "What the fuck are we standing in line for behind all these N– – – ers?" Out of nowhere two big uniformed police officers showed up and escorted Leo and Tom back to the boat, with a stern message of, "Don't even think of putting one foot on the dock, and especially don't consider sailing out of here after dark. We have a fast patrol boat fitted out with plenty of artillery."

After another three days of sitting, Leo finally got his meeting with the magistrate—and alone. He explained how he had met the Englishman, that he needed a crew and that he stupidly took him on without checking his credentials. The magistrate kindly agreed to let Leo and crew leave. If he would like to stay a few days in St. Thomas, the magistrate added, Leo should sail out about 20 miles, throw Tom overboard and return if he wished. Leo did make it home, and did throw Tom overboard, but on shore somewhere.

Leo sold the Tullen Tie soon after and I was with him when the new owner took possession of the boat. What I remember most is that after handing over the keys to the new owner it was a long walk from the pier back to the car. He was quiet, and not once did he look back. Leo has since re-married and settled down on a lovely island in B.C. called Marshall Island, in a little spot called Sointula. Al retired from insurance, re-married and moved to Brighton, Ont., and moved again since. Al sailed a Tanzer 27 for a while but has since downsized to something smaller. I too sold my 30 ft. Excalibur (steel) and downsized to 17 ft. and sold that too. I re-married and we're now living in Nanaimo, B.C. (and loving it).

I still keep in touch with Al and Leo, and at one time hoped that when Leo got home, we three old friends from the Tullen Tie could sail out to the middle of Lake Ontario and just sit and stay a few days, drink, sleep, reminisce and dig into my world-famous spaghetti dinner. But that never happened and never will. After all these years, the two of them have not said one word to each other. What a bloody shame.

I've tried not to dwell too much on the sea legends, sea language, superstitions of sea monsters, giant squids or octopus that can pull down a ship, or beliefs that people have in mermaids or sirens, but to stick to the real sea and the power of it.

Most of us prefer to stay on land, knowing more about it makes it feel safer. It doesn't move, although occasionally it does. On land, we are told daily what the weather will be and do, and we can prepare for it. But the sea can be calm, placid, a pretty blue and quite tranquil until it decides to move. I used to stare at the horizon from the deck of Tullen Tie and see that the rim of the earth drops off on both sides of you, proving the earth is really round. This same ocean that just an hour previously was the most peaceful, relaxing, the most serene thing you've ever laid eyes on, wakes up with a roar and screaming winds; the swells turn into mountains of water with white horses' tails breaking on every crest. Later, after the storm has left its mark and blown itself out, the sea takes on the colour of a beautiful steel blue grey, only to be replaced with fog. By midnight you can have a gale blowing, the sound of which is so loud, nobody on deck will hear you. In the morning you're becalmed, with not a whisper or breath of air.

This is the fascination of the sea. It is completely unpredictable, and at the same time, the most fascinating, horrendous thing you ever laid eyes on. Let's face it, that's why we went out there in the first place.

Appendix A: Planning your trip

I'm sure some of you have heard the saying, "Sailing can be like standing under a cold shower tearing up $100 bills." On any trip away from land, the farther out you go the more important the preparation should be. Of course, everybody should start with a list. A typical list usually reads: What's this going to cost? Provisioning: meals, supplies, storage, etc. Foul weather gear: This includes a lot of stuff like footwear, accessories and goes on and on. Government: Customs. Find out about immigration. Computer & Internet: E-mail access. Health supplies For heavy-weather sailing: Reefing, sea-anchor, etc. Navigation: Charts, coastal and offshore. Offshore insurance: You probably can't afford it. Self-steering: Auto pilot or wind vane. Weather: Plan a passage plan. If possible, get a piracy report for the water you plan to be in.

Obviously, the list will go on and on, and for each of these few things I've written here, you will need columns of details. One of the very important pleasures involves staying warm and dry. Think of surfing down 40-ft. waves at 20 knots, plus the cold water coming over the deck again and again. I had top and bottom underwear that resembled a fisherman's net. This "netting" keeps the outer clothing away from the body and breathes. Believe me, it works. Stay away from cotton clothing. Cotton will soak up sweat and stay damp for the entire trip. There is a thermal stretch fabric on the market that is apparently quite good. The material moves moisture away from the skin and traps air in the weave to keep you warm. Now, the mid layer of clothing is really the insulating layer.

When you're out shopping, look for fleece-lined jackets or vests. Fleece pants are a must, if you can find any. Myself, I believe in wool for almost everything. Wool can be wet, but you can still feel warm. Last, and equally important is, the outside waterproof layer. Insist on a breathable, fully waterproof lined jacket with a hood, and with inner cuffs and outer wrist tabs to help keep water out. If available, get one with fleece-lined hand-warmer pockets and visibility reflective strips front and back. If you're a warm-weather sailor get a second jacket without fleece lining. But again, make sure it's breathable, light and waterproof. Invest in a good pair of waterproof breathable boots (you'll be glad you did). A strobe light and whistle are also a must for your life jacket.

The Food: The supply of food was certainly well put together by Ruth on the Tullen Tie. Since it turned out to be such a cold trip and nothing spoiled, more eggs would have been nice, also potatoes, sausages, bacon in tins, more fruit choices in tins. The reason I mention this last item is that, because of the constant taste of salt on your lips, anything with a sweet taste was the most wonderful experience of the day. The brown sugar was a big hit. We could have used a jar or two of candies (I would take plastic over glass where possible.) Jars of toffees, corn syrup, maple syrup and that kind of thing would have been heaven. We would have liked more hot cereal choices. The same goes for different tins of pasta sauces for my world-famous spaghetti. In tropical waters, some sailors dip the eggs in hot wax so they last longer, but as I said before, in this cold weather that was not a problem. I only wished we'd had more eggs.

Taking a room full of food is not necessary, and you don't have the space anyway. When you're shopping for the boat, don't go to the supermarket after a big dinner, because then you'll sail away with a few cereals and beer nuts. Another good piece of advice is, don't scrub and wash the fruits and vegetables before packing. This speeds up the spoilage. Store all your loose foods in airtight plastic containers, or in some cases air containers (where needed) with lids on everything. Keep garlic in a cool, dark place. The bilge is like your home basement, so it's a good spot for drinks, butter in plastic containers (but margarine does last longer). Think plastic for everything except maybe the egg container. Cardboard is more forgiving, but keep it away from your bilge pump.

Take Worcestershire sauce, Tabasco sauce, soy sauce, balsamic vinegar, olive oil to enrich your soup. Pack some hard cheeses and a hand grinder for the spaghetti. A note about cheese: To prevent cheese mould, take ordinary kitchen paper and moisten with cider vinegar and re-wrap in a breathable bag, and then keep in a cool, dark place. Cured ham or an all-beef salami hung somewhere below can make a nice treat. Cheeses, margarine, butter, all in plastic will keep 10 to 15 days, if you're in the Northern Atlantic they'll last a lot longer. Virgin olive oil is especially good to have on board for many things,. Bring some spices, buy lots of rice, couscous, and don't forget the plastic containers. You don't want a 10-pound bag of rice in your bilge pump. In canned meats, you can have Irish stews, corned beef, wieners in a tin. You can even buy a chicken in a can. Jams and peanut butter, honey is wonderful, coffee, tea, hot chocolate, soups in cans and instant powered soups, Rye Krisps will last you for a circumnavigation, sardines, herrings, onions, nuts, cookies, the list goes on and on. Forget the hand soaps; if you're sailing in salt water, they do nothing for you. Use liquid detergents for hands, face and your dishes. Single-ply (layer) toilet paper is best. Don't load up with curry if you're a little delicate. The stove needs some respect. Some like to tie the pots to the stove, others don't. I prefer to tie the pots and the lids. I figured it better for me to jump out of harm's way and not have the pot follow. The stove, of course, is gimbaled. When not in use we always kept it in one position with a hook; That way, it prevents it from trying to destroy itself from crashing back and forth continuously in rough weather.

Don't forget the rule: One hand for yourself, one hand for the boat. On the Tullen Tie, we had two propane tanks. The same white tanks everyone uses at home for the barbeque. The spare was well tied to the steering pedestal. The other was bolted down in the rear lazarette, which was well vented to the outside of the boat. It was only turned on when the stove was needed. After each and every usage, the tank valve was always closed first; this way the propane line will be empty of propane to the stove. The stove is turned off after the flame goes out. This is probably enough about provisions and clothing and I know if someone is really serious about an offshore trip, there are books galore on what to take, eat, wear, and other subjects.

Appendix B:

Some of my favourite sea-faring books

Probably the first great sailor who left shore single-handed was Joshua Slocum, a New Englander, who was the first to circumnavigate the globe in a small sailboat. The Americans have adopted him as one of their own, but in truth, Joshua was born on Brier Island, Nova Scotia, in 1844. In other false news, some books will have you believe that Sir Francis Chichester was the first to circumnavigate the globe. This is not so. His claim to fame for this feat came many years after Joshua's, and Chichester had the newest and best of sailing items at his disposal: things like roller reefing and electronics galore to relate wind changes and weather patterns. What helped get Chichester knighted was his age of 63, which of course is very admirable indeed. Instead of all the modern conveniences of today, the only item Joshua had on board was a sextant, and a wind-up clock with only one hand.

I'm sure that within a few miles of your home there's a dreamer who's in the process of building his boat with thoughts that, one day, he too will have his adventure of a lifetime. These minute shipyards are usually in a barn, a shed, a backyard or some sort of temporary structure consisting of framework covered in plastic building material. Naturally, the size of your boat will also dictate where it can be built. One of my friends, Dieter, spent a few years building his dream, a 42-ft. steel hull design by Thomas Colvin. Dieter was renting space in a field with a lot of other dreamers at the Toronto lakeshore. Another, Geoffrey Turner, who for years shared a studio with me, was working on his 36 ft. wooden double ender in a three-car garage he was renting.

Every penny Geoffrey earned went into the boat, and a beautiful ocean-going vessel it turned out to be--all wood and varnish, it would most certainly make anyone proud. The hand-poured lead ballast alone weighed 9,000 lbs. The sails cost $12,000, and apparently that was a wholesale price thanks to a friend. As they say, this was a "one-off" boat, gleaming varnish, bronze ports and fittings, built to be very personal.

While all this is going on, thousands of us (who are not building) spend countless hours looking at ads in every yachting magazine, sending for folders, going to boat shows, prowling around marinas, yacht clubs, attending boating lectures and in general just hanging around boats all the time. I know, I for one would even spend my winters wandering around boat yards, only to look at boat hulls covered in tarps. The dream of far away places never stops. Most of us will never leave our own province. Geoffrey named his boat "Daydream," an appropriate moniker. Others will keep the dream a secret for fear it doesn't happen. That way, there is no embarrassment, and one will never have to explain. The same applies to departure times. Once you've committed yourself, you better be ready to go, because you'll be bombarded with, "When are you going?" "What went wrong?" "Why are you still here?" So, tell friends, relatives, whoever, only a week before, and then slip away.

In the meantime, for me, I get great enjoyment and a thrill in just reading about others who got away. Their sea stories, adventures, trying to analyse the voyages of the people who have succeeded, and others who failed with their voyages, and why. On top of this, some have never been heard from again. What sort of sailors take to this kind of life, to be faced with storms, cyclones, hurricane-force winds, sometimes being dismasted, taking on water? Who knows? Are they romantics, adventurers, heroes or just a bunch of dropouts, bums not willing to work? Or are they a little "tetched?" In truth, it's all of these things. This naturally includes men and women, married, single, it doesn't matter. Sometimes, it's just couples who need to go blue water cruising as a way of life.

Eric and Susan Hiscock have cruised extensively on all their boats, all named Wanderer, numbered from One, Two, Three up to Wanderer IV, built of steel and 49 ft. overall. They also must have missed Wanderer Three a lot because it was their home for 17 years. They went to sea for tranquillity and the freedom of long ocean passages, not like some others who go to sea for the publicity and glory, or prize money such as the likes of Chichester or Chay Blyth. These last two and many others are definitely into another kind of sailing.

Worthwhile reading on this subject includes anything by Miles and Beryl Smeeton. Living on a farm in British Columbia, the Smeetons felt homesick for their native England, took a year's absence and went home for a visit. While visiting, they saw a beautiful Bermudian ketch with the name Tzu Hang, and it was for sale. Years later they discovered that the name Tzu Hang meant "The wooden ship of Kwan Yin, or Kannon Sama," the names of the goddess in Chinese and Japanese. Miles and Beryl had never sailed before, but bought the boat anyway and sailed Tzu Hang back to British Columbia via the Azores, the West Indies, Panama and the west coast of North America.

In 1955 they sold the farm and with Clio, their only daughter, headed for Australia. The journey that followed was enough for a very fat book. Clio was sent back to England and John Guzzwell (another sailor) became a crew member. Guzzwell was a very able seaman who owned a well-known boat called Trekka. Nearing the horn, a giant wave pitch-poled Tzu Hang, throwing Beryl into the sea and dismasting the ship. The doghouse top was gone and the inside of the boat was a broken mess. Somehow Smeeton and Guzzwell rescued Beryl, who was badly injured. After setting up a jury rig they slowly made their way to a Chilean port. This kind of terrible mishap would happen again to Miles and Beryl when they were alone on Tzu Hang; Again, mast gone, hatch gone, broken spars, lost rigging, etc., and still they carried on.

If I had to pick but one name that I have enjoyed reading about most, it would have to be the Frenchman, Bernard Moitessier. I've admired his calmness, his logic on sailing, the many good books he's written--I guess it all boils down to his general lifestyle. In early March 1969, Moitessier, on board his 39-ft. steel ketch named Joshua (after Joshua Slocum), had just rounded Africa's Cape Horn and was now ready for the long uphill trip to jolly old England. In doing so, he would finish first in The Sunday Times Golden Globe Race around the world. Joshua was far ahead of every other entry and if nothing went wrong, winning would be a sure thing. With winning, Moitessier would receive the 25,000 pounds Sterling cash prize, the trophy, adulation and a good chance for another million dollars in endorsements, books, public appearances, and of course beating the English. For Moitessier, as for the others, it was a hard race, but his mind was made up. He changed course and headed east along the Roaring Forties and had now crossed his outbound track. Moitessier was now on a second non-stop circumnavigation, and in doing this was out of the Times race. He already had a letter written for his publisher, which he hoped to deliver via a passing ship. He insisted he was of sound mind and his letter apparently said, "Why am I doing this? Imagine yourself in the forest of the Amazon. Suddenly you come upon a small temple of an ancient lost civilization. You are not simply going to go back and say, 'I have found a temple, a civilization nobody knows.' You're going to stay there and try to decipher it. Then you discover that 100 km. on is another temple, only it's the main temple. Would you return?" Yet, for Moitessier to have not done what he did, would have been out of character for him. So, with that in mind, he turned around and sailed back to Tahiti.

A good friend of Bernard Moitessier at the time was Jean-Michel Barrault, who spent five months alone at sea. He was a man who faced a multiplicity of technical problems but had shown his physical stamina. He had run risks that most would not have faced, but above all had sought his own truth, had silenced the sounds of the world and talked to the waves, with the flying spume, the torn clouds, the albatross and the petrels. He had lived in the Roaring Forties, not as a stranger but deep in the beauty of the ocean. "I shall always cherish the memory of these gigantic waves, of this incredible beautiful sea," he wrote. What was waiting for him in Plymouth, England, was the other side of glory, the tumultuous crowds, the lack of respect for the individual, prying, the rape of his realized dream. He was not ready to accept this.

Moitessier's first boat was a Siamese Junk called "Marie-Thérèse." On board, he found himself 85 days out of Singapore on the Indian Ocean, near the Chagos reefs, bound for nowhere. He had no chronometer and no transistor radio, which might have helped him find his longitude. But, he was happy and learning. He was young, healthy, a swimmer and he spoke French, English, German, Dutch, Vietnamese and Siamese. Also, he had a talent for writing and much more. One night, with a lurch, he was thrown against a bulkhead. Marie-Therese was aground on a reef in three feet of water. Moitessier swam ashore and in the early morning was back with a large crew of natives with plans to rescue the Marie-Thérèse, but through the night she had disappeared into the sea without a trace. Being stranded and broke, he now wrote for a local newspaper so he could eat and make some money to buy his next boat. He also worked as a commercial fisherman with scuba gear until, in January 1953, a shark took a piece of his foot off. After healing for a month he was able to walk again and went back to work. His bank account started to look better, so he started work on Marie-Thérèse II, a 28-ft. double ender ketch rigged. In 1955 he was ready to go again.

He sailed for a few years to get used to the new boat and get a little money together, then around 1958 he was off again on his way to Grenada. He fell asleep at the tiller, woke with a violent crash and Marie-Thérèse II was on the rocks. This time, he was stranded and broke in the West Indies, half a world away from the previous sinking. Moitessier had never in his life been so totally depressed. Now he was spending most of his time in saloons begging for drinks. In this state, and penniless, he was seriously thinking of building a boat out of paper. The local newspaper was to supply all the paper. He was already started on this, when luckily he got a job on a freighter bound for Europe.

Eventually he got himself back to Paris, worked as a boat salesman and finished his first book. The book turned out to be a best-seller. The book also made a lot of money and established Moitessier as one of the best blue water sailors of the world.

A successful manufacturer, one Mr. J. Fracaul, who employed 250 workers in a metal working company and happened to be a sailor himself, invited Moitessier to visit his plant, and offered to build Moitessier a boat for just the cost of material. This new boat was now a 39-ft. steel hull called "Joshua." In the few years that followed, Moitessier met up with his old childhood sweetheart, Françoise, who now had three children from a previous marriage. They married and he was suddenly a father of three. The kids went to a boarding school, and Moitessier and Françoise set sail in 1963 for Tahiti. Later they travelled through the West Indies, and still later took on Cape Horn once again-- without any mishaps. A good read is Moitessier's second book titled "Cape Horn: The Logical Route."

There are so many other good books to read about interesting sailors, male and female, and to try and list them all would take forever, so here I'll only mention a handful. Naomi James was one of the first women to sail single-handedly around the world, with just two years of sailing experience. David Lewis spent years studying the Polynesian explorers, and using the same techniques. Lewis was also the first person to sail solo to Antarctica. Margaret and Hal Roth have sailed the world over and you could never meet a nicer couple. They, too, have published numerous books. They've been shipwrecked and carried on like the others before them.

An interesting book of Nicholas Tomalin, "The Strange Last Voyage of Donald Crowhurst," is a must read. This story centres on the 1968 Golden Globe race. Donald Crowhurst, sailing a trimaran, tries one of the biggest hoaxes in marine history. Instead of sailing around the world, he stays put in the middle of the Atlantic Ocean. An ambitious electrical engineer, he radios back false reports of his progress. Partway down the Atlantic he realizes his boat, Teignmouth Electron, is not worthy of sailing around the Cape of Good Hope. After 111 days of radio silence he suddenly makes contact again to announce he's rounded the cape and was now in the Atlantic. Others in the race, thinking he's going to win, start to push themselves harder. Crowhurst was not exceptionally skilled as a sailor but he needed the money badly. His plan was to come in second place behind the winner. The winner did come along but his boat was wrecked and Crowhurst was then in place to win. Finally Crowhurst, feeling very guilty about his deceit, didn't finish but instead stepped off his boat and was never seen again. The boat was later found floating in the Atlantic and, with notes left on board detailing a full confession--a lot of it complete gibberish, and raving on with depression and guilt about his fraud, it recreates his tormented and troubled voyage. This book, a true "sailor's classic," is still in print. It's impossible not to feel some sort of compassion for the man and for what he went through. The winner of the 1968 Golden Globe race was Robin Knox Johnson, who, after hearing of Crowhurst's financial problems and death, donated his winnings to Crowhurst's wife and children.

John Rousmaniere book "Fastnet, Force 10," is set as the standard for all sailing disaster stories. What makes this a great read on the Sydney Hobart tragedy, is that Rousmaniere is not only a wonderful writer, he was in the race. The tally at the end: 15 dead, 24 crew-members abandoned ship, five yachts went down, and 136 sailors were rescued. Rousmaniere does his best to explain what caused the tragedy and how maybe, just maybe, this could have been avoided.

Then there is "The Incredible Voyage" by Tristan Jones. I first encountered it when I was working in Detroit at an art studio for about two months, retouching car photos for the new folders that come out every year. The work was good and the money was better. But the evenings were long, especially when working alone every night, watching TV in a motel room. I'd swear that every evening, somewhere in the States, there is a big fire and it's always on the TV news. I drove to the mall for a change of scenery and found on display a new book titled "The Uncreditable Voyage" by a sailor named Tristan Jones. I bought the thick book and every night before going to sleep, I'd read until I nodded off. While reading one night I found myself at the part where Tristan had just taken possession of "Sea Dart," a well-used mahogany marine plywood boat a mere 20 ft. long on the waterline. He felt the price was right, the hull was sound and the boat boasted a great feature for salt water sailing: it was sheathed in 20 layers of cascomite, a silk and rubber coating that protects the bottom from the ravages of the teredo worm, a tropical borer that is the curse of wooden boats.

Sea Dart had been built in a small yard in England. I continued to read until I again dozed off. In the wee hours, because of drink, I had to go to the bathroom, and on the way back I decided to have a look outside my motel window. The first thing that went through my mind was, how much did I drink? Outside my motel window on a flat bed truck was "Sea Dart." It seemed on this day in July 1977, Tristan Jones and his Sea Dart were here on a book promotion tour. I met Tristan the following morning outside, while he was waiting for a limo to take him to some TV station for an interview. We chatted for a while until the limo pulled up and an arrogant woman rolled down her window and said, "Mr. Tristan, we're running late, let's get going." Tristan's reply, I remember, was something like, "You're late, I'm not and I'm talking to someone." With that, he kept talking to me, which made me a little uncomfortable. I politely said to Tristan, "Why don't you go, and later if you're available, we'll have a drink or two in the bar." His reply was "Good idea, but I'm not getting into the car until Miss America here calms down." We did meet in the bar, and the bugger wouldn't let me pay for any drinks.

Tristan Jones was born at sea aboard a British ship, alongside a remote island called Tristan Da Cunha. He was a wiry little man who probably didn't weigh more than 120 lb., and displayed more confidence than anyone I've ever known.

In that year when I met him, he had sailed a record 345,000 nautical miles in boats smaller than 40 ft. He has crossed the Atlantic 18 times under sail, nine times alone, and has sailed at least 180,000 miles single-handed. He once sailed from the Dead Sea to Lake Titicaca in a single voyage. To survive and carry on, he has literally hauled his tiny sloop through the South American pampas and back to the sea. Now, there are some out there who think this has been somewhat exaggerated.

I've mentioned this last part because there's more. Getting from the Pacific side to the Atlantic side through the middle of South America would have entailed a lot of physical pulling of Sea Dart through snake-infested waters. I remember Tristan telling me in the bar that evening how uncomfortable he was drinking in a room with so many green plants around. After you've read his book, I'm sure you will agree it's one hell of an adventure. By the way, on the little boat, he did take photos to confirm his stories. What an odd feeling it was, sitting in the little sloop on a flat bed truck looking at stained black and white photos of Tristan's trip. One bit of advice he gave me related to sailing in unknown waters with night arriving shortly. "If you can't arrive in daylight," he warned, "then stand off well clear and wait until dawn. After all, that's one of the things God made boats for, to wait in." He signed my book, I thanked him for the drinks and bid him good-night.

As Lin and Larry Pardey have said, "We will continue cruising for as long as it stays fun." I had the pleasure of meeting the Pardeys at a book signing and dinner in the 1980s. At the time they were into their fifth boat (all had been named Seraffyn). The Pardey's logic to sailing is not about how much expensive equipment you have on board, but whether you really need all that stuff. If a sailor relies too much on his radios, flares, radar, emergency things in general, he may be inviting disaster. Their thinking is, use your common sense because if the gadgets break down, you're finished. You've got to be knowledgeable first and take advantage of the electronics and mechanics last. An example: Do not count on your safety harness to keep you attached to the boat. Do learn first the how, why and what of not falling overboard in the first place. Of course, you definitely should have your safety harness on. Just don't count on everything being fool proof. That is all the Pardeys were trying to point out.

When I personally think back to all the trips across Lake Ontario with my good friend Geoffrey in the Scarlet Pimpernel, it makes one shudder. There were no life jackets, no radio, no compass, no flashlight, no life raft, no flares, nothing. But we had Scotch, Rum, Vodka, Coke, ice, gourmet meals and television. Mooring lines on the Pimpernel could be one piece of nylon tied to a piece of manilla rope, which was tied to a piece of yellow poly, but you never saw a prettier 28-ft. double ender on Lake Ontario. I remember one holiday with Geoffrey on his new and bigger boat called "Daydream." Dieter had joined us and we were mooring over on the American coast when a beauty of a storm came up. We had lightning that made the evening look like the fourth of July. The three of us sat around down below reminiscing of sailing trips past, and that led to a discussion about safety features on boats. Geoffrey's new Daydream had the tallest mast in the marina. Dieter asked about the lightning rod at the top of the mast. Geoffrey then hauled out the literature to show he bought the best there was, including the copper cable for grounding to the keel. Next Geoffrey peeled back the beautiful Indian carpet under our feet and then the hardwood hatch to show the still shiny copper wire all nicely rolled up in its packaging. Shiny it was, but still not bolted to the keel, and we three had been resting our feet over this bare wire for hours. According to the later newspaper reports, this was the worst storm of the summer so far. Somewhere up front in the bow was a brand new VHF radio still in its box.

Later, when I read the Pardey's book "The Self Sufficient Sailor" I thought, If Lin and Larry Pardey had been with us on this trip, they probably would have jumped overboard while under way. The Pardeys have sailed thousands of miles and in doing so have learned and shared their knowledge with others. It was Larry Pardey who always said, "if you can't repair something, maybe it shouldn't be on board."

Sterling Hayden (actor and sailor) wrote a book called "Wanderer." I think Sterling was certainly a better sailor than he was an actor, although he did bring a lot of pleasure in the movies. When you put the pieces of his life together, you wish some of this would rub off on you. The book "Wanderer" has been out of print for many years now, but if you can locate one or borrow one, please do. As they say in moviedom, "I give it two thumbs up."

During World War II, Sterling assisted the Yugoslavian partisans fight against the Germans. He was also involved with the Communist party for six months. This last big mistake would haunt him for many years later on. He turned snitch, and named-names to the F.B.I. This, too, was a dumb thing to do, but it allowed him to work again. Many years earlier when he was at the peak of his career as a big earner and superstar, he walked out on Hollywood. He also walked away from a shattered marriage, defied the courts and found himself broke. As an outlaw with the courts, he set sail with his four children in the schooner Wanderer. By law, he wasn't allowed to take his children away from the United States, but he did anyway. He figured once they got to the South Seas, the children would get a better education with him than staying in school.

We all know Hayden the actor, who was in such notable films *Dr. Strangelove, Johnny Guitar* (a cult film in France), *The Godfather,* John Huston's *The Asphalt Jungle, King of the Gypsies* and more. But a lot of people don't realize he was more of sailor than anything else. Ships took over his life when he was 12 years old. Sterling signed on fishing boats for no pay and, because most fishermen were generous, they would hand him ten bucks or so, which was good money back then. Hayden was crew on the Gloucesterman vessel "Gertrude L. Thebaud." The Thebaud was in many races against the Bluenose from Lunenburg, Nova Scotia. Much as Gloucester fishermen hated to admit it, the truth of the matter was that the Bluenose, for over 20 years, consistently took the lead of any vessel Gloucester Mass. put forward as a challenger. If you should find your way to Lunenburg, by all means, visit the museum in the big red building down by the shore. There, you will see a photograph of Sterling Hayden with the crew of the Gertrude L. Thebaud. Another excellent book to read is a piece of fiction by Sterling called "Voyage." This book became a best seller. Sterling Hayden spent the last of his days living most of the time on a Dutch canal barge in Paris till his death in 1986. He was born in 1916. "Wind is to us what money is to life on shore," he once wrote.

There are literally hundreds of worthy sailors through the years who need mentioning, names like Eric Tabarly, who won many races, H.G. "Blondie" Hasler and Montreal-born Yves Gélinas, who did a circumnavigation. Ellen MacArthur, who is in her early 30s as I write this, was born in landlocked Derbyshire, England, and sailed her first boat, a dinghy, when she was 8. At 18 she single-handedly sailed around Britain and won the BT/JA young sailor of the year award. In France came her success in the Route du Rhum Transatlantic race. Her biggest challenge was the gruelling Vendée Globe 2001, in which she became the youngest woman to race around the world alone. She finished in second place after 94 days at sea.

Sir Peter Blake was one of sailing's greatest figures. Born in 1948 in New Zealand, he was sailing at the age of 5. In 1974, he undertook his first around-the-world race. In 1983 Peter was awarded the MBE by the Queen. Eight years after that was presented with an OBE, becoming Sir Peter Blake. He also won the Whitbread race of 1989 and the Jules Verne trophy in 1994 for setting the best time around the world in a catamaran. In 1995 he headed New Zealand's successful "Black Magic" syndicate to win the America's Cup for New Zealand. Sadly, Sir Peter was killed by pirates on his 119-ft. yacht "Seamaster," while anchored on the Amazon 1,660 miles north of Sao Paulo.

Sir Chay Blyth sought his first big sea-bound challenge in 1966 when he rowed the Atlantic Ocean with Capt. John Ridgway. Next, in 1970, he set off from Southampton, England, in his yacht "British Steel" to become the first person to sail alone non-stop around the world in a westerly direction, against prevailing winds and currents. On another gruelling race around the world, this time with paratroopers, he won with an average speed of 7.82 knots. Then came a two-handed transatlantic race with Rob James. The list goes on.

Discussions about Slocum and Chichester continue, as to who did what and when first. Both were great men but from different times. Slocum's circumnavigation was completed in 1898. Slocum had also done it the hard way, sailing from east to west. Chichester, like most sailors, took the easier route. Slocum weathered storms and many frightening navigational pitfalls. He severely ran aground on the coast of Uruguay. Later on, he was off the hazard-strewn Patagonian Island at night, in an area that's full of so many rocks and foaming water and breakers that it's known as the milky way. His navigational aid was that battered old tin clock I mentioned earlier, with the minute hand missing. His dead reckoning as to where he might be, was just a matter of the island he just left and where the next one should be. He outran a pirate felucca off the African coast and this made him worry all the way through Tierra del Fuego about more intruders. Most know the clever story of how he had carpet tacks strewn all over the deck at night to keep unwanted Fuegian guests away while he slept. Slocum had been alone for so long now that he took on an imaginary crew-member. Throughout his book, this imaginary Spanish señor often shares his duties with Slocum, until his last landfall. There is a passage in the book where the pirates with paddles are slowly overtaking him. Slocum went below to get his gun and then from the cockpit yelled below, as if there were more crew on board. Firing the gun from the cockpit, he jumped below, ran forward sticking his head out the forward hatch, fired again, and ran aft again to fire the gun--mostly for the sake of noise. He has had various pets along the way to help his sanity: a rat, a coconut crab, a centipede and a goat that ate through all his mooring lines. Somewhere along the way, there had been a problem with the authorities when he reached shore and exposed himself to a little girl. I feel any young lad out there who is interested in sailing and adventure should first read Slocum's "Sailing Alone Around the World." It's been around now for over 100 years and still feels new..

Sir Francis Chichester (1901-1972) is well known for his adventures as a deep-sea yachtsman. He named his sailing vessels after Gypsy Moth, a small double winger he flew solo to Australia in 1929. Being an expert on air navigation, he became a recreational sailor after World War II, going on to win the first single-handed transatlantic race in his sloop Gypsy Moth III. That race had but five sailors. Chichester in Gypsy Moth III (39'7" in length), "Blondie" Hasler in Jester (25'9"), Valentine Howells in Eira (25'), Dr. David Lewis in Cardinal Vertue (25'3"), Jean Lacombe in Cap Horn (19'7"). Hasler came in second in his modified Folk-boat, a full eight days later than Chichester. David Lewis was third and was dismasted in his Laurent Giles-designed boat. Howells reached New York in 63 days, and Lacombe staggered in 69 days after leaving Plymouth.

In 1966, sailing in Gypsy Moth IV, Chichester set out from England on a voyage that beat the sailing times of earlier clipper ships on their way to Australia. This was another first for Chichester. He continued on this journey completing a circumnavigation of the globe in 274 days. In 1970, sailing Gypsy Moth V, he attempted to sail 4,000 miles in 20 days, but fell short of his goal by one day. He was knighted by Queen Elizabeth II using the same sword that had been used to knight Sir Francis Drake by Elizabeth I. As Chichester aged, and because he had done so much for sailing, the media had played down the stories of how he would sail away from England's shores and put out a distress call on the V.H.F. The coast guard, naturally, always found him and he was fine every time. A question asked of Chichester in the early years after a long race always elicited the same answer:

"When were your spirits at the lowest ebb?" "When the gin ran out," was his reply.

    I'd like to mention just a few other books I've read, which have kept me interested in the sea all these many years. I've always had hopes and dreams that some day in a small way, I too could witness some adventure. I would first suggest reading anything about David Lewis. He passed away long ago but packed into his life as much adventure as he possibly could. He is most remembered for making known the old traditional systems of navigation used by the Polynesian peoples. Lewis was a short, sturdy and tough man. He left New Zealand in 1938 to finish medical school in England and joined the British paratroop regiment as a medical officer. After the war, he married and worked as a doctor. This marriage didn't last, as many more later on didn't last. Apparently he was an unashamed womaniser, and women took to him. He was always attracted to sailing and since he was between wives, this seemed a proper time to go. After his single-handed transatlantic race he returned to England and medicine, but not for long. It appears his bedside manner was not normal: While examining a patient, he was generally dressed only in his bathing suit, for he was now living on Danger Island in the Hawkesbury river. He looked up to see the hens in his house, dirtying the carpets, and hollered out, "You Bastards." It was also said by those who knew him best, that no ship of his ever left port that was not in all respects ready for sea. It therefore was no surprise when "Cardinal Vertue" broke her mast at the start of the 1960 single-handed transatlantic race.

    There were other incidents too. The rig of "Rehu Moana" fell down on her maiden voyage and "Isbjorn" foundered before the first

Antarctic voyage, thereby probably saving David Lewis's life. "Ice Bird," another Lewis boat, capsized often. The vessel "Dick Smith Explorer" was rolled twice in the Ross Sea. "Cyrano" sailed better sideways than forward and put Lewis in hospital with stomach ulcers. "Taniwha" broke her foremast on her first voyage and went down.

Lewis, a typical Polynesian sailor, would get messed up because of no preparation, but he always managed to get himself and crew back somehow. He retired to New Zealand to write his autobiography, "Shapes on the wind." His friend said of him, "He was the most wonderful scallywag I have ever met. His love for the ocean can only be balanced by the beautiful women he knew." With his eyesight failing and eventually becoming blind he returned to Tin Can Bay, where he died.

More good reading includes "Survive the Savage Sea" by Dougal Robertson,. "Woman Alone: Sailing Solo across the Atlantic" by Clare Francis, "Oars across the Pacific" by John Fairfax and Sylvia Cook., "The Circumnavigators" by Donald Holm, "The Proving Ground" by G. Bruce Knecht and "Alone against the Atlantic" by Gerry Spiess (in his 10-ft. long "Yankee Girl"). There are, of course, hundreds of titles out there, but these are a few of my very favourites.